COMEDY WRITING
FOR LATE-NIGHT TV

COMEDY WRITING
FOR LATE-NIGHT TV

How to Write Monologue Jokes, Desk Pieces,
Sketches, Parodies, Audience Pieces,
Remotes, and Other Short-Form Comedy

JOE TOPLYN

TWENTY LANE
MEDIA

Published by Twenty Lane Media, LLC
P. O. Box 51
Rye, New York 10580
www.twentylanemedia.com

Cover design by Derek Murphy

ISBN: 0615953891
ISBN-13: 9780615953892
Library of Congress Control Number: 2014901808
Twenty Lane Media, LLC

For Sherry, the lovely and talented editor of this book
and of the rest of my life

And for Andrew and Jeffrey, who love to laugh

CONTENTS

CONTENTS

CONTENTS

ACKNOWLEDGMENTS

I WANT TO THANK Dave Letterman and Jim Downey, who together gave me my first break in television. I want to thank everybody I ever worked with on comedy/talk shows for teaching me so much. My thanks go to Dan Dratch for introducing me to Ali Farahnakian, and to Ali for welcoming me into the Peoples Improv Theater, where I created the class on which this book is based. My thanks also go to all my students, who helped me refine this material. I'm grateful for the immense talent of all the writers whose work I've included as examples in this book; I wish I could give credit to each of you individually. Finally, thanks to John Morreall for his guidance on theories of laughter; to Karen Shatzkin for her legal advice; to Strat, Dave, Lise, Steve, Alexa, Eric, and Rob for their valuable contributions; and to Jay Leno and Conan O'Brien for their gracious support.

INTRODUCTION

THIS IS THE FIRST BOOK about how to write for one particular television genre that occupies over thirty hours of national broadcast and cable time every week. It's the only book about how to write comedy for a television series that airs not just twenty-two new episodes a year, as a sitcom does, but up to ten times that number.

This book is devoted to writing for late-night comedy/talk shows. Those are the shows that air from 11:00 p.m. until 2:00 a.m. or so and blend comedy, variety, and talk. Shows like that include the ones hosted by David Letterman, Jay Leno, Conan O'Brien, Jimmy Fallon, Jimmy Kimmel, Craig Ferguson, Arsenio Hall, and Seth Meyers.

Writing for a comedy/talk show is very different from writing for a sitcom or for a one-hour drama. Comedy/talk shows require very specialized writing techniques because they contain very specialized material. There are no topical Monologues or Audience Pieces in sitcoms. There are no Desk Pieces or Pedestrian Games in one-hour dramas.

If you want to learn those specialized writing techniques you could spend countless hours studying comedy/talk shows, taking apart their comedy pieces and reverse engineering them to figure out how they

1

work. You could take a class on comedy/talk shows like the one I teach at the Peoples Improv Theater in New York City. Or you could read this book, which contains the distillation of what I've learned in over fifteen years of writing and producing comedy/talk shows, including three of the shows I referred to above: *Late Night with David Letterman, The Tonight Show with Jay Leno,* and *Late Show with David Letterman.*

WHO THIS BOOK IS FOR

This book is intended for more people than you might expect. It is, of course, for those of you who want to get hired onto the writing staff of a late-night comedy/talk show. It will teach you everything you need to know to prepare your all-important submission packet, the comedy/talk show equivalent of a sitcom spec script. It will also give you tips on how to use that packet to go after a writing job. I've even included a complete sample submission packet in Appendix A so you can see what one looks like.

But this book isn't just a detailed how-to manual for late-night television. It's also an all-purpose guide to writing short-form comedy, which I define as comedy pieces under about ten minutes long. That's because all the comedy on a comedy/talk show is short-form: Monologue jokes are each only a few sentences long and even more elaborate comedy segments like Desk Pieces and Story Sketches are each under about seven minutes. And short-form comedy pieces like the ones on late-night comedy/talk shows appear in many other contexts, too.

So you also need this book if any of the following describes you:

You want to write for comedy/talk shows that aren't in late night. Daytime comedy/talk shows like *The Caroline Rhea Show,* which I worked on, or *The Ellen DeGeneres Show* feature many of the same types of comedy pieces covered in this book. The daypart is different, the audience is different, but the same writing principles apply.

You want to write for other comedy shows besides comedy/talk shows. The techniques in this book apply to writing comedy for any television show. I've personally used these techniques to write jokes and scenes in sitcoms (*Doctor, Doctor*; *Hangin' with Mr. Cooper*); to write sketches for a sketch show (*In Living Color*); to help create a pilot for a comedy game show (*The Late Game*); and even to craft comedic scenes and dialogue for a one-hour detective show (*Monk*). Other alumni of comedy/talk shows have gone on to write feature films and even reality shows. (Note that writers on reality shows seldom have the official title of "writer" but they do write.)

You want to write comedy for the Internet. The same types of short-form comedy that you see on comedy/talk shows you'll also find all over the Internet. For example, here are some of the types of short-form comedy I'll cover in this book and where they appear online:

- The websites Funny or Die and CollegeHumor are packed with Commercial Parodies, Taped Joke Basket Sketches, and other short-form comedy. So is the YouTube channel Official Comedy, for which I was head writer.

- Story Sketches populate YouTube channels like Annoying Orange, which features a web series that was adapted into a TV series on Cartoon Network.

- The website I Can Has Cheezburger? deals in Found Photo Comedy based on real, unaltered photographs of animals.

- The website Cracked features the online equivalent of Art Card Pieces like "17 Awesome Technologies We Secretly Suspect

They're Hiding." (One such technology is "Diapers for pigeons who perch on statues.")

- Twitter is home to tons of Monologue-style jokes, each edited down to 140 characters or less, including spaces.

You want to create funny items to sell or give away. If you can write a Desk Piece for a comedy/talk show you can create funny consumer products like calendars, tee-shirts, bumper stickers, posters, novelty gifts, and greeting cards. For example, one holiday season I wrote the official greeting card sent out by the staff of *Late Night with David Letterman*. The outside of the card invited the recipient to "Charge Yourself a Lovely Holiday Gift...It's On Us!" Printed below was an embossed (fake) replica of CBS newsman Dan Rather's American Express card along with the instruction "Detach carefully along perforations."

You want to advertise or promote something using comedy. The writing techniques employed on comedy/talk shows are also frequently used in advertising and promotion. For example, on *Late Night* Dave Letterman entertained millions with his videos of a hydraulic press crushing offbeat objects like bowling balls. Years later, the Blendtec company gets millions of views for its online marketing videos that show its blenders grinding up unexpected items like golf balls.

You want to write comedy for radio. Many radio shows air Commercial Parodies and Story Sketches (like fake interviews) similar to the ones on comedy/talk shows. For example, Jones American Comedy Network, which supplies comedy bits to radio stations, produced what writers call a Commercial Parody for a fake product called "Frogaine," which is like Rogaine but for growing afros.

You want to write comedy for print media. Many newspapers and magazines run short comedy pieces—such as a side-by-side comparison of the features of two items—that could easily have been Text Pieces on a comedy/talk show. And *MAD Magazine* publishes pieces like "Pet Peeves of Major League Batboys" and "Other Ways the U.S. Postal Service is Cutting Back." What are those if not print media versions of *Late Show with David Letterman* "Top Ten Lists"?

You want to add topical comedy to your stand-up act. The topical jokes that comprise a Monologue on a comedy/talk show are structurally different in key ways from the jokes told by many professional stand-up comics. To write those topical jokes so you can include them in your act you'll need the techniques described in this book.

You want to add comedy to a speech. A speech can have comedic elements and those comedic elements are often similar to those on a comedy/talk show. For example, I once wrote a speech for an actor friend that included a comparison between the actor's on-screen persona and the way he is in real life—what I call in this book a Text Comparison Piece.

You want to know more about what it's like to work on a comedy/talk show. Throughout this book I illustrate points I'm making with tales of my adventures in the late-night trenches. Among those tales is my account, included in Appendix B, of how *The Tonight Show with Jay Leno* survived an early, savage beat-down by *Late Show with David Letterman* to become the number one comedy/talk show in late night.

If you want to do any of the above, this book is for you.

ON TEACHING COMEDY WRITING

Some comedy professionals apparently don't think comedy can be taught. For instance, actress-comedian Lucille Ball has been quoted as saying, "People either have comedy or they don't. You can't teach it to them."

I respectfully disagree. That's like saying, "People either have music or they don't. You can't teach it to them." I believe that anyone who takes, say, piano lessons and practices diligently learns something about music and becomes a better musician. Not a professional musician maybe, but a musician who can play recognizable tunes and entertain people.

Likewise, I believe that if you do nothing but read this book you'll learn a great deal about short-form comedy and about how to make people laugh. I also believe that anyone who studies comedy/talk shows, puts the lessons in this book into practice, and writes some new material every day can learn to write like a late-night comedy writer. And enthusiasts with some real talent have a good chance of making money from their writing.

So my version of Lucy's quotation is, "You can't teach people to have comedic talent but you can teach them comedy writing." Not as punchy but, I think, more accurate.

Even so, why would I want to teach comedy writing? After all, teaching comedy writing is bound to involve analyzing comedy, and as writer E. B. White is quoted as having said, "Analyzing humor is like dissecting a frog. Few people are interested and the frog dies of it."

I respectfully disagree with E. B., too. I think anybody who wants to learn how to write comedy will be very interested in analyzing it. That's because analyzing a joke or a comedy piece allows you to see how it works. And when you see how comedy works—the techniques that went into creating it—you'll learn how to create effective comedy yourself. Plus it can be satisfying and fun to figure out how a writer, a magician of words, pulled off the clever trick of making you laugh.

So the way I teach late-night comedy writing is to analyze each type of comedy piece in turn. I'll give you guidelines, rules, and techniques to help you create your own versions of it. And I'll illustrate my points with many examples taken from actual late-night shows.

I encourage you to analyze the comedy you see on late-night shows yourself as you read this book. Also study the shows' jokes and other comedy pieces online, where you can take your time. Dissect the comedy and see the principles that I cover in this book in action. Sure, E. B., the frog will die of it; the comedy we analyze won't be as funny anymore. But it will have died so that new comedy can live.

ABBREVIATIONS OF NAMES OF SHOWS

Since I do include a lot of examples of comedy in this book, to save space when I note where the examples came from I've abbreviated the names of many of the shows. Here are the abbreviations I use:

JKL:	*Jimmy Kimmel Live*
LLSWCF:	*The Late Late Show with Craig Ferguson*
LNWCO:	*Late Night with Conan O'Brien*
LNWDL:	*Late Night with David Letterman*
LNWJF:	*Late Night with Jimmy Fallon*
LSWDL:	*Late Show with David Letterman*
TSWCO:	*The Tonight Show with Conan O'Brien*
TSWJL:	*The Tonight Show with Jay Leno*

Whenever I refer to a show that isn't on this list—like *Conan* on TBS—I give its entire name.

A NOTE ABOUT GENDER

Because the English language doesn't have a singular, gender-neutral pronoun meaning "he or she," I have a problem when I write, "When a writer writes about gender-neutral pronouns, he has a problem." The problem is, of course, that not all writers are male. So why will I often resort in this book to using "he" in a sentence like that? Because the alternatives tend to be awkward, impractical, or not widely accepted. And because the vast majority of writers for late-night comedy/talk shows are male.

Why is the hiring in late night so skewed toward men? Lynn Harris suggests one theory in an article on the Salon website. She writes that, according to some late-night writers and producers, "there are far fewer women applicants; that's in part a problem with late-night's principal farm team—stand-up comics—who, for reasons that could fill a whole separate article, also heavily skew male." But the causes of the gender disparity in late night are unclear.

What does that mean for a woman who wants to get hired to write for a late-night comedy/talk show? She should do the same thing a male prospective writer should do—write an excellent submission packet and get it into the hands of somebody who can hire her. Women shouldn't let the statistics discourage them. I believe that if a pleasant woman and a pleasant man each submit a packet to a late-night comedy/talk show and the packets are of equally high quality, the woman will have the edge in getting hired.

That's because I believe the hosts, head writers, and producers of those shows are embarrassed that they have so few female writers on their staffs. They are tired of being perceived as sexist. They don't want to see more articles like the one by Bill Carter that appeared in *The New York Times* under the headline "Among Late-Night Writers, Few Women in the Room."

So how does any writer—female or male—create an excellent submission packet for a late-night comedy/talk show? Read on.

THE ELEMENTS OF A LATE-NIGHT COMEDY/TALK SHOW

COMEDY/TALK SHOWS ARE relatively inexpensive. A week's worth of episodes—that is, five hours—costs about as much to produce as one hour of a prime-time drama series. That's why comedy/talk shows have always been popular with television programmers looking to make money in late night, which has far fewer viewers, and therefore attracts far fewer advertising dollars, than prime time. Comedy/talk shows have been fixtures of late night almost since the dawn of television.

Here's a partial list of late-night comedy/talk show hosts, past and present:

Byron Allen	Dick Cavett	Spike Feresten
Steve Allen	Chevy Chase	Craig Ferguson
W. Kamau Bell	Stephen Colbert	Zach Galifianakis
Joey Bishop	Carson Daly	Whoopi Goldberg
David Brenner	Rick Dees	Tom Green
Johnny Carson	Jimmy Fallon	Kathy Griffin

Merv Griffin	David Letterman	Chris Rock
Arsenio Hall	George Lopez	Pat Sajak
Chelsea Handler	Bill Maher	Ross Shafer
D.L. Hughley	Seth Meyers	Sinbad
Magic Johnson	Dennis Miller	Jon Stewart
Craig Kilborn	Conan O'Brien	Wanda Sykes
Jimmy Kimmel	Jack Paar	Alan Thicke
Jay Leno	Joan Rivers	Keenen Ivory Wayans

And that list doesn't even include comedy/talk shows aired primarily in daytime like the ones hosted by Roseanne Barr, Wayne Brady, Ellen DeGeneres, Bonnie Hunt, Megan Mullally, Rosie O'Donnell, and Caroline Rhea.

Each of those hosts is unique but their shows have all been surprisingly similar. That's because all comedy/talk shows tend to share certain key elements. Those elements were first devised by a late-night pioneer, Steve Allen. As Ken Tucker wrote about Steve Allen on the *Entertainment Weekly* website, "He invented the late-night TV talk show as we now know it, with the introduction of *The Tonight Show* in 1953. The whole megillah was Allen's creation—the desk, the band, the opening monologue, the wacky skits, the going up into the audience to answer questions, the guest chatter."

Why have the basic elements of a comedy/talk show changed so little since the days of Steve Allen? Because they add up to a show that works. A show with those elements, if it's well-executed, can be produced entertainingly and inexpensively every weeknight for years.

Here are the elements that are common to most comedy/talk shows. As I discuss each one, I'll focus on how it relates to writing the comedy on the shows.

THE HOST

The host presents the comedy, interviews the guests, and introduces the other performers. But more than that, he's the most important factor in determining how popular the show will be. That's because, in general, the more people who like the host, the more people will watch his show on a regular basis. In an article in *Esquire* magazine Johnny Carson was quoted as saying, "It's all about the guy sitting behind the desk."

Networks want lots of people to watch their shows. The bigger the viewership, the higher the ratings and the more money advertisers will shell out. That's why networks tend to give comedy/talk shows to hosts who they think are likely to have broad appeal. Because all late-night hosts are expected to have this same broad appeal, they all have basically the same persona. It's a time-tested persona that has proven very popular in all sorts of media, that of a likeable, playfully irreverent everyman.

If you don't believe that every late-night host has basically the same persona, consider the Monologue jokes included as examples in this book. It's almost impossible to identify which host told each joke just by having someone read it to you. The Monologue jokes are largely interchangeable between shows, as are most of the other comedy pieces I'll cite as examples.

By contrast, consider Jeff Foxworthy's "You might be a redneck" persona, and Lewis Black, with his angry rants. You'd probably be able to identify their jokes pretty easily. That's why, as talented and successful as those comics are, they're less likely to be asked to host a nightly comedy/talk show on a major network.

But even though all late-night hosts play basically the same charac-ter, those characters aren't identical. A host's on-camera personality is influenced by his real-life personality, which may be quite different. "The guy sitting behind the desk" is not the same as "the guy sitting in his office after the show." And the guy sitting in his office after the show is the person with the most say in what comedy material gets on the show; he's the person his writers have to please.

So to write comedy that gets produced and aired you have to be very familiar with the subtle quirks and preferences of the host. Specifically, you have to be able to answer questions like these:

What types of comedy is the host willing to do? The comedy pieces that a host has performed in the past are the best predictors of the types of comedy he'll perform in the future. So study the show's comedy archives because not all hosts are willing to get laughs in the same ways. For example:

- Dave Letterman builds a comedy segment around watching cos-tumed superheroes parade one-by-one into a restaurant across the street from his studio. Jay Leno probably wouldn't have done that.

- Craig Ferguson puts on fake ears and a comb-over wig and portrays Prince Charles in a sketch. Dave Letterman would never do that.

- Dave Letterman and Jimmy Fallon both play games where they ad-lib with members of the studio audience. Conan O'Brien and Craig Ferguson don't.

- Jay Leno ad-libbed with pedestrians in comedy pieces taped on the street, like his "Jaywalking" pieces. Jimmy Fallon and Craig Ferguson don't do that. Dave Letterman used to, but doesn't anymore.

What's the "voice" of the host? How informal is his wording? How sarcastic is he? What words will he and won't he say? What is his approach toward political topics? Hosts differ subtly in these areas. For example:

- Dave Letterman tends to speak with a certain quirky formality, as when he says, "I don't think there's a man, woman, or child alive today who doesn't enjoy a refreshing beverage." And after I joined Dave's writing staff I discovered that he liked the terms "molly bolt" and "spackle," so I worked them into his material whenever I could.

- Conan O'Brien had a character on *Late Night* dubbed "The Masturbating Bear." Dave would probably never even say the word "masturbating" on his show.

- Jay Leno once told a Monologue joke containing the words "anal leakage"; I'll tell you the joke in Chapter 5. Except for maybe Jimmy Kimmel, would any other host have told that joke?

- Craig Ferguson tends to do political jokes that don't rely on an in-depth knowledge of the issues and instead pay off with easily accessible pop culture references.

How edgy is the host's comedy? When it comes to doing material about sensitive topics like race, sex, and death, different hosts draw the line in different places. For example, on *Lopez Tonight* George Lopez performed a comedy piece in which he invited the audience to guess whether an attractive Asian woman had ever given a "happy ending" and whether an African-American man had ever been in jail. Most other hosts probably wouldn't have done that piece.

Does the host ever draw on his personal life for his comedy? Some hosts do but others don't. For example, Jay Leno often referred to his vast collection of motor vehicles; he even incorporated his cars in his comedy pieces. Conan O'Brien has played the guitar on his show. But Dave Letterman doesn't go out of his way to share his hobbies with his audience.

If you submit a writing packet to a particular show and your material isn't a good fit for the host—and by extension for the show—you won't impress the staff members who read it. Head writers are looking for writers who can turn out comedy material that requires very little editing to get it to the point where the host is happy with it.

So, as best you can, figure out what the host of the show you're writing for wants in his comedy. Learn his unwritten rules; I'll tell you how in Chapter 14, on Submission Packets. Remember, you're writing for a character as well defined as any character on a long-running sitcom or one-hour drama; better defined, in fact, because the performer has created the character himself.

Another important character on a comedy/talk show is:

THE SIDEKICK

The sidekick is a supporting performer who shares the stage with the host and interacts with him throughout the show. He is Robin to the host's Batman. Not every comedy/talk show has a sidekick but almost all do. Dave Letterman and Seth Meyers have as their sidekicks their bandleaders, Paul Shaffer and Fred Armisen respectively. Jay Leno also had a bandleader sidekick, Rickey Minor. Conan O'Brien has Andy Richter and Jimmy Fallon has Steve Higgins, both sidekicks who also serve as announcers. Jimmy Kimmel has a parking lot security guard, Guillermo Rodriguez. Chelsea Handler has her assistant, Chuy Bravo. Craig Ferguson's sidekick is a robot skeleton named Geoff Peterson.

The sidekick serves three main purposes on a show:

> **The sidekick participates in the prepared comedy.** The writers can incorporate the sidekick into scripted and semi-scripted comedy pieces, which gives them another creative option in coming up with material.

> **The sidekick adds to the impromptu comedy.** The ad-libbed interactions between a host and his sidekick can be very funny. Even a camera shot of the sidekick reacting to something can get a laugh from the audience.

> **The sidekick makes the host look better.** He does this in several ways:

> - The sidekick laughs at the host's jokes, encouraging the audience to laugh, too.
>
> - The sidekick clarifies for the audience things the host says that may be hard to follow.
>
> - The sidekick makes the host more relatable to the audience by giving the host someone to share his thoughts with.

When writing for a sidekick, bear in mind that the sidekick, like the host, is playing a character. Research the show to be sure your material is consistent with the sidekick's persona. As one example, *LSWDL* bandleader Paul Shaffer portrays an old-school, show business hipster who oozes false sincerity and owns an extensive collection of gaudy sunglasses and jackets. So I wrote a sketch in which Paul sang an original song defending his flashy wardrobe choices in the style of Rat Pack members Frank Sinatra, Dean Martin, and Sammy Davis Jr. The sketch worked because it was a surprise but still consistent with Paul's on-camera persona.

Besides the host and sidekick, the cast of characters on a comedy/talk show can also include:

OTHER STAFFER-PERFORMERS

Think of a comedy/talk show as a sitcom set in a workplace, like *The Office* or *Parks and Recreation*. The host is the lead character in the sitcom, the sidekick is the lead character's best friend on the job, and certain members of the comedy/talk show's staff are the secondary characters who populate the workplace. Among those staffer-performers could be the members of the band, crew members, or even the writers themselves.

A sitcom with, say, six regular characters offers the writers many more story options than a sitcom with only two regular characters. Likewise, a comedy/talk show that supplements its cast of host and sidekick with several other staffer-performers offers the writers many more directions to go in with the comedy. That's important because the writers have to produce reasonably fresh comedy five nights a week, month after month. For example, Dave Letterman wouldn't be able to do his "Staff Show-and-Tell" sketch without a sizable cast of characters, each of whom has a fairly well-defined persona that the writers can play off.

A typical way comedy/talk shows use staffer-performers is as surrogates for the host in Field Pieces. Dave Letterman frequently sent easy-going stage manager Biff Henderson out into the field to anchor comedy pieces like "Biff Henderson at Spring Training." Jay Leno dispatched his excitable intern Ross to cover red carpet events. And Jimmy Kimmel had his cousin Sal conduct Hidden Camera Pranks.

So if you're writing for a particular show make sure your material fits the established personas of any staffer-performers, too. The announcer on *LSWDL*, Alan Kalter, is red-haired and hot-tempered. The announcer on *LNWCO*, Joel Godard, enjoyed the company of young Asian men. You wouldn't want to get those two announcers confused.

Not all the characters on a comedy/talk show are on the show's staff. Every night a show also features:

THE GUESTS

Guests can be celebrities, musicians, stand-up comics, specialty acts such as ventriloquists, or civilians (also known as non-pros, that is, people who aren't show business professionals). A comedy/talk show books guests because:

- Watching the host interview guests can be entertaining.
- Budgetary restrictions and limited production time dictate that the show can't consist entirely of comedy. So guests fill out the rest of each episode.
- Certain guests (fewer than you might expect) will give the show a "ratings bump," attracting a larger-than-average number of viewers. An extreme example of this phenomenon, described in Appendix B, is when a visit by newsworthy actor Hugh Grant helped boost *The Tonight Show with Jay Leno* to number one in the weekly ratings, where it remained for many years.

Sometimes writing comedy based on what a celebrity is known for can backfire. One morning on *LNWDL* I wrote a Cold Opening for a guest scheduled to appear on that night's show. The guest was Tony Perkins, famous for playing the deranged Norman Bates in Alfred Hitchcock's classic *Psycho* and its sequel, *Psycho II*. My Cold Opening revolved—naturally enough, I thought—around Tony in that iconic role. I gave my script to the segment producer assigned to Tony, who said that he'd ask the actor whether he wanted to do it.

A few hours later I got a call from the segment producer. He said Tony Perkins was on the phone and wanted to talk to me. This was unheard of. Celebrity guests don't call writers on late-night comedy/talk shows, especially writers they've never met. The segment producer put the call through. Tony told me, quite calmly, that he was very upset that I wanted him to perform in a comedy piece where he played Norman Bates. At first I thought Tony had a dry sense of humor and was just having fun with the young writer. But as Tony talked it became clear he was totally serious. Tony said he was coming on the show to promote his new movie, *Crimes of Passion*, and he found it hard to believe that I wouldn't respect that he was trying to change how people perceived him. I apologized profusely and the call ended. I let the segment producer know what had happened and we both shook our heads.

Of course, *Crimes of Passion* bombed and less than two years later Tony Perkins was on-screen as Norman Bates again in *Psycho III*, which he also directed. Too late for my little Cold Opening, Tony learned to take advantage of his persona.

Years later this incident inspired a scene in an episode I wrote of *The Larry Sanders Show*. In the scene, William Shatner, the original Captain Kirk, gets offended when he's asked to perform in a *Star Trek* sketch.

Writers almost never provide material for guest interview segments, which are also known as "panel." Instead, guests are handled by segment producers in the talent department. A segment producer conducts a pre-interview of each guest to find out what the guest wants to chat about with the host and to elicit entertaining anecdotes. The segment producer then types up notes for the host listing suggested questions. The host usually has these notes on his desk during panel but even if he does he may ignore them and ask his own questions. The segment producer also writes the introduction that the host reads right before the guest walks out.

Occasionally, though, writers do create comedy for celebrity guests to perform; I'll talk more about that in the next chapter, where I detail what the writers write. When a writer scripts a piece for a celebrity, the piece should reflect the celebrity's persona. It should be consistent with what the celebrity is known for. That way the audience won't be confused.

For example, actor Robert DeNiro performed a Cold Opening I wrote for *The Chevy Chase Show* in which he arrived at the studio not in a limousine, but (apparently) clinging to the undercarriage of a van. The joke rang true because that's how DeNiro's ex-convict character hitched a ride in the then-current movie *Cape Fear*.

Other key participants in a comedy/talk show aren't in front of the cameras. They are:

THE STUDIO AUDIENCE

The studio audience factors into the writing in two ways:

The studio audience has a big influence on what comedy pieces are produced. That's because the studio audience is a surrogate for the home audience and the home audience drives the ratings. So the laughter of the studio audience helps the show's staff decide what kind of comedy they should air to keep the home audience happy and the ratings up. If a certain joke or comedy piece gets laughs (or "plays") in the studio, the staff will want to do other jokes or pieces like it in the future. If a joke or comedy piece doesn't get laughs (or "dies"), the staff will want to avoid doing similar jokes or comedy pieces again; either that, or the writers can guess what went wrong and try to fix the problem next time.

Even though the studio audience is a surrogate for the home audience it's not identical to the home audience. The two audiences have different characteristics that can cause them to react to comedy in different ways. For example, a joke that refers to an obscure landmark in the city where the show is produced might play in the studio (because many studio audience members live in that city) but not at home. And a joke that relies on a small visual detail in a video clip might play at home but not in the studio because many studio audience members couldn't see that important detail on the overhead monitors. But the similarity between the two audiences is close enough that from now on when I just say "audience" I'll be referring to both.

The studio audience can directly participate in some comedy pieces. Those pieces are called, appropriately, Audience Pieces. Audience Pieces give the writers another way to vary the comedy and to keep the show fresh week in and week out. I'll discuss Audience Pieces in detail in Chapter 12.

So the writers on a comedy/talk show often have to take into account many different participants in the show: the host, the sidekick, other staffer-performers, the guests, and the audience. And those participants may all have slightly different tastes in comedy. Sometimes a writer comes up with a joke that he's sure the audience will think is hilarious but the host doesn't like it, and vice versa. But even though the target for the writers is the intersection of several overlapping circles in a Venn diagram, the circle that counts the most is the one labeled "Host." If the host really wants to do something on his show, the other performers in the show will usually find a way to do it. Conversely, if the host really doesn't want to do something, the other performers are probably making a mistake if they try to talk him into it.

Another key ingredient in the comedy mix isn't even human:

THE DESK

The desk is where the host spends most of his time during the show, performing comedy, interviewing guests, and presiding like a ringmaster over the other activities inside and outside the studio. For that reason the desk, and the sofa or chairs next to it where the guests sit, are collectively referred to as "homebase."

Some shows, like *The Arsenio Hall Show* and *Lopez Tonight*, never had desks. *The Jay Leno Show*, Jay's nightly show at 10:00 p.m., started out without a desk, in part to differentiate the show from Jay's *Tonight* show. But most late-night comedy/talk shows have featured a desk since Steve Allen set the pattern in the 1950s.

Why is that? Does a comedy/talk show have a desk just because it's traditional, a trademark of the format that the audience would miss if it weren't there? I believe that's true but I think there are two additional reasons, one psychological and one practical.

The psychological reason for a desk: The host has to manage pretty much everything that happens in front of the camera and that's a difficult assignment. He has to perform comedy, interview guests, ad-lib jokes, and keep the audience under control. A big, handsome desk bestows an air of authority on the host that makes it a little easier for him to do his job. A desk gives the host an edge when it comes to commanding respect and attention. It signals to audience and guests, "The guy sitting here is in charge."

In other words, a host sits at an expensive desk for the same reason the CEO of a large corporation often rules his empire from behind an enormous desk and a judge sits at an elevated desk—"the bench"—in the courtroom. The need to project power and credibility is also why hosts tend to dress like CEOs in custom-tailored suits instead of in tracksuits and sneakers.

The practical reason for a desk: The host has to deal with a fair amount of paperwork and paraphernalia during the show. For example, he usually needs notes when conducting an interview, the notes prepared by the segment producer. If the host isn't comfortable memorizing his notes or reading them off cue cards, he can keep them on his desk as if it were a speaker's podium. The desk can also hold water glasses, pencils, and props the host might need for an interview, like photographs or a book.

But from a writer's standpoint the desk is important because it allows the host to perform a wider range of comedy. Specifically, the desk allows the host to do Desk Pieces that involve physical items. (I'll cover Desk Pieces at length in Chapter 7.) The host can, for example, conceal props behind his desk until it's time to reveal them for a joke.

The host can also use the desk to display items more effectively, as Jay did during "Headlines" on *TSWJL*. Inserting each newspaper clipping, mounted on cardboard, into a holder on the desk let the camera operator get a steady close-up of the clipping. This close-up reinforced the joke because it let the audience easily see the clipping while Jay read it aloud. A desk is so important to performing "Headlines" and other Desk Pieces that one was eventually brought on a part-time basis onto the previously desk-free set of *The Jay Leno Show*.

SUMMARY

All late-night comedy/talk shows tend to share certain key elements:

The Host—Get to know his on-camera persona really well because all the comedy revolves around "the guy sitting behind the desk." Be able to answer the following questions:
- What types of comedy is the host willing to do?
- What's the "voice" of the host?
- How edgy is the host's comedy?
- Does the host ever draw on his personal life for his comedy?

The Sidekick—He plays three roles on the show:
- To participate in the prepared comedy
- To add to the impromptu comedy
- To make the host look better

Learn the details of the sidekick's on-camera persona because your writing must reflect it.

Other Staffer-Performers—As secondary characters in the workplace sitcom that is the show, they expand the options for written comedy. Make sure the material you write for them fits their personas.

The Guests—When you write comedy for a celebrity to perform, keep it consistent with what the celebrity is known for. If you don't, the audience will be confused.

The Studio Audience—Their laughter has a big influence on what comedy pieces are produced. Study what jokes and comedy pieces make the studio audience laugh and write more material like that. Also consider having the studio audience participate in the comedy.

The Desk—It lends the host an air of authority and makes it easier for him to carry out the activities of the show. Among those activities are comedy pieces that involve physical items, such as many Desk Pieces.

The writers have to factor in the particular characteristics of all of these show elements when they write. But exactly what parts of the show do they write? I'll tell you that next.

2

WHAT THE WRITERS WRITE

WHEN I FIRST JOINED the writing staff of *Late Night with David Letterman* a few of my acquaintances who weren't in the entertainment industry seemed surprised that the show had writers. Either they hadn't watched the show much or they thought Dave just strolled in front of the cameras and made everything up as he went along.

The fact is, the host of a comedy/talk show does have to make up a lot of things as he goes along; he has to improvise constantly. That's one of the reasons hosting a show is so tough. But the host doesn't make everything up. Many of the things he and the other performers on the show say and do are scripted in advance by the writers.

Here are the parts of a late-night comedy/talk show that are written, that is, the comedy pieces on the show. (Comedy pieces other than the Monologue are also sometimes referred to as "bits.")

COLD OPENING

A Cold Opening (or "Cold Open") is a short—usually under a minute—comedic scene that appears at the very beginning of an episode, even before the opening title sequence. Comedy/talk shows that have Cold Openings—and not all of them do—tend to have them infrequently. But a good Cold Opening can get a show off to a fast, funny start and entice a casual viewer to keep watching.

A Cold Opening is almost never produced in front of the studio audience because it's almost always about something that supposedly took place right before the show started, which would mean it took place outside the studio. Because most Cold Openings take place outside the studio they're usually prerecorded; since the audience can't tell exactly when the Cold Opening was produced, why not prerecord it to make sure you get it right?

A Cold Opening almost always features the host. It can also include a guest who's going to appear on that night's show. A funny Cold Opening with a celebrity guest can be a particularly effective way to hook channel surfers into watching more of the show. To get a guest to participate in a Cold Opening, or in any other sketch, the writer needs the guest to approve the material; the talent department handles that process. Once the host and the guest have signed off on the Cold Opening the writer produces it.

Cold Openings involving guests have to be easy to produce because many guests arrive at the studio less than half an hour before the show starts, which doesn't leave much time to shoot and edit the scene. So Cold Openings with guests typically require only one or two shots with no complicated editing and no fancy makeup effects or elaborate costumes.

Cold Openings with celebrities are not only good for the show, they're also a thrill for the writer, who gets to work directly with a big star. That's one reason I wrote and produced four different Cold Openings for Arnold Schwarzenegger, which aired on *LNWDL* and *TSWJL*. I loved writing for Arnold because he has such an outsized, well-defined persona, a hallmark of a great comic character. Arnold also has a terrific sense of humor and was willing to do whatever goofy stuff I asked him to.

One Cold Opening I did for *TSWJL* has Jay meeting Arnold outside the studio right before the taping. Arnold apologizes for almost being late, saying his flight was delayed and he rushed right over from the airport. Jay tells Arnold that it's not a problem and suggests that Arnold could have at least taken the time to unfasten his seatbelt. A wider camera shot reveals that muscleman Arnold is still strapped into his airliner seat, which he has apparently ripped from the floor in his haste to exit the plane.

I'll talk about how to write self-contained, funny scenes like the ones that make good Cold Openings in Chapter 9, about Joke Basket Sketches. A Cold Opening can also be a Stunt, which I'll cover in Chapter 12.

MONOLOGUE

The Monologue is a series of verbal jokes delivered by the host right after he makes his entrance at the start of the show. During the Monologue the host always stands at a specific spot (referred to as the "Monologue Mark") to make things easy for the camera operators.

The Monologue ideally energizes and engages the studio audience and gets them in the habit of laughing. It also lets the host gauge how tough the crowd is going to be that night so he can adjust his delivery.

The writing staff writes the Monologue. Writers also help the host select the jokes for the Monologue and put them in an effective order.

Occasionally a Monologue joke has a punch line that isn't strictly verbal. Such a punch line might consist of, say, a short video clip, an altered photograph, or a fake book. These Monologue jokes with visual punch lines are also written.

I'll talk a lot more about writing Monologue jokes in Chapter 5.

MAIN COMEDY PIECE

After the Monologue and before the first commercial break tends to come the Main Comedy Piece. It can be a Desk Piece, an Audience Piece, a prerecorded Field Piece, or one of the many other comedy pieces I'll be covering in the following chapters. This main, top-of-the-show comedy piece is created by the writing staff.

GUEST SEGMENT EXTRAS

As I mentioned, the writers are almost never involved in the panel segments, where the host interviews the guests. But there are exceptions. Sometimes a writer can script a comedy extra for a guest. Such an extra can add entertainment value to what would otherwise be a fairly predictable encounter.

For example, when I was a new writer on *LNWDL* I learned that singer Tina Turner was going to be a guest. I remembered seeing, in a store window on my walk to work, a ridiculous product called "The Tuna Turner," a plastic container with a crank that could be used to blend the ingredients for tuna salad. Dave and the talent department went for my idea to present the gadget to Tina on the show. A couple of days later, there was the legendary Tina Turner at homebase, giddily cranking The Tuna Turner and making tuna salad while the band played Tina's hit "River Deep—Mountain High."

Writers can sometimes get deeply involved in producing a guest segment. This tends to happen when a guest wants to perform a scripted comedy piece instead of just sitting down and chatting. Shortly after I started at *LNWDL* actor/comedian Steve Martin told me about an idea he had for his upcoming appearance on the show. Steve would display for Dave his collection of supposedly priceless Ming vases and the vases would, one-by-one, accidentally get broken. I pitched Steve some jokes for the sketch, which he liked, and ended up co-writing the piece with him. One of the jokes: Steve tapped a vase with his fingernail so the audience could hear the bell-like tones that the high-quality porcelain produced. The boom mike inched closer to pick up the sound and nudged the vase off its pedestal so that it shattered on the floor. The sketch ended with Steve trying out Dave's new tennis cannon, firing tennis balls at the remaining unbroken vases.

I played an anonymous security guard in the sketch. For some reason I was positioned upstage, directly in the line of fire of the tennis cannon. As balls streaked toward my face I had to decide what was best for the sketch, to break my tough-guy character and get out of the way or to get my nose broken. I decided to split the difference and only moved as much as necessary to avoid injury. As it was, a ball grazed my cheek, a physical reminder of the judgment calls that comedy/talk show writers frequently have to make on the fly.

A Guest Segment Extra can take many forms. It can involve the guest participating in a Story Sketch, a type of piece I'll cover in Chapter 10. It can have the guest perform a Stunt; I'll talk about Stunt Pieces in Chapter 12. It can consist of the guest delivering the type of joke you might find in a Desk Piece (Chapter 7) or a Joke Basket Sketch (Chapter 9). In short, any type of joke or short comedy piece that the host could conceivably perform could also be performed by a guest as a Segment Extra.

BUMPERS

A bumper is a still photo or other video element that briefly appears right before and/or after a commercial break. Comedy/talk shows almost always use bumpers to buffer the transition between the main content of the show and the commercials. For example, the host might "throw to commercial" by saying "We'll be right back," at which point the director will transition to a bumper consisting of the show's logo superimposed over a live shot of the band playing. After a few seconds the commercial will begin.

Writers sometimes use bumpers to add jokes to the show. For example, a writer might create a series of bumpers entitled "Audience Fun Facts" which consists of text jokes superimposed on live shots of the audience. A sample Audience Fun Fact for a show in a notoriously chilly studio might be: "83% of tonight's audience is only applauding to prevent frostbite." Once you know how to write Desk Pieces (Chapter 7) and Joke Basket Sketches (Chapter 9) you'll also be able to write the short jokes that make good comedy Bumpers.

SECOND COMEDY PIECE

Some comedy/talk shows schedule a Second Comedy Piece to appear about halfway through the show. The idea is that the increasingly sleepy viewers at home will look forward to this booster shot of comedy and stay awake for it.

The Second Comedy Piece is usually shorter than the Main Comedy Piece and completely unrelated to it. The "Top Ten List," for example, served for a time as the Second Comedy Piece on *LSWDL*.

But the Second Comedy Piece could also be the second installment of a Story Sketch, of a Field Piece, or of some other scripted activity that began earlier in the show. For example, *LSWDL* once aired this comic variation on the reality show "Survivor": A stagehand, George, was supposedly stranded downstairs in the boiler room of the studio for the entire show. The first installment of this sketch, near the top of the show, had Dave talking with George via a camera in the boiler room. The second installment, in effect the Second Comedy Piece, showed George complaining about how hungry he was. In the third installment, toward the end of the show, George described how he chewed off and ate his own foot.

A simple comedy piece like that which plays out in multiple installments over the course of an episode is called a "runner," which is short for "running joke."

COLD CLOSE

A Cold Close is the opposite of a Cold Opening. That is, a Cold Close is a short comedic scene that appears at the very end of an episode, during or possibly even after the closing credits. I'll cover Cold Closes in detail in Chapter 9.

Here's a Cold Close I wrote for *LNWDL*: A prerecorded scene shows Dave, Paul, and the other band members lounging around homebase. Everybody wears handguns in shoulder holsters. Dave explains how he solved the murder of one of the guests on that night's show. The Cold Close parodies the kind of epilogue that tied up loose ends at the conclusion of some 1970s detective shows like *Charlie's Angels*. My Cold Close ends with Dave and his buddies sharing a laugh and a freeze frame as cheesy crime show music comes up.

My experience with the "Detective Show Cold Close" reflects one reason that Cold Closes rarely appear on comedy/talk shows: preserving time for them at the end of an episode can be difficult. That's because comedy/talk shows are, for the most part, shot "live-to-tape." That is, they aren't aired live but they're produced as if they were airing live, recorded straight through with no stops and with commercial breaks that are the length of the actual commercial breaks. A live-to-tape show is also edited very little, if at all, before it airs. Live-to-tape production gives the show some of the exciting unpredictability of a live show, including the unpredictability of how long each segment of a finished episode will turn out to be.

The detective show Cold Close was scheduled to be on the show twice before it actually ran but was bumped (i.e., cut) each time because the rest of the show ran too long. And because the dialogue in the Cold Close referred to the specific guests on that night's show, each time the Cold Close was rescheduled it had to be rewritten and reshot. Eventually that Cold Close made it onto the show but I decided never to write another one. Getting my material on the show was hard enough without signing up for that kind of aggravation.

SUMMARY

The possible comedy pieces on a late-night comedy/talk show are these:

Cold Opening—This short comedic scene appears before the opening title sequence. It's almost always prerecorded and almost always features the host. If the scene involves a guest it has to be easy to produce since the guest's time (and possibly patience) is limited.

Monologue—The host delivers this series of verbal jokes right after he makes his entrance at the top of the show. Sometimes a joke will have a visual punch line.

Main Comedy Piece—The writers spend most of their time on this piece and on the Monologue. In the chapters to come I'll detail the many options for this piece.

Guest Segment Extras—These pieces can be used to boost the entertainment value of panel segments. Any type of joke or short comedy piece that the host could conceivably perform could also be performed by a guest as a Segment Extra.

Bumpers—Writers can inject more comedy into the show through these transitional video elements that air before and after commercial breaks.

Second Comedy Piece—Shorter than the Main Comedy Piece, it could be the second installment of a scripted piece begun earlier in the show.

Cold Close—This short comedic scene, the opposite of a Cold Opening, airs during or even after the closing credits.

The job of a writer on a late-night comedy/talk show is to write those pieces. You might be curious about how that job compares to writing for another type of comedy show, a situation comedy. I'll talk about that next.

3

COMEDY/TALK SHOWS VERSUS SITCOMS

L ET'S SAY YOU want to write comedy for television but aren't sure whether to pursue a job on a comedy/talk show or on a situation comedy. To help you decide, here's how the two types of shows compare from a writer's standpoint.

OPENNESS TO NEW WRITERS

No television writing job is easy to get. But comedy/talk shows tend to be more open than sitcoms to hiring writers who don't have agents, or even any previous television experience. The reason is probably because most comedy/talk shows have more than a dozen writers on staff, whereas most sitcoms have under a dozen. That means hiring a new writer onto a comedy/talk show entails less risk. If the new writer doesn't work out, there are relatively more writers around to take up the slack until he can be replaced.

TOPICALITY OF THE WRITING

If you like writing about current events, a comedy/talk show is for you. Every day you can make fun of what just happened in the world. The pace is fast and the feedback is almost immediate. You can write a joke in the afternoon about some dumb thing a celebrity did that very day and watch it get a laugh on the show a few hours later.

By contrast, sitcoms air several weeks or more after they're produced and can live on for years in syndication. Sitcom writers usually avoid including jokes based on current events because topical jokes would make their episodes seem dated and stale almost immediately.

Even sitcoms that incorporate a lot of humor based on pop culture, like *Family Guy,* mostly stick to jokes about evergreen topics. An evergreen topic is a topic that stays fresh, sometimes because it's based on a lasting pop culture phenomenon. One example of an evergreen topic is how Apple is always coming out with a new electronic device that immediately makes the one you just bought obsolete.

I'll cover topical humor extensively in Chapter 5 on Monologue Jokes.

DEGREE OF CREATIVE CONTROL

Most sitcom episodes are written by the writing staff as a group. Typically all the writers sit around a table and brainstorm possible story ideas. At some point the show runner chooses one of the story ideas and the entire writing staff "beats out" (outlines) the episode together. Then the writer who will get the "written by" credit for the episode takes the story outline and turns it into a full script. When the credited writer's draft is finished the writing staff "tables" it, that is, rewrites it. The dialogue may change. Individual scenes may change. The entire story may change. But the writing credit won't change. This means that by the time a script is finished, the credited writer of an episode may not have written a single word of it.

What's more, the credited writer, unless he or she is an upper-level producer, will probably also have little or no say in the casting of the episode, the set design, or any other production element. In short, the typical sitcom writer has very little control over how his or her work appears on television.

The writing process on comedy/talk shows is very different. For one thing, there's very little group writing. Although writers can always choose to collaborate on any given comedy piece, about ninety percent of the writing on a typical comedy/talk show is done by individual writers working by themselves.

There are two main reasons for that:

- A comedy/talk show requires a large volume of material to be written and produced every day on tight deadlines. When you have to "feed the beast" like that, writing around a table isn't efficient. Dividing and conquering gets more work done more quickly.

- The comedy on a comedy/talk show consists of short bits—from jokes to sketches—that aren't tied together by any episode-long story. Because the writers don't have to worry about whether their material dovetails with a story as they would on a sitcom, they can work independently.

Because the beast has to be fed every day, a writer's material for a comedy/ talk show is rewritten very little. There simply isn't enough time to do a lot of rewriting. If a joke or comedy piece needs a lot of editing to get it in shape for the show it will often be passed over in favor of material that's ready to go.

And if a comedy piece is selected to appear on the show, the writer of the piece can produce it himself. In fact, he's expected to produce it himself, to save time. This means the writer can, for example, write a Commercial Parody and supervise its preproduction (choosing the actors, sets, props, graphics, makeup, and wardrobe), its production (giving suggestions to the director or maybe even directing it himself), and its post-production (selecting stock footage, music, and sound effects, and supervising the editing). Of course, the head writer, producers, and host may have suggestions that have to be incorporated into the finished piece but usually the writer can see his Commercial Parody aired almost exactly as he envisioned it. (By the way, if you do get hired to write for a comedy/talk show and you have no production experience, don't worry; you'll quickly pick up whatever you need to know from your coworkers.)

What all this means is that writers on comedy/talk shows, even new writers, have much more creative control over their material than do sitcom writers. To have the same amount of creative control on a sitcom you'd have to be running the entire show. So writing on a comedy/talk show is a great way to learn, on a small scale but relatively quickly, how to be a television producer.

WORKING HOURS

On any television show the amount of time that a writer is expected to spend at the office is inversely correlated with how well-run the show is. On a well-run comedy/talk show or sitcom the writers arrive at the office around nine in the morning and are out of there by seven in the evening. On a poorly-run comedy/talk show the writing staff might still be at their desks at ten o'clock at night. On a poorly-run sitcom the writers may not stagger homeward until well after midnight. So in general, a writer's working hours are a little more manageable and predictable on a comedy/talk show than on a sitcom.

COMPENSATION

On the home page of the website of the Writers Guild of America (www.wga.org) there's a link to the Schedule of Minimums. (You'll find it in the "Quicklinks" box.) The schedule spells out how much unionized television shows, a category which includes all the respectable shows, have to pay their writers.

If you dig down into the Schedule of Minimums you'll find that the minimum weekly salary for a writer on a five-episodes-per-week comedy/talk show and on a network prime-time sitcom is about the same. It's good that the pay is about the same because a new comedy writer shouldn't be choosing between types of shows based on money but based on the other factors in this chapter, which more directly translate to job satisfaction. And in either case the money is great—around $4,000 a week.

Late one night after working all day on a sitcom, I arrived home to see an unfamiliar car cruising my deserted neighborhood very slowly. I was suspicious because a follow-home robbery had taken place on my block the week before, so I sat in my car to see what the other driver would do. As I watched, something flew out of his car and landed on a neighbor's lawn. A pipe bomb? No, the driver was delivering the morning newspaper. We writers had been kept at the office until 5:00 a.m. So, a bit of advice: If you have a choice, only work on shows where the show runner has a personal life. In my experience, show runners who have no reason to go home will create reasons to stay at the office with their surrogate families, their writers.

TRANSFERABILITY OF SKILLS

One factor to consider when you're weighing any job opportunity is what else that job prepares you to do. If you want a long career, it's good to develop options early on. So let's take a look at how transferable a writer's skills are to other television genres in both the sitcom and the comedy/talk show scenarios.

A successful writer for a comedy/talk show is an expert on short-form comedy, that is, material ranging in length from individual jokes to sketches. Short-form comedy writing skills are also particularly useful on these other types of shows:

- Sketch shows like *Saturday Night Live*
- Comedy clip shows where a host or announcer tells scripted jokes about unscripted video clips. Such shows include Comedy Central's *Tosh.0*, *Fashion Police* on E!, and Animal Planet's *The Planet's Funniest Animals*.
- Game shows that incorporate jokes, like *Hip Hop Squares* on MTV2, an updated version of the game show *Hollywood Squares*

Of course, the ability to write short-form comedy is also valuable when writing dialogue and individual scenes in sitcoms. But writing a sitcom demands additional skills, too, mainly the ability to structure a story that will hold an audience's interest for half an hour. Even though a comedy/talk show writer does learn basic story skills while writing sketches, sitcom storytelling is on a whole other level that demands additional study and practice.

That's why even after having won four Emmys for working on a comedy/talk show I still needed to demonstrate that I was "good with story" to get my first job on a sitcom. So I wrote a spec episode of the sitcom

"Cheers" and used that as a writing sample. (A spec is a script that you've written without being paid in the hopes that it will help you get paid work; "spec" is short for speculative.)

In short, comedy/talk show writing skills do somewhat translate to other television genres. Now, how well do sitcom writing skills translate to other genres? Well, a successful sitcom writer can craft a well-structured, half-hour story featuring sharply defined characters and lots of laughs. That makes it a short step from writing a sitcom to writing a feature film comedy: just expand the story. It's a slightly longer, but still possible, step to go from writing a sitcom to writing a one-hour drama: expand the story and skip most of the comedy.

But what about going from sitcom writing to writing for a comedy/talk show? Sitcom writers would find their experience very useful in writing sketches with storylines but probably less useful in writing more joke-intensive pieces. Put another way, your spec episode of the sitcom *The Big Bang Theory*, as hilarious as it may be, will not show the head writer of a comedy/talk show how well you can write topical Monologue jokes, Desk Pieces, jokes about video clips of pedestrians, games involving the studio audience, and other mainstays of the genre.

So whether you start out writing for a comedy/talk show or for a sitcom you'll have to learn additional skills if you want to cross over successfully to a different television genre. You're also going to need at least one excellent writing sample that shows you have the skills the new genre requires, whatever that genre is.

Take all of the above factors into account if you're trying to decide between pursuing a writing job on a comedy/talk show or on a situation comedy.

SUMMARY

Compared with sitcoms, comedy/talk shows tend to be:

- More open to new writers
- More fast-paced and topical
- More the product of individual writers working by themselves
- More predictable and manageable in terms of hours spent at the office
- About the same when it comes to weekly compensation

No matter where you start your writing career, you'll need additional skills and a solid writing sample or two to make a successful move to a different television genre.

Teaching you how to create an excellent writing sample for a late-night comedy/talk show is one of the goals of this book. I'll tell you how to write the various types of comedy pieces that go into those shows and how to assemble your versions of those comedy pieces into a submission packet. You'll also find out how to use that submission packet to get a writing job.

But before I get into specific writing techniques, I think it's important for you to know why those techniques work because if you understand why they work you'll be able to use them more effectively. So let's take a brief look at why people laugh.

4

WHY PEOPLE LAUGH

I F YOU'RE WRITING for a comedy/talk show you want the studio audience to laugh at your work. You don't want them to just chuckle or applaud, although you'd rather they do that than groan, or not react at all. You want people to actually laugh, the harder the better. The spontaneous laughter of the audience at something you've written is the sign that you've done your job.

So, what makes people laugh? If we knew that, comedy writing would be easier, wouldn't it? But nobody knows exactly. Psychologist Patricia Keith-Spiegel lists dozens of theories of humor that have been proposed over the centuries and sorts them into eight categories. Yet none of those theories seems to apply to every situation where people laugh.

Two theories, though, go a long way toward explaining why audiences laugh at the comedy in a comedy/talk show. I'll be referring to these two theories again and again because they underlie most of the writing techniques I'll be teaching you. These two theories are the *Surprise Theory* and the *Superiority Theory*. Here's my interpretation of what those two theories mean and how they might have their roots in early human behavior.

THE SURPRISE THEORY

The Surprise Theory of Laughter says that we laugh when we're surprised that an incongruity turns out to be harmless.

This is the sort of theory proposed by neuroscientist V.S. Ramachandran, researcher Thomas Veatch, and psychologists Peter McGraw and Caleb Warren. Say you're a caveman enjoying a languid prehistoric afternoon with your cave family. You notice a clump of tall grass rustling not far away. The air is calm so it's odd that the grass is moving. Something's not right. Is a saber-toothed cat about to leap out and rip your family to pieces? Your stress level shoots way up. Then a sudden gust of wind flattens the grass and reveals a couple of monkeys havin' monkey sex. You utter a shout of surprise and relief, announcing to your family that there's no danger after all. That's a caveman laugh.

Now flash forward several dozen millennia and consider how that behavior of our primitive ancestors might translate into our laughing at a joke today. According to the Surprise Theory, a joke creates an incongruity, a dissonance. Specifically, the last part of the joke, the punch line, isn't what the audience expected after they heard the first part of the joke. The punch line doesn't fit tidily into the rest of the joke so when the audience first hears the punch line they feel a little threatened. Their brains tell them, "Something's wrong here," and their stress level rises. But as the audience mentally processes the apparent incongruity they suddenly make sense of it and get a pleasant surprise—the realization that there's no threat after all. It was a false alarm. The incongruity was harmless. And the audience laughs to signal that all is still right with the world.

You can see the Surprise Theory in action in this joke from *LNWIF*:

> "A couple got married at the Texas State Fair this week. It was so sweet...the bride was wearing something old, something new, something fried, and something dipped in chocolate."

When an audience member hears "something fried, and something dipped in chocolate" her first thought is, "Hey, that doesn't make sense. It's supposed to go 'Something old, something new, something borrowed, and something blue.'" A split-second later she realizes that the punch line actually does make sense because at the Texas State Fair there's a lot of that kind of junk food. Relieved that there's no threat to the established order of her universe, the audience member laughs.

THE SUPERIORITY THEORY

The Superiority Theory of Laughter says that we laugh when we suddenly feel superior to someone else.

This theory is supported by Albert Rapp and the philosopher Thomas Hobbes. Imagine that you, the caveman, are once again lounging around with your cave family when your luck runs out—this time a saber-toothed cat really does charge up and attack you. A violent struggle ensues. You pummel the cat with your stone axe and it falls down dead. Victorious, you roar in triumph.

The Superiority Theory suggests that laughter in the present day has its origins in that prehistoric victory yell. In the context of a comedy/talk show, this theory explains why an audience member tends to laugh when she sees someone being embarrassed or humiliated: the audience member feels like a winner in comparison.

The Superiority Theory explains, for example, why the "Jaywalking" Field Pieces on *TSWJL* made the audience laugh so hard. When a pedestrian answered Jay's question "What countries border the United States?" by responding, "Australia...and Hawaii," the audience roared with laughter because they knew the correct answer and that poor, foolish pedestrian didn't. The audience felt superior.

The Superiority Theory also explains why the questions that Jay asked in those "Jaywalking" pieces were so easy. If the questions had been difficult, say about the periodic table of the elements, most of the audience wouldn't have known the answers either. That means most of the audience couldn't have felt superior to the pedestrians and wouldn't have laughed.

Both theories of laughter—Surprise and Superiority—come into play in more layered comedy pieces such as Sketches. For example, *LNWCO* once aired a Commercial Parody for a fake product called "Atomic Clog-O," which removes a stubborn clog from your bathroom drain using a small atomic bomb. The audience laughs because it feels superior to the gullible homemaker in the commercial who is shown using that absurd product. The audience also laughs with surprise at all the harmless incongruities built into the script, like the instruction "Place an ordinary household lead shield in front of you and you're ready to go!"

Notice that you could say that the Superiority Theory is explained by the Surprise Theory: we laugh when we suddenly feel superior to someone else because we're pleasantly surprised that whatever incongruous event made us feel superior didn't hurt us. We laugh, for instance, at a pedestrian who makes a mistake in "Jaywalking" because the mistake is an incongruity—Hawaii isn't a country!—but we ourselves didn't make that embarrassing mistake so it's harmless. But even though there is some overlap between the theories I'll keep them separate because often one theory does a better job than the other of explaining why a particular writing technique works. And as I mentioned, if you understand why a technique works you'll be able to use it more effectively.

SUMMARY

Two theories explain why people laugh at the jokes on comedy/talk shows:

- **The Surprise Theory of Laughter** says that people laugh when they're surprised that an incongruity built into the joke turns out to be harmless.
- **The Superiority Theory of Laughter** says that people laugh when they suddenly feel superior to someone else.

In the following chapters you'll learn many specific writing techniques that systematically exploit those two theories to produce laughter. I'll begin with techniques for writing the piece that begins most comedy/talk shows: the Monologue.

5

MONOLOGUE JOKES

THE MOST INDISPENSABLE comedy segment in a late-night comedy/talk show is the host's Monologue. I can't think of a late-night comedy/talk show since the days of Steve Allen that didn't begin with some kind of Monologue. In almost all cases the Monologue is a topical Monologue, a series of unconnected verbal jokes based on the news of the day.

WHY COMEDY/TALK SHOWS ARE SO TOPICAL

Most of the comedy in late-night shows, not just the Monologue, is based on current events. This topicality reduces the value of late-night shows to the companies that own and air them because it gives the shows a relatively short shelf life. The episodes wouldn't hold up in the ratings if they were rerun years later because the comedy would be too dated to be funny.

Why, then, do comedy/talk shows contain so much topical comedy? There are two main reasons, one emotional and one practical:

The emotional reason: Topical comedy helps make the host relatable to viewers. When you get together with coworkers at lunch or with your family around the dinner table, what do you tend to talk about? What happened since the last time you met, what happened today, what's happening now, right? That's why a host who gives you his funny take on the news and helps you make sense of it seems like a friend, relatable. And because you enjoy spending time with your friends, topical comedy helps draw you back to that host's show night after night.

The practical reason: Basing comedy on current events makes it easier to keep the comedy funny. Late-night shows air new episodes four or five nights a week, week in and week out. That means the writers have to constantly generate new comedy material, up to twenty minutes worth a night. One way to help keep the material fresh, and therefore funny, is to base it on the news because the news is mostly different every day. If a late-night host filled his show with comedy about personal topics like his relatives or about generic topics like airline travel he'd run out of fresh material fast.

Topical comedy is woven throughout every comedy/talk show but it exists in its purest, most concentrated form in the Monologue.

WHY LEARN HOW TO WRITE MONOLOGUE JOKES?

Some comedy/talk shows have writers on staff who work practically full time on the Monologue. All day long these Monologue specialists absorb vast amounts of news from the Internet, print publications, television, and wherever else they find it and transform it into topical jokes for their shows.

It's a tough job. Jay Leno performed an unusually long Monologue on *TSWJL* that consisted of about thirty jokes. To get thirty jokes approved, his writing staff had to submit hundreds. That meant that each of Jay's

Monologue specialists was expected to turn in about twenty to fifty jokes a day. On a good news day—when the news was heavily laden with gleaming nuggets waiting to be refined into comedy gold—one especially prolific *Tonight* show scribe would write up to a hundred jokes. And the job is even more demanding on a slow news day because the Monologue won't be getting any shorter. A former writer for Johnny Carson said this about writing a topical Monologue: "Doing this every day is like taking a [dump] when you don't have to."

Writing high-quality Monologue jokes in large quantities is so difficult that you may be thinking that the task isn't for you and, therefore, that you don't have to know how to do it. Can't you just learn how to write Desk Pieces and Audience Pieces and all the other kinds of late-night comedy and leave the Monologue writing to the specialists?

No, you can't. A prospective writer for a comedy/talk show needs to know how to write Monologue jokes. Here are three reasons why:

On some comedy/talk shows every writer is expected to contribute to the Monologue. Some shows have tighter budgets and smaller writing staffs so they can't afford to dedicate writers exclusively to the Monologue; every writer has to pitch in. In fact, those shows usually request that you include a page of Monologue jokes in your submission packet. That means that writing candidates who demonstrate the ability to write strong Monologue jokes improve their chances of landing a job on those shows.

Monologue-type jokes are the building blocks of many other comedy pieces. That's because many comedy pieces on comedy/talk shows are "joke baskets"; a joke basket piece gathers together a series of interchangeable jokes under a single topic, such as "Thank You Notes" on *LNWJF*. And each joke in a joke basket is created using the same techniques you'd use for a Monologue joke. So a late-night writer needs to know how to write Monologue jokes in order to be able to write a lot of the other comedy on the show.

Most of the writing techniques that apply to Monologue jokes also apply to jokes in general. A well-crafted joke is a well-crafted joke, whether it's on a comedy/talk show or in a newsletter, blog, stand-up act, radio show, sitcom, or feature film comedy. Writers who can create solid Monologue jokes will have an easier time advancing their careers in comedy no matter what direction those careers take.

So pretty much every comedy writer needs to be able to write Monologue jokes. But don't worry because there's a formula for it.

THE MONOLOGUE JOKE FORMULA

How can there be a formula for writing Monologue jokes? Isn't humor subjective? Don't different people laugh at different jokes? Yes, humor is subjective and different people do laugh at different jokes. But different people also laugh at many of the same jokes and those are the jokes that go into a late-night Monologue.

The host of any nationally broadcast late-night show wants to tell jokes that almost everybody in the audience will laugh at. After all, if almost everybody is laughing then the ratings for the show are more likely to stay high and the host is more likely to keep his job. This desire of every host to make everybody laugh leads every writer for every host to write Monologue jokes the same way.

Don't believe that every late-night writer writes Monologue jokes the same way? Then have somebody read you some jokes that were transcribed from various late-night Monologues—you can find them online—and try to guess which host delivered them. You'll see that it's difficult, which proves my point that Monologue jokes are basically interchangeable between shows. The jokes were all designed to make a mass audience do the same thing—laugh—which is why they were all created using the same time-tested techniques.

Collectively these techniques add up to a formula for writing Monologue jokes. And because these techniques are so versatile and so powerful, they're also used to create many other forms of comedy. I'll be referring to these Monologue joke techniques again and again throughout this book so in this chapter I'll devote a lot of attention to explaining them.

Let's start by talking about the basic structure of a Monologue joke.

THE THREE PARTS OF A MONOLOGUE JOKE

In Western culture all stories with mass appeal, whether dramatic or comedic, have a three-act structure. The first act introduces a relatable hero who wants something very much. The second act makes it increasingly difficult for the hero to get what he or she wants. And the third act shows how the hero either succeeds or fails to get what he or she wants. Audiences seem to enjoy watching three-act stories, where somebody they can identify with achieves a goal despite huge obstacles, because stories like that make them feel better about themselves.

The idea of the three-act story structure actually dates back to the ancient Greek philosopher Aristotle, who discussed it in his *Poetics*. Since Aristotle's time, a lot has been written about the use of the three-act structure in screenwriting. I only mention the structure here because a Monologue joke is a tiny story, intended to entertain a mass audience, and that may be why it has three parts.

The three parts of a Monologue joke—in their order of appearance in the joke—are (1) the topic, (2) what I call the angle, and (3) the punch line.

1. **The topic** is the news item that the joke is based on.
2. **The angle** is the particular direction that the joke takes.
3. **The punch line** is the surprise at the end of the joke.

Other writers may have different names for the three parts of a Monologue joke, or may believe that a Monologue joke has more or fewer than three parts. For example, the topic and angle taken together are often referred to as the setup. But I prefer my terminology because I think it leads to simple, clear explanations of how Monologue jokes work and how to write them.

Now let's look at these three parts of a Monologue joke in more detail, along with the techniques used to create them.

THE TOPIC

The process of writing a Monologue joke starts with picking a topic. The topic is the first part of the joke. It's a concise statement of the news item that the joke is based on. To give you some examples, here are the topics of six jokes taken from the Monologues of various late-night comedy/talk shows:

- "Two Oklahoma women were caught shoplifting two thousand dollars' worth of merchandise stuffed in the rolls of their body fat." [*Conan*]

- "Charlie Sheen is on the show tonight to talk about his hit TV show *Anger Management*." [*TSWJL*]

- "Denny's has a new sandwich called the Fried Cheese Melt, which comes with deep-fried mozzarella sticks inside a grilled cheese." [*LNWJF*]

- "Bernie Madoff's underpants were sold at an auction." [*LSWDL*]

- "Carl's Jr. is selling a foot-long burger." [*LSWDL*]

- "A company in North Carolina is selling a sixty-dollar IQ test that people can give their dogs." [*LNWJF*]

I'll finish telling these jokes later in the chapter. For now, let's just focus on the topics. Professional comedy writers singled out those topics for Monologue jokes because they each had six specific characteristics. Each of your Monologue joke topics should have those six characteristics, too. Here they are.

THE SIX CHARACTERISTICS OF A GOOD TOPIC

1. A good topic is factually true.

A good topic is not something that sprang from your imagination. It is based on a real story that was reported by at least one reputable news source.

It is so important for topics to be true that comedy/talk show hosts will often ask the writer of a joke with a dubious topic whether the topic is true before they'll even consider delivering the joke. And some Monologue writers, anticipating the host's doubt, will add the notation "true" next to jokes they submit that have hard-to-believe topics. For example, here's a joke from *LLSWCF* that I would add the notation "true" to: "Scientists in Scotland say they're inventing an invisibility cloak. If you want to make a Scotsman invisible, just give him a talk show on CBS at 12:30." [Host Craig Ferguson, a Scotsman, is describing his own show.]

Why does the topic have to be true? The reason is because if the audience suspects that the host made up the topic they'll be distracted; they'll be wondering whether the host lied instead of paying attention to the joke. Also, if the audience thinks the joke is about something fictitious they won't care about the joke because it can't possibly be relevant to them. They'll tune it out, and as a result the laugh won't be as big. Returning to the prehistoric analogy in the previous chapter, if the tall grass isn't really rustling, the caveman will ignore it and won't even see the laughable amorous monkeys when they're revealed.

To help reassure the audience that a questionable topic is true you can begin the joke with a few details that ground it in reality. For example, you could state the source of the story or when or where it took place, using words like "According to a new poll..." or "Yesterday in Tennessee..." Such touches of specificity subtly validate the topic in the audience's minds. The host himself might also validate a suspect topic by leading into the joke with "This is true" or "Did you hear about this?"

2. A good topic is not intentionally funny.

A good topic is a serious, straight statement of fact. It shouldn't be embellished with any comedy at all. For example, you wouldn't want to reword the sample topic above to read "Carl's Jr. may have to change its name to Calories Jr. because it's selling a foot-long burger."

The reason, again, is to avoid distracting the audience. If there is any humor in the topic the audience will be busy mentally processing that humor when they should be paying attention to the rest of the joke. As a result they may not absorb all the information they need to appreciate the actual punch line and may not laugh when it arrives. Continuing with my prehistoric analogy, the caveman won't notice the rustling grass and mating monkeys if he's watching a silly wolf cub chase its own tail.

3. A good topic can be and should be stated in only one sentence.

Sometimes a topic can consist of two sentences if you have to convey a lot of essential information and the resulting joke is worth it. But in general one sentence is the limit for a topic. If you make the audience sit through a long, complicated, multi-sentence topic they may get confused or their attention may wander. In either case they won't be fully prepared to laugh at the punch line.

I'll talk more about the importance of brevity in the next chapter, "How to Edit Jokes."

4. A good topic is a news item that will capture most people's interest.

The topic has to stimulate the curiosity of a mass audience. If the audience isn't curious about the topic, if they don't care about it, they'll decide from the start that the joke doesn't relate to them and they won't listen closely to it. They won't be taking it in as it's told and they won't laugh when it ends.

Going back to my prehistoric analogy, the topic of a Monologue joke should grab an audience member's attention the way rustling grass would grab the attention of a caveman, and for the same reasons. The rustling grass is out-of-the-ordinary and means something to the caveman, namely the possibility that a predator is hiding in the grass ready to tear him apart. The topic of a Monologue joke should be out-of-the-ordinary and mean something to an audience member—the possibility that something happening in the world could affect his or her life.

But how can you tell whether any given news item will capture enough people's interest to justify writing a joke about it? Here are four ways to identify news items that may be compelling enough to become the topics of successful Monologue jokes:

a) Focus on stories that are getting a lot of coverage in the media.

What are the top stories on television news shows, on Internet news sites, in the newspaper, and on the radio? If a story is being featured by several news outlets, that means that several teams of news professionals have decided that the story will interest most of their audience. So you should consider making that story the topic of a joke.

Don't limit yourself to "hard news" stories. What about that movie that opened last weekend? That TV series that was just cancelled? That celebrity who got arrested today? Any pop culture item, if it's covered widely enough in the media, is a candidate for a joke topic.

Be attuned to every facet of pop culture. Watch shows like *Entertainment Tonight* and *Access Hollywood*. Read mass-circulation magazines like *People* and *Entertainment Weekly* and scan their websites along with pop culture websites like TMZ and PerezHilton. Check out what topics are trending on Twitter. Explore YouTube to see what Internet videos have gone viral.

You could even tune into the late-night comedy/talk shows to see what topics they're using as joke material. If one of those topics seems to have staying power ("legs") you might base some of your own jokes on it. Note that a topic is a news event, which is in the public domain, so plagiarism wouldn't be an issue. (It would be an issue, however, if you copied an entire joke. I'll talk more about plagiarism in Chapter 14.)

There's another reason to choose well-covered news stories for your joke topics, besides the fact that most people will probably be interested in those topics: your audience will know enough about the topics to understand your jokes without your having to do too much explaining. For example, you could mention Bernie Madoff in your topic without also having to lengthen the joke to include the facts that he ran a Ponzi scheme and scammed people out of billions of dollars. The shorter the joke, the better; I'll cover this point more in the next chapter.

b) Focus on stories that even people who aren't media professionals are talking about.

Your friends, your family, your coworkers...what news items are they bringing up in conversation? What articles and video clips are your friends sharing on Facebook? What blog topics are attracting the most comments? What current events do strangers at a party care enough about to want to discuss? Those are all stories you should consider for joke topics.

c) Focus on stories that you yourself have an emotional reaction to.

Have you ever heard or read a news story and had one of these reactions?

- "That's interesting."
- "That's dumb."
- "That's surprising."
- "That's annoying."
- "That's weird."
- "That's hypocritical."
- "That's disgusting."

An emotional reaction like one of those to a news story is a sign that the story has hooked you. It has grabbed your interest. And if the story has grabbed your interest the chances are excellent that it will grab many other people's interest, too. So add that story to your list of potential joke topics.

d) Consider "Odd News" stories.

Odd News stories are about events that are out-of-the-ordinary and attention-getting but not significant enough to rate extensive coverage by the national media. You can easily find Odd News stories online by typing "odd news" into your favorite search engine. You can also go directly to websites like Fark that specialize in aggregating Odd News items.

Here are a few examples of headlines taken from the Odd News page of the "Yahoo News" website:

- "Woman says she found snake in bag of potatoes from Walmart."
- "World's most expensive coffee is defecated from an animal."
- "After car crash, Australian woman has French accent."

The fact that stories like those are included on an Odd News webpage means that the professionals curating the page think the stories are of general interest. And that means that the stories have excellent potential as joke topics even though they weren't widely reported.

Writers on late-night comedy/talk shows often turn to Odd News for joke topics on slow news days, when there aren't enough suitable, high-profile stories to fill out a full-length Monologue.

5. A good topic is something that your audience will let you joke about.

A mass audience won't let you joke about certain topics. Many topics are so tragic, disturbing, or offensive that the negative emotions they bring out in most people tend to overwhelm any urge to laugh. Among these problematic topics are death, mental illness, natural and manmade disasters, rape, and child abuse.

If a mass audience hears a joke about one of those traditionally taboo topics the subtleties of the Surprise Theory of Laughter come into play. The audience might be surprised by the incongruity in the punch line but they won't laugh because the incongruity isn't harmless. The incongruity harms them because it makes them think, "If I laugh at that punch line I'm a horrible person."

To be sure, some comics who host niche television shows, say on Comedy Central, do make jokes about dead children and other sensitive topics. But those hosts aren't expected to attract a mass audience and the viewers they do attract know what they're in for. By contrast, the hosts of major comedy/talk shows like the ones I'm focusing on want to avoid repelling too many viewers with troublesome joke topics. High ratings mean money, prestige, and job security so those hosts want every viewer they can get. Since the big-time hosts have a strong incentive to avoid difficult topics, anybody writing for those hosts should avoid them, too.

But some news stories about sensitive topics are too high-profile to rule out immediately. If the entire country is riveted by a particular current event, the instinct of a comedy/talk show writer is to try to mine it for material even if it has unsavory elements.

So here are four tips on how and when to write jokes about a tricky but hard-to-ignore topic:

a) Steer clear of the most disturbing aspects of the topic.

If the news story has some humorous elements and you don't rub the collective face of the audience in the unsettling details, your jokes on the topic are more likely to get laughs.

For example, late-night hosts told dozens of jokes about pop singer Michael Jackson after he was arrested for suspected child molestation. Here are just a few examples:

- "Michael Jackson was arrested yesterday. According to the Santa Barbara Police, Michael Jackson is five foot eleven and only weighs a hundred twenty pounds. Michael is able to keep his weight down because he only orders off the children's menu." [*LNWCO*]

- "Police swarmed all over the Neverland Ranch for twelve hours, about sixty investigators, and found a lot of items that needed explaining...like the wedding photo with Lisa Marie Presley." [*LSWDL*]

- "I guess they got Michael on that new law—three tykes and you're out." [*TSWJL*]

How could jokes about an alleged serial child molester have gotten laughs? Because those jokes didn't call up any upsetting mental images of the alleged heinous acts themselves. Also, late-night audiences were already inclined to laugh at Michael Jackson—Jacko!—whose many eccentricities had made him comedy fodder for years.

Contrast Michael Jackson with Jerry Sandusky, the Penn State football coach who was also accused of serial child molestation. Even before Sandusky was found guilty of the crimes, late-night hosts mostly avoided telling jokes about the case. Unlike Michael Jackson, Jerry Sandusky didn't wear a sequined glove and cavort with a pet chimp named Bubbles. No aspect of the Penn State story was even remotely funny.

b) Remember that comedy equals tragedy plus time.

You've probably heard that formula before. It means that even a tragic event can become the topic of jokes if enough time has passed. Months or years after the tragedy the graphic details may be forgotten and the emotional scars may be mostly healed. A host can then tell a joke about the event without the audience thinking "too soon" and turning on him.

For instance, people occasionally die in Amtrak accidents when trains derail, crash, or hurtle off bridges. But as long as a decent amount of time has elapsed since the last train fatality, an audience will laugh at a joke like this one from *TSWJL*: "Amtrak marked their thirty-fifth anniversary today. To celebrate, they had an upside-down cake."

c) Remember that comedy also equals tragedy minus emotional connection.

You probably haven't heard that formula before because I made it up. It means that audiences are more willing to laugh about a tragic event if they have little emotional connection to it.

Of course, anyone's death is sad but a joke like this went over big on one late-night show: "Yesterday the founder of the [company name] movie theater chain passed away. Funeral services will be held today at 11:45 a.m., 2:30 p.m., 5:15, 8:00, and 10:45." The host may have received a letter of complaint from a grieving relative but the audience allowed itself to laugh because the founder had died a natural death, they didn't know him personally, and they had little emotional connection to the event.

This formula even applies to nonhumans. That's why the audience laughed at this joke on *TSWJL*: "Paul, the octopus who predicted the outcome of all those World Cup games, died this week. In lieu of flowers, the family has asked that people send lemon wedges and tartar sauce." Millions of viewers have deep emotional ties to animals like dogs and cats but apparently not to cephalopods.

d) Don't make fun of people for things they can't help.

I don't know who originally said that but it's a good rule of thumb for comedy. In general you want to avoid writing jokes about people's physical deformities, speech impediments, mental illness, birth defects, war wounds, and so on. The audience won't be on your side and they won't laugh.

This rule of thumb even applies to celebrities. In general, celebrities make excellent targets for jokes because audiences are fascinated by them and know everything about them. Plus, the Superiority Theory of Laughter implies that if the audience suddenly feels superior to someone more powerful than they are—like a celebrity—then their laughter will be even louder. But if celebrities are in the news for things they can't help, comedy writers should tread very carefully.

Pop singer Britney Spears is a good example. Over the years she had been the subject of countless late-night jokes about her short-lived marriages and her careless childrearing practices. But after she had her head shaved and was taken to a hospital in an ambulance the late-night hosts backed off. Their perception, and the audience's, was that Britney might have some psychological problem that was temporarily beyond her control.

Contrast Britney with actor Charlie Sheen. Charlie trashed his hotel room and gave interviews that made him sound deranged but late-night hosts never stopped telling jokes like this one from *TSWJL*: "I turned on the TV today and there's nothing but CSI. CSI is on every single channel. Not the crime show...Charlie Sheen Insanity." Hosts didn't let up on Charlie because they felt that the audience would attribute his bizarre behavior not to psychological problems but to substance abuse. That is, the general feeling was that Charlie could, in fact, help himself if he wanted to.

Fat jokes seem to fall in a grey area. Even though people can have unavoidable medical reasons for being overweight, late-night hosts routinely joke about plus-size celebrities like actress Kirstie Alley and New Jersey Governor Chris Christie. Why? Because their audiences let them get away with it.

The four tips above will help you decide how and when to write jokes about problematic but high-profile topics. But how can you know in advance whether your audience will find a joke acceptable? How can you predict whether your head writer will think you're an insensitive jerk for submitting a particular joke? You could first try out any questionable joke on friends of yours whose opinions you trust, but in the end you'll have to make a judgment call. I would say that if you have any doubt about whether a particular joke crosses the line, don't submit it anywhere. Substitute a different joke.

Here's how a typical late-night show handles a tricky topic. The writers submit jokes on the topic that they believe might be acceptable. The host discusses the jokes with the writers who help him assemble the Monologue. If the host decides a joke is worth the risk he'll tell it on the show and see how it does. If the audience reaction is positive, the next night the host might perform two jokes on the topic. If those play well too, the next night he'll do more jokes on the topic, assuming it has remained a major news story. He might even do an entire comedy piece on the topic.

For an inside look at this process in action see Appendix B. It describes how *The Tonight Show with Jay Leno* found comedy in a topic arising from a double homicide—the trial of football player and actor O. J. Simpson.

6. A good topic is something that your host is willing to joke about.

Since the host of a comedy/talk show plays a version of his real self when he performs, it's only natural that he would filter his jokes through his real personality. That's why some topics may be perfectly acceptable to an audience but off-limits to a host. For example, one comedy/talk show host is a vegan and won't tell any jokes involving milk, cheese, or meat. Another host wouldn't perform a joke I wrote about actor Steve Guttenberg because the *Police Academy* star was a neighbor of his.

Unless you're on staff you can't know for sure what the host's taboo topics are. As an outsider all you can do is study the show, note what topics are conspicuously absent from the comedy, and make an educated guess.

To recap, a good topic for a Monologue joke has to meet six conditions. It must be:

1. factually true
2. not intentionally funny
3. only one sentence long
4. a news item that will capture most people's interest
5. something that your audience will let you joke about
6. something that your host is willing to joke about

Let's take another look at the joke topics I listed earlier in this chapter and see how they stack up against that list of conditions. Here are the topics again:

- "Two Oklahoma women were caught shoplifting two thousand dollars' worth of merchandise stuffed in the rolls of their body fat."

- "Charlie Sheen is on the show tonight to talk about his hit TV show *Anger Management*."

- "Denny's has a new sandwich called the Fried Cheese Melt, which comes with deep-fried mozzarella sticks inside a grilled cheese."

- "Bernie Madoff's underpants were sold at an auction."

- "Carl's Jr. is selling a foot-long burger."

- "A company in North Carolina is selling a sixty-dollar IQ test that people can give their dogs."

Each topic is factually true, even the Bernie Madoff one. Each topic is one sentence that isn't trying to be funny. Each topic is most likely acceptable to the host and to the vast majority of Americans. And finally, each topic would probably capture the interest of the typical viewer. Shoplifting merchandise in their body fat? That's disgusting. Crazy Charlie Sheen has a hit show? That's interesting. A cheese-in-cheese sandwich? That's disgusting, too. Somebody bought a con man's underpants? That's weird. A foot-long burger? That's dumb. An IQ test for dogs? That's dumb, too.

Professional Monologue writers zeroed in on those news items out of the thousands available at the time because they knew those items could be joke topics with all six necessary characteristics. Once they picked those topics the writers then took the next step in turning them into Monologue jokes. They thought about angles.

THE ANGLE

The angle is the middle part of the joke. It's the particular direction the joke takes in getting from the topic to the punch line. Like a good topic, a good angle is at most one sentence long; it may even be only a phrase. Returning to my prehistoric analogy, the angle is the equivalent of the observant caveman pantomiming to his family that the rustling grass means a saber-toothed cat is hiding there.

Here again are the sample Monologue jokes I've been analyzing, this time with the angles of the jokes added and underlined.

- "Two Oklahoma women were caught shoplifting two thousand dollars' worth of merchandise stuffed in the rolls of their body fat. <u>The cops said...</u>"

- "Charlie Sheen is on the show tonight to talk about his hit TV show *Anger Management*. <u>In fact, they're adding a new character this year...</u>"

- "Denny's has a new sandwich called the Fried Cheese Melt, which comes with deep-fried mozzarella sticks inside a grilled cheese. <u>It's so good, it'll have all your friends saying...</u>"

- "Bernie Madoff's underpants were sold at an auction. They were from..."

- "Carl's Jr. is selling a foot-long burger. You may know it better as..."

- "A company in North Carolina is selling a sixty-dollar IQ test that people can give their dogs. If you spend sixty bucks on a dog IQ test..."

If you visualize the topic of the joke as a circle (T), the angle of the joke is a line starting from that circle that guides the audience in a specific direction toward a punch line. See the diagram below.

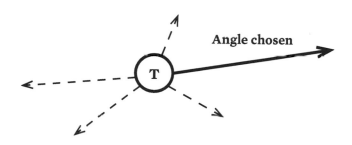

Note that the angle that the writer chooses is only one of many possible angles (represented above by dashed lines) that he could have chosen. Each alternate angle could lead to a different punch line. For example, the angle chosen by the writer of the shoplifting joke means that the joke will be about something "the cops said." The joke won't be about what merchandise was stolen, what happened to the merchandise, or how the women prepared for the crime. But each one of those other angles could be used to write a different joke based on the shoplifting topic, as you'll see below.

In fact, the writer of that shoplifting joke may have submitted several versions of it to the host, each one with a different angle and punch line.

It's perfectly okay for a writer to submit multiple jokes on the same topic. Hosts can be hard to predict, so as long as you think each version of a joke is "pitchable," i.e., worth considering, why not let the host choose between them? Instead of retyping the topic for each version, some writers just type "[Same topic]" followed by the alternate angle and punch line.

So if several possible angles might work with a topic, how does the writer choose which one to use in writing a joke? There are two ways:

- Come up with a punch line for the joke and then write an angle that points from the topic to that punch line. That is, the punch line comes first, then the angle.

- Apply several different angles to the topic and select the angle that leads to the best punch line. That is, the angle comes first, then the punch line.

Either way, a writer can't decide what angle to use in his joke until he decides on a punch line. So let's talk about punch lines.

THE PUNCH LINE

The punch line is the third and last part of the joke, the word or phrase that results in a laugh. According to the Surprise Theory of Laughter, the punch line introduces an incongruity into the joke which—surprise!— turns out to actually make sense. Put another way, the punch line is the surprising revelation of a harmless truth. In my caveman analogy, the punch line is the equivalent of the rustling grass suddenly flattening to reveal not a saber-toothed cat but two monkeys having sex.

So it stands to reason that if a punch line is a surprising revelation of a harmless truth, it must be (1) surprising and (2) true. Let's look at those two requirements more closely.

1. A punch line has to be surprising.

The same Aristotle who proposed the three-act story structure also said, "The secret to humor is surprise." The principle that humor depends on surprise underlies everything from the punch line of a joke to a sight gag in a movie comedy. I'll refer to the surprise principle again and again in this book.

The surprise in a Monologue joke occurs because the topic and angle prime the audience to think in a certain direction but suddenly, incongruously, the punch line veers off in a different direction. Comedy writer Gene Perret points out that a joke can be represented by a line with a sharp turn at the end. Here's my version of the joke diagram:

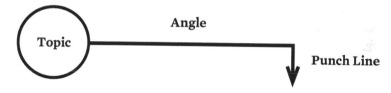

The more abrupt the turn, the more surprising it is to an audience member who is mentally traveling along the line of the angle. And the more surprising the turn is, the bigger the laugh it'll produce. In my prehistoric analogy, the caveman won't roar as loudly when the wind flattens the grass and reveals the monkeys if, moments earlier, he heard the sounds of hot monkey love emanating from behind the grass.

2. A punch line has to be true.

You've probably heard the saying, "It's funny because it's true." It means that a punch line will get a big laugh only if it makes a point that most of the audience agrees with. Jay Leno put it well when he said to me, "Tell people what they already know."

For example, if the punch line of a joke implies that a certain celebrity smokes a lot of marijuana, the audience won't laugh unless they already agree that the celebrity does smoke a lot of marijuana. The caveman won't roar with primitive laughter when the wind flattens the grass if he doesn't believe those really are two monkeys going at it.

The requirement that a Monologue joke must tell people what they already know may seem paradoxical. After all, shouldn't comedy/talk show hosts be irreverent and open up the eyes of the audience to things they may not already see? Isn't it true that, as Joan Rivers was quoted as saying, "A comedian's job is to say the emperor's not wearing any clothes"?

Yes, a comedian should be outspoken, puncturing hypocrisy and taking shots at emperors, venerable institutions, and celebrities. But if the comedian tries to educate his audience they won't laugh. That little boy in Hans Christian Andersen's story who announced that the emperor had no clothes didn't get a laugh at first. Instead, he provoked a discussion among the confused spectators, who still wanted to believe that the emperor was fully clothed. The job of a comedy/talk show host isn't to get his audience to discuss his jokes. His job is to make his audience laugh, immediately and loudly, and to do that he can't say the emperor's not wearing any clothes. Instead, he has to tell the audience something they already know. The audience has to agree that his punch line is true.

Note that the punch line doesn't have to be factually true. The audience only has to accept that it's true for the punch line to get a laugh. For example, when George W. Bush was President most audience members of comedy/talk shows agreed that he was stupid. Even though an IQ test may have revealed that President Bush was, in fact, of above-average intelligence, for comedic purposes most people were willing to accept that he was an idiot. Similarly, when Bill Clinton was President most audience members agreed that he was a sex addict.

The fact that almost everybody, regardless of their political leanings, accepted that those Presidential traits were true made possible the hundreds of Bush-is-dumb and Clinton-is-horny jokes that saturated late night. If the audience had disagreed about whether those characterizations were accurate they would have reacted along party lines. Only about half the audience would have laughed at a Bush-is-dumb or a Clinton-is-horny joke. The other half would have just sat there, silent and annoyed. And a late-night host can't afford to have half his audience not laughing at a joke.

How do you decide what an audience will accept as true? The same way you decide what topics an audience will let you joke about: keep your fingers on the pulse of public sentiment, watch late-night shows to see what their audiences are buying, and first try out any questionable joke on your trusted friends. Then make an educated guess.

Now I'll tell you about six techniques for creating a punch line that's both surprising and true.

THE SIX PUNCH LINE MAKERS

Most of the Monologue jokes on comedy/talk shows have punch lines that were created using one of six techniques. All of these techniques work by manipulating elements of the topic in a surprising way to say something true.

I call these six techniques Punch Line Makers. Here they are, listed roughly in the order of how often they're used, from most frequently to least frequently.

■ PUNCH LINE MAKER #1: Link two associations of the topic.

This technique consists of four steps:

1. Identify two handles of the topic.

As I mentioned, good topics for Monologue jokes grab your attention. The most attention-grabbing elements of the topic, the words or phrases that are most responsible for making the topic interesting, I call the handles. The handles are the details that stand out the most in the topic. They can be people, places, things, or actions. Many topics have two handles. Decide what they are.

Take the topic, "Two Oklahoma women were caught shoplifting two thousand dollars' worth of merchandise stuffed in the rolls of their body fat." The fact that the two people mentioned are women, the fact that they're from Oklahoma, and the fact that the merchandise is worth two thousand dollars don't particularly stand out.

The two elements that do stand out and make this news story interesting and worthy of being a joke topic are the fact that the women were caught shoplifting and the fact that they hid the merchandise in the rolls of their body fat. So the two handles of this topic are "caught shoplifting" and "rolls of body fat."

2. Brainstorm a list of associations for each handle.

An association is something that comes to mind when you (and ideally most other people) think about a particular subject. An association could be a person, place, thing, action, adjective, event, phrase, quotation, expression, or concept, among other things. Come up with a list of associations related to each of the two handles of the topic.

Continuing with our shoplifting joke example, here are lists of some associations that the joke writer might have generated for the two handles:

Caught shoplifting

Crime preparations
Security cameras
Police
Get arrested
"You have the right to remain silent."
Get searched
"We can do this the easy way
                      or the hard way."
Stolen merchandise
Value of merchandise
Collect the evidence
Press charges
Handcuffs
Fingerprinting
Mug shots

Rolls of body fat

Obese
Overeating
Too many calories
Doesn't exercise
Sweaty
Disgusting

Heavyweight
Enormous breasts
Double chins
"Muffin top"
Huge clothes
Clothing too small
Size XXXXL
A plus-size celebrity

3. Link together one association from each list to reveal a truth.

Run the two lists through your head, pairing each association in one list with each association in the other list. Find a couple of associations that you can cleverly link together to make an observation that most people would accept as true. That observation will become your punch line.

In our example, the writer mentally paired the "caught shoplifting" associations with the "rolls of body fat" associations, spinning the lists together like two discs in a combination lock. One pair clicked: "We can do this the easy way or the hard way" and "disgusting." The writer linked the two together to craft the punch line, "We can do this the easy way or the disgusting way." That punch line would strike most people as true because it would be fairly disgusting to have to retrieve merchandise from between somebody's sweaty rolls of bare flab.

4. Write an angle that points from the topic to the punch line.

Write a phrase or sentence that guides the audience logically and efficiently from the topic to the punch line you've just created. That phrase or sentence will be the angle of your joke.

Because the punch line in our example—"We can do this the easy way or the disgusting way"—is something the police would say, the most logical, efficient angle for the joke was, "The cops said..." Putting the topic, angle, and punch line together we get this joke as aired on *Conan*:

> "Two Oklahoma women were caught shoplifting two thousand dollars' worth of merchandise stuffed in the rolls of their body fat. The cops said, 'We can do this the easy way or the disgusting way.'"

Since this punch line was created from two associations that most people would agree relate to the topic, the punch line will strike an audience as true. And since the punch line combines those associations in an unexpected way, it will also surprise the audience. This punch line is both surprising and true and that's why the joke got a laugh.

At this point you might be asking yourself, "Out of all the hundreds of ways to pair up the associations on both lists, how can I possibly find that one pair that will produce a punch line?" The answer is that there isn't just one pair that can produce a punch line. Other pairs of associations can be linked to create other, different punch lines.

For example, below are three other jokes that could be spun out of those same two lists of associations. (These other jokes are represented by dashed-line arrows in the diagram about angles earlier in this chapter.)

- "Two Oklahoma women were caught shoplifting two thousand dollars' worth of merchandise stuffed in the rolls of their body fat. Luckily, they were arrested before they could use the merchandise—thong bikinis." In this case I linked "stolen merchandise" with "clothing too small."

- "Two Oklahoma women were caught shoplifting two thousand dollars' worth of merchandise stuffed in the rolls of their body fat. Even worse, before they stole the merchandise it was worth ten thousand dollars." Here I connected "value of merchandise" and "sweaty."

- "Two Oklahoma women were caught shoplifting two thousand dollars' worth of merchandise stuffed in the rolls of their body fat. To bulk up for the crime they also shoplifted two thousand dollars' worth of burritos from 7-Eleven." This one connects "crime preparations" with "overeating."

As you can see from that exercise, the more associations you can generate for each handle of a topic, the easier it is to create multiple jokes from that topic. I'll discuss this concept in more detail towards the end of this chapter.

You might also be asking yourself whether it's necessary to

Even after years of creating jokes I would still occasionally write down lists of associations. When I was with *LSWDL* I kept written lists of dozens of associations for three particular topics we kept returning to over and over for comedy: President Clinton, Michael Jackson, and New York City. Whenever I learned of a new detail associated with one of the topics—the small room next to the Oval Office where President Clinton had sex with intern Monica Lewinsky, for example—I'd add it to the appropriate list. The lists were a real time-saver when I wrote jokes about those topics, say for a "Top Ten List." Instead of repeatedly combing my brain for the same associations I could just scan the lists.

actually write down the two lists of associations. The answer is no. When the process becomes more instinctive you'll be able to generate a list of associations in your head and try out each one mentally as you think of it. That's the way professional Monologue writers work. But writing down the associations can help you at first while you're still learning these techniques.

Before I move on, take a look at a few more late-night Monologue jokes that were created using Punch Line Maker #1:

- "China started conducting its nationwide census this week. That's right, parents will be required to list each child's age, grade, and occupation." [*LNWJF*] This punch line combines the "China" association "child labor" with the "census" association "occupation."

- "Paris Hilton is banned from the Wynn Hotel and Casino in Las Vegas. I'm not sure what Paris is banned for but I think we can rule out card counting." [*TSWJL*] This punch line links the "Paris Hilton" association "dumb" to the "casino" association "card counting."

- "ABC is developing a new drama about pilots and flight attendants. The show is scheduled to air at 8:00 p.m., so it'll probably get going around 9:43." [*LNWJF*] This punch line combines the "new drama" association "time slot" with the "pilots and flight attendants" association "late departure."

- "Starbucks may start selling beer and wine at its coffee shops. Apparently, Starbucks is having trouble finding sober people willing to pay nine bucks for a cup of coffee." [*Conan*] This punch line links the "Starbucks" association "expensive coffee" to the "beer and wine" association "impaired judgment."

■ PUNCH LINE MAKER #2: Link the topic to pop culture.

More specifically, link an association of the topic to something that the association suggests in popular culture. This is a variation of Punch Line Maker #1. It entails four steps:

1. Identify a handle of the topic.

For example, take the topic "Charlie Sheen is on the show tonight to talk about his hit TV show *Anger Management*." One obvious handle of the topic, a distinctive detail, is *"Anger Management."*

2. Brainstorm a list of associations for the handle.

Continuing with the example, associations for *"Anger Management"* include words and phrases like "rage," "cursing," "short temper," "throwing things," "classes," and "Adam Sandler movie."

3. Try to identify something in pop culture that each association suggests.

Take each association on your list in turn and see if it calls to mind some person, place, or thing in pop culture. If it does, that pop culture reference could be the basis for your punch line. The writer of our sample joke made a connection between "rage" (or one of the other "angry behavior" associations) and Rutgers University basketball coach Mike Rice, who was in the news because of a video that showed him verbally and physically abusing his players. So the punch line became Mike Rice.

4. Write an angle that points from the topic to the punch line.

In our example the punch line, Mike Rice, is a person. Since the topic refers to a TV show, *Anger Management*, the most efficient angle to connect the two was something like, "In fact, they're adding a new character this year..." Putting the topic, angle, and punch line together we get this joke that aired on *TSWJL*:

> "Charlie Sheen is on the show tonight to talk about his hit TV show *Anger Management*. In fact, they're adding a new character this year—Rutgers coach Mike Rice."

So instead of deriving the punch line from two associations of the topic, as you do using Punch Line Maker #1, this technique connects one association of the topic to something in pop culture that isn't even mentioned in the topic. The connection yields a surprising punch line that, because it strikes the audience as true, makes them laugh.

Here are more examples of jokes written using Punch Line Maker #2:

- "A new study showed that heavy drinkers live longer than non-drinkers. Finally, some good news for David Hasselhoff." [*TSWJL*] The handle of the topic is "heavy drinkers." An obvious association of the handle is "heavy drinker." This association suggested the actor David Hasselhoff, who was in the news for a video that showed him trying to eat a hamburger off the floor while roaring drunk.

- "Everybody's excited about college basketball's tournament. You know who is a big fan of the Syracuse Orangemen? John Boehner." [*LSWDL*] The handle of the topic is "college basketball." One association of the handle is the name of a college basketball team—the "Syracuse Orangemen." "Orangemen" suggested Speaker of the House John Boehner, who is well-known for his orange tan.

- "There's a Nerf automatic dart gun that fires sixty darts in twenty seconds. Our kids are so fat now that it takes sixty darts to take them down." [*TSWJL*] One handle is "sixty darts." An association of that is "tranquilizing a large beast," which suggested a punch line about a well-publicized problem in the U.S.—childhood obesity.

- "NBC is creating a new reality dating show that is being described as a cross between *Survivor* and *The Bachelor*. It's called *Who Wants to Date Charlie Sheen?*" [*LNWJF*] One handle is *Survivor*. An association of the handle is "dangerous situations." This association suggested a punch line about actor Charlie Sheen, who had a reputation for violence and had been arrested for assaulting his wife.

Note that the host himself is a part of pop culture so you could also consider using him in the punch line. It's okay—many hosts make jokes at their own expense because they know that self-deprecation can make them even more likeable. Here's an example that Jay Leno told about himself on *TSWJL*: "According to the tabloids, while Brad Pitt was in France, Angelina Jolie was in Los Angeles partying with a handsome hunk. Nonsense...We had one drink!"

■ PUNCH LINE MAKER #3: Ask a question about the topic.

With Punch Line Makers #1 and #2 you create a punch line first and then back into an angle. By contrast, with this technique you start with an angle and then move forward into a punch line. Writing a joke using this technique involves three steps:

1. Ask questions about the topic.

Comedian Judy Carter credits comic Steve Marmel with this suggestion (and I'm paraphrasing here): ask questions about the topic that begin with "who," "what," "when," "where," "why," and "how." In other words, ask questions as if you were a reporter gathering more information about the topic. Each one of those "Five Ws and an H" questions represents a possible angle on the topic.

To illustrate, take this topic: "Denny's has a new sandwich called the Fried Cheese Melt, which comes with deep-fried mozzarella sticks inside a grilled cheese." One question the writer might have asked about that topic is, "What are people saying about the new sandwich?"

2. To get a punch line, answer each question using associations of the topic.

Take each question and try to answer it in a surprising way by using associations of one or two handles of the topic. The funniest one of those answers is your punch line.

Continuing with our example, the writer might have tried to answer the question "What are people saying about the new sandwich?" by using some associations of the handle "Fried Cheese Melt." Possible associations include "high cholesterol," "clogged arteries," "heart attack," and "defibrillator," and a sub-association of "defibrillator," which is "Clear!" Since "Clear!" could answer the question the writer asked, he made that his punch line.

3. Write the angle so it flows naturally from the topic.

Guided by the "Five Ws and an H" question that inspired your punch line, write an angle that's consistent with the content and tone of the topic. An angle that sounds like a natural continuation of the topic will help misdirect the audience and maximize the surprise of the punch line.

Going back to our example, the writer needed an angle that implied that the punch line would reveal what people are saying about the new sandwich. The angle also had to convey enthusiasm, so that the morbid picture painted by the punch line would be a surprising contrast. One angle that does those jobs efficiently is "It's so good, it'll have all your friends saying..." Adding that angle to the topic and punch line yielded the complete joke as aired on *LNWJF*:

> "Denny's has a new sandwich called the Fried Cheese Melt, which comes with deep-fried mozzarella sticks inside a grilled cheese. It's so good, it'll have all your friends saying, 'Clear!'"

Note that more than one "Five Ws and an H" question can lead to a solid punch line. In the case of our example, the topic also invites the question, "What other new item is Denny's selling?" You could answer that question by combining the "Denny's" association "Grand Slam Breakfast" with the "Fried Cheese Melt" association "bypass surgery." This could yield a different joke:

> "Denny's has a new sandwich called the Fried Cheese Melt, which comes with deep-fried mozzarella sticks inside a grilled cheese. It goes really well with their other new item, the Grand Slam Bypass."

Or you could ask the question, "What else does the sandwich come with?" Combine the "Denny's" association "place mat" with the "Fried Cheese Melt" association "write your will" to arrive at a third possible punch line and joke:

> "Denny's has a new sandwich called the Fried Cheese Melt, which comes with deep-fried mozzarella sticks inside a grilled cheese. It also comes with a special place mat and a crayon so you can write your will."

So if the topic is fertile because it has a lot of associations, asking questions can lead to multiple jokes based on the same topic.

Here are more examples of jokes that were written using Punch Line Maker #3:

- "Kia is recalling their logo on their hoods. Not because they injure anyone, it's just that the owners are embarrassed to have it on there." [*TSWJL*] This topic invited the question, "Why is Kia recalling their logo?" The answer, the basis of the punch line, arose from the association of "Kia" in the topic with "embarrassing."

- "A couple in Toronto had their Facebook friends vote on the name of their newborn daughter. So congratulations to the couple and their baby girl, 'Like.'" [*LNWJF*] The obvious question was, "What name did their friends choose?" The punch line came from the association of "Facebook" in the topic with "like."

- "New York City is considering a law to ban people from wearing costumes in Times Square after a man dressed as the Cookie Monster shoved a little boy. In his defense, Cookie Monster said, 'Boy not give up cookie.'" [*LNWJF*] The topic prompts the question, "Why would the man do that?" An association of "Cookie Monster" in the topic is "craves cookies," which is the basis of the punch line.

- "Quentin Tarantino has had to alter *Django Unchained* so it can be shown in China. It will be *Django Escapes the iPad Factory*." [*Conan*] One question you could ask is, "How did Tarantino alter the movie?" An association of "Django Unchained" is "escapes slavery" and an association of "China" is "poor factory conditions." The answer to the question, the punch line, links the two associations.

■ PUNCH LINE MAKER #4: Find a play on words in the topic.

Seventeenth-century poet and playwright John Dryden called the pun the "lowest and most groveling kind of wit." But Dryden didn't have to squeeze out fifty jokes a day five days a week. The fact is that a play on words like a pun can be a very effective device for combining associations in a surprising way to create a punch line.

This technique is similar to Punch Line Maker #1 and entails four steps:

1. Identify two handles of the topic.

For example, take the topic about that notorious Ponzi scheme operator: "Bernie Madoff's underpants were sold at an auction." The two most distinctive elements of the topic—the handles—are "Bernie Madoff" and "underpants."

2. Brainstorm a list of associations for each handle.

In our example, associations of the handle "Bernie Madoff" include "Ponzi scheme," "cheat," "fraud," "arrested," and "scam." Associations of the handle "underpants" include "briefs," "Fruit of the Loom," "elastic waistband," "Jockey," and "tighty-whities."

3. Link together one association from each list to create a play on words.

A play on words can be created if you have one of two basic situations:

- two different words that sound similar
- one word that has two different meanings

Either type of play on words will work for a punch line. Continuing with our example, the "Bernie Madoff" association "fraud" sounds like "fruit" in "Fruit of the Loom." Substituting one word for the other yielded the play on words—and the punch line—"Fraud of the Loom."

4. Write an angle that points from the topic to the punch line.

"Fraud of the Loom" is supposedly a brand of underpants so the most effective angle would lead the audience to expect that the punch line will answer the question, "What company made the underpants?" The angle "They were from…" would do that job efficiently, so adding that to the topic and punch line gave the writer on *LSWDL* the final version of the joke:

> "Bernie Madoff's underpants were sold at an auction.
> They were from 'Fraud of the Loom.'"

Here are more examples of jokes with punch lines created using Punch Line Maker #4:

- "An airline in Sweden plans to host the first-ever in-flight gay wedding in December. The entire flight crew is excited for the event, although the right wing isn't happy about it." [*LNWJF*] One association of the handle "airline" is "right wing." "Right wing" is also an association of the handle "gay," since right-wing politicians are traditionally opposed to gay marriage. This double meaning of "right wing" gives the punch line its surprise.

- "In high school Kim Jong-un starred in a production of the musical *Grease*. That's also where Kim met his first wife, Olivia Newton Jong." [*Conan*] The handle "Kim Jong-un" has the association "Jong." The handle *Grease* is associated with the actress "Olivia

Newton John." "Jong" sounds like "John," so the writer mashed the two names together for a play on words in the punch line.

- "The folks at Google are testing a car that drives itself, without a human. You thought it was bad when your computer crashed." [TSWJL] "Crash," with two different meanings, is an association of both the handle "Google" and the handle "car."

- "Scientists in Utah have discovered a new species of dinosaur believed to have the most horns of any dinosaur in history. Experts called it the horniest dinosaur ever—and then Larry King said, 'Well, I had a good run.'" [LNWJF]

This last joke demonstrates a variation on the play-on-words technique. In this case the writer started with the handles "dinosaur" and "horniest" and then came up with different meanings for both those words, namely "out-of-date" and "lustful." Turning to pop culture for a celebrity who's commonly considered to be out-of-date and lustful produced Larry King, the TV interviewer who has been in show business for over fifty years and has been married eight times. So the writer used Larry King and a double play on words to arrive at the punch line. This joke shows that it's possible to blend two Punch Line Makers—in this case #2 and #4—when you're writing a joke.

■ PUNCH LINE MAKER #5: Visualize the topic.

The previous technique involved a play on words. This technique involves what I call a play on images. It consists of three steps:

1. Form a mental picture of the topic.

Base your mental picture on a handle or handles of the topic. Take the topic, "Carl's Jr. is selling a foot-long burger," for example. A handle of the topic, a detail that makes the topic interesting, is "foot-long burger." So imagine what a foot-long burger looks like.

2. Write a punch line about a different perspective on that mental picture.

A different perspective on the mental picture is a different way of looking at it. You can get that different perspective in one of two ways:

- Think of something different that resembles the mental picture.
- Exaggerate some association of the mental picture. That is, think of associations of the mental picture and take one to an extreme.

In our example, the truth is that a foot-long burger probably resembles a meatloaf. So the writer based the punch line on the idea that a foot-long burger is a meatloaf.

3. Write an angle that points from the topic to the punch line.

For the punch line in our example, the writer needed an angle that would lead the audience to expect an answer to the question, "What's that burger called?" Adding the angle "You may know it better as..." to the topic and punch line resulted in this joke as aired on *LSWDL*:

> "Carl's Jr. is selling a foot-long burger. You may know it better as a meatloaf."

Here are more jokes with punch lines that were constructed using Punch Line Maker #5:

- "The French Senate has outlawed the burka, giving hope to U.S. lawmakers that one day soon, we will outlaw the Snuggie."

[*TSWJL*] If you visualize the handle "burka" in the topic you imagine a cloak that covers your whole body. This cloak looks like a different, but also controversial, garment—a Snuggie. The punch line points out that resemblance and the angle smoothly continues the topic's theme of a government outlawing things.

- "Tom Cruise made his first public comments about his divorce from Katie Holmes. He said, 'I didn't see it coming.' Apparently Katie kept her divorce papers on top of the refrigerator." [*Conan*] The writer visualized Tom not being able to see something. One association of Tom Cruise is "really short" so the writer exaggerated that and imagined Tom being so short that he couldn't even see the top of a refrigerator. That gave the writer the different perspective he used in the punch line.

- "*Time* magazine is now ranking the best tweets of the year and, according to *Time*, the best tweet for 2010 was written by John McCain. Experts say it's even more impressive because McCain thought he was opening his garage door." [*Conan*] The writer visualized McCain tapping away at a smartphone. One association of McCain is "really old" so the writer apparently imagined McCain as being so exaggeratedly old and feebleminded that he's mistaking his smartphone for something it resembles—his garage door opener. That different perspective became the punch line.

- "It's rumored that Shaq and his girlfriend are engaged. When he proposed, Shaq got down on one knee and said, 'Hey, you down there. Will you marry me?'" [*LNWJF*] Visualizing the engagement of basketball player Shaquille O'Neal produced a mental picture of him proposing on one knee. Shaq is really tall, over seven feet. Exaggerating that association led to an image of the kneeling but still giant Shaq towering over his average-sized fiancée. The punch line grew out of that different perspective.

It's okay to take your mental pictures to extremes. For instance, when Pringles Potato Chips first came out with a new version containing a substance called olestra, Jay Leno told a joke on *TSWJL* that went something like, "A warning on the new fat-free Pringles Potato Chips says that they may cause anal leakage. Finally you have a use for that can." Apparently the writer imagined a naked guy with uncontrolled diarrhea standing there with a can of Pringles and then adjusted that mental picture to have the guy position the can under his rear end. And it turns out that the joke might have been even more nauseating. Some years later I told it to somebody who had actually been involved in launching Pringles with olestra. The person told me that the FDA was very close to requiring that the Pringles label warn against "fecal seepage." But Jay might have drawn the line at that wording.

■ PUNCH LINE MAKER #6: State the obvious about the topic.

Do that by providing the obvious answer to an obvious question suggested by the topic. This technique leads to punch lines that get laughs because they're surprisingly direct. The audience expects the punch line to make a sharp turn the way punch lines usually do but instead, unexpectedly, it charges straight ahead. The technique, which is related to Punch Line Maker #3, involves three steps:

1. Ask an obvious question suggested by the topic.

That is, ask the "Five Ws and an H" question that you think is most likely to pop into the heads of audience members when they hear the topic.

To illustrate, take this topic: "A company in North Carolina is selling a sixty-dollar IQ test that people can give their dogs." The audience would probably ask themselves, "Who would buy that?"

2. Write a punch line based on the obvious answer to that question.

Think of how the audience would most likely answer that obvious question. That is, think of the answer that the audience would consider to be the most obvious. That answer, in some form, could be the basis of a punch line.

Continuing with our example, the audience would probably agree that a sixty-dollar IQ test for dogs is a waste of money. Therefore they would probably respond to the question "Who would buy that?" with the answer, "An idiot." That suggests that the punch line should be some clever way of saying "an idiot," like "someone who should take an IQ test."

3. Write an angle that points from the topic to the punch line.

Write an angle that implies that the punch line will answer the obvious question suggested by the topic. In the case of our example that obvious question is, "Who would buy that?" so the angle should mean, "Here's who would buy that." Adding an angle like that to the topic and punch line led to this joke as aired on *LNWJF*:

> "A company in North Carolina is selling a sixty-dollar IQ test that people can give their dogs. If you spend sixty bucks on a dog IQ test, maybe <u>you</u> should take that IQ test."

Here are more examples of Punch Line Maker #6 in action:

- "The tax cut deal means tax cuts for the rich and benefits for the unemployed. If you work for a living, you're screwed." [*TSWJL*]

The topic is "The tax cut deal means tax cuts for the rich and benefits for the unemployed." An obvious question suggested by that topic is, "What if you aren't rich or unemployed?" The obvious answer in the minds of the audience, most of whom work for a living and think their taxes are too high, would be, "You're screwed." So that becomes the punch line.

- "In October, a monument will be unveiled in South Carolina honoring the band Hootie and the Blowfish. No word yet as to why." [*LNWJF*] An obvious question about that monument erected in South Carolina is, "Why?" Most likely few people in the audience are big fans of Hootie and the Blowfish so the audience's answer to that question would be, "Who the heck knows?" The punch line reflects that answer.

- "A rattlesnake handler in Texas is recovering in the hospital after being bitten for the twelfth time. If you're a rattlesnake handler and you've been bitten twelve times, are you really a handler? Aren't you just a guy who doesn't know how to pick up snakes?" [*TSWJL*] The topic suggests the obvious question, "How could a rattlesnake handler get bitten twelve times?" The audience would probably answer, "He couldn't." And that's basically what the punch line says: that guy is no rattlesnake handler.

- "A man is trying to organize zeppelins, blimps, and other dirigibles for a race around the world. This would be a huge story if it was 1907." [*TSWJL*] This topic raises the obvious question, "Who would be interested in that weird race?" The answer in the audience's minds would probably be, "People who are really excited by zeppelins, blimps, and dirigibles," namely people living in the early 1900s. The angle and punch line reflect that answer.

PUTTING THE PUNCH LINE MAKERS TO WORK

You now have six techniques for creating punch lines. If you're trying to write a joke on a particular topic, which technique should you use? Start with Punch Line Maker #1 and if that doesn't seem to be getting you anywhere, go down the list and try the other techniques. See which one results in the funniest punch line. If none of the Punch Line Makers yields a winner within a reasonable amount of time, don't keep banging your head against the topic. Maybe it isn't as fertile as it seemed to be. Move on to another promising topic.

What makes a topic fertile for joke writing? As I suggested earlier in this chapter, the more associations a topic has the more fertile it will tend to be. That's because, as you've probably noticed, the associations of a topic play a huge role in creating punch lines based on that topic. A topic with two handles, each of which has a lot of associations, offers many possible combinations that could spark a punch line. A topic like that might give you the feeling joke writers often have that "there has to be a joke in there somewhere."

So as you're poring over the day's news, direct your brainstorming efforts first at topics that not only have all six characteristics of being a good topic but also have a couple of handles with a lot of associations. After you've gained some experience, fertile topics like that will start to leap out at you from the vast sea of news items.

The joke-writing process may seem mechanical at first but as you practice the techniques in this chapter over and over they'll become more instinctive. You'll train your brain to automatically generate and weigh various possibilities until a punch line clicks into place. In other words, you'll begin to think like a professional Monologue writer.

THE ROUGH DRAFT

Okay, you've picked a topic and you're building it out with an angle and a punch line. Jot down the parts of the joke as you put it together so you don't forget them. Don't worry about how sloppy the wording is because you can tidy that up later. I tend to scribble down the basics of a new joke using pencil and paper, subconsciously giving the creative, right side of my brain permission to run free. When all the raggedy pieces are lined up in front of you and doing basically what you want them to do, you have the rough draft of a Monologue joke.

SUMMARY

A prospective writer for a comedy/talk show has to know how to write topical Monologue jokes because:

- On some comedy/talk shows every writer is asked to contribute to every comedy piece, including the Monologue.
- Monologue-type jokes are the main ingredients of many other pieces on a comedy/talk show.
- Most of the techniques used to write Monologue jokes also apply to writing jokes outside of comedy/talk shows.

Writing Monologue jokes is easier when you know the formula. It starts with the three parts of a joke: the topic, the angle, and the punch line.

The topic—It's a concise statement of the news item that the joke is based on. A good topic has six characteristics:

1. A good topic is factually true.
2. A good topic is not intentionally funny.
3. A good topic is only one sentence long.

1. A good topic is a news item that will capture most people's interest. Here are four signs that the news item will do that:
   - The media are covering it extensively.
   - Even people who aren't media professionals are talking about it.
   - You yourself have an emotional reaction to it.
   - At least one media outlet carries it as Odd News.
5. A good topic is something that your audience will let you joke about. You may be able to write acceptable jokes about an otherwise objectionable topic if you:
   - Avoid calling to mind the most disturbing aspects of the topic.
   - Remember that comedy equals tragedy plus time.
   - Remember that comedy also equals tragedy minus emotional connection.
   - Don't make fun of people for things they can't help.
6. A good topic is something that your host is willing to joke about.

The angle—It's the middle part of the joke and sets the particular direction the joke will take in getting from the topic to the punch line. It's at most one sentence long.

Any given topic can spawn more than one joke, each with a different angle. Sometimes you create the punch line first and then construct an angle to get to that punch line. Other times you try different angles first and see which inspires the funniest punch line.

The punch line—It's the word or phrase at the end of the joke that results in a laugh. The punch line must be surprising. It must also be true in the sense that the audience must agree with what the punch line is saying.

The six Punch Line Makers allow you to create punch lines that are both surprising and true. They are:

- Punch Line Maker #1: Link two associations of the topic.
- Punch Line Maker #2: Link the topic to pop culture.
- Punch Line Maker #3: Ask a question about the topic.
- Punch Line Maker #4: Find a play on words in the topic.
- Punch Line Maker #5: Visualize the topic.
- Punch Line Maker #6: State the obvious about the topic.

To create a punch line based on any given topic, start with Punch Line Maker #1 and go down the list. Your task will be easier if your topic is fertile, that is, has a lot of associations. Once you've worked out the three parts of your joke, jot them down in a rough draft.

Now it's time to fire up the left side of your brain, the more analytical side. If you used pencil and paper for your rough draft you may want to switch to a computer for this step, to signal to your brain that it needs to start thinking a different way. You still have work to do because the rough draft of a joke is like a rough diamond. It's valuable as it is, but to maximize its value you have to cut it a certain way, minimize its flaws, and polish it to a sparkling brilliance. Only then will it have the powerful impact on people that you want it to have. You need to edit your joke. I'll show you how in the next chapter.

6

HOW TO EDIT JOKES

L ET'S TALK ABOUT basketball for a second. If you're playing in a professional basketball game it's not enough just to have possession of the ball. You have to put that ball in the basket. You have to score. And to do that you need top-notch ball handling skills.

Scoring with a joke is a little like sinking a basket. It's not enough just to have a rough draft of the joke, although that's an essential first step. You then need to move that joke past distractions, confusion, boredom, and other obstacles in the audience's brains to get a laugh. To do that with a joke you don't need ball handling expertise; you need word handling expertise. You need the ability to shift words around in a joke, substitute words, cut words, and all in precisely the right way. In other words, you need pro-level joke editing skills.

In this chapter you'll learn time-tested editing techniques for making jokes as funny as they can possibly be. I'll describe these techniques using topical Monologue jokes as examples but they also apply to editing any jokes you write for a comedy/talk show, like the jokes in a Desk

Piece or a Story Sketch. In fact, I recommend using these all-purpose joke-polishing techniques whenever you write comedy in any context.

I call these twelve editing techniques Joke Maximizers.

THE TWELVE JOKE MAXIMIZERS

These techniques are the joke editing equivalents of the behind-the-back, between-the-legs, and cross-over dribbling moves in basketball. Most of these Joke Maximizers work by helping to maximize the surprise produced by the punch line.

■ JOKE MAXIMIZER #1: Shorten as much as possible.

As Shakespeare wrote, "Brevity is the soul of wit." So make the joke as short as you absolutely can. Try hard to limit the topic and the angle to one sentence each as I recommended in the previous chapter. Eliminate all unnecessary words from the joke, even all unnecessary syllables, until any more cutting would hurt the joke. A tight, economical joke will do the following:

- It will keep the audience from getting bored and possibly getting annoyed that you're taking too long to get to the punch line. An annoyed audience member whose attention is drifting will be less likely to laugh.

- It will keep the audience from getting distracted by words that aren't essential to the joke and will keep them focused on precisely the words that are essential.

- It will maximize the surprise of the punch line—and the size of the laugh—by not giving the audience time to "get ahead of" the joke and to guess the punch line prematurely.

As an example of how shortening a joke can make it much funnier, consider this hypothetical rough draft:

> "Last Tuesday, the official newspaper of the Vatican, *L'Osservatore Romano*, published an editorial in which chief editor Raimondo Manzini condemned the sport of boxing. The scathing editorial appeared in the newspaper the day after the Vatican lost fifty thousand Euros betting on the Corrales-Castillo fight in Las Vegas, Nevada."

There's a great joke in there somewhere but it's obscured by a thicket of unnecessary verbiage. With all superfluous words and syllables pruned away, here's the joke as it was actually delivered on *LNWCO*:

> "This week, the official newspaper of the Vatican condemned the sport of boxing. This was after the Vatican lost a bundle on the Corrales-Castillo fight."

See how shortening the joke pumps up the laugh? You might ask yourself whether the joke should be shortened even more by eliminating the words "this week." I'd say no. I'd keep those two words in the joke to subtly reassure the audience that the incident actually took place; you may remember that I mentioned adding details like that in the previous chapter, where I discussed how important it is for a joke topic to be factually true.

■ JOKE MAXIMIZER #2: End on the laugh trigger.

Decide which word (or possibly two adjacent words) in your punch line is the most unexpected—the most surprising—in the context of the joke. This word will do the best job of activating the laugh so I call it the laugh trigger. Now reword your joke if necessary to put the laugh trigger at the very end. Doing that will maximize the joke's potential by making it harder for the audience to predict where the joke is ultimately going.

As an example, let's look at a joke from *LNWJF*:

> "This weekend is the New York City Marathon, the one race in America that has yet to be insulted by Mel Gibson."

The audience laughs because they agree that actor Mel Gibson has made racist comments. "Mel Gibson" is the laugh trigger because those are the two most unexpected words in the punch line "has yet to be insulted by Mel Gibson." Until the audience hears "Mel Gibson" they don't have enough information to laugh, so it's hard for them to get ahead of the joke. That's why those two words were put at the very end.

For comparison, let's move the laugh trigger away from the end of the joke. I'll reword the punch line to put it into the active voice, which is usually preferable to the passive voice in any kind of writing. The joke might go like this:

> "This weekend is the New York City Marathon, the one race in America that Mel Gibson hasn't insulted yet."

Not quite as funny, right? The reason is because when the audience hears "race" and then "Mel Gibson" they can get a little ahead of the joke. They can guess that the punch line will involve a play on words about Mel Gibson's perceived hostility towards people of other races. That means when the joke ends the surprise won't be as big as it could be and the laugh will be softer.

Sometimes it's hard to decide which word in the joke would make the best laugh trigger if you have a couple of candidates. In that case, write the joke both ways, read both versions aloud, and see which sounds more effective. Like many situations in comedy writing, it's a judgment call.

■ JOKE MAXIMIZER #3: Backload the topic.

That is, make sure the topic begins with the least important information and ends with the most important information. You want the least essential words in the topic to be out of the way before they can distract the audience from the meat of the joke. And you want the most essential words in the topic to be as close as possible to the angle and the punch line that depend on them. That way, those words will be fresh in the audience's minds when the joke really needs them. For example, take this joke from *LNWJF*:

> "A company in Seattle just came out with a new bacon-flavored soda. So if you love the taste of bacon and you love the taste of soda, you're about to realize how much you love them separately."

The least important information in the topic—"A company in Seattle"—is at the very beginning of the joke. Those details have some importance because they give the news story the ring of truth but they're not as essential to the joke as the information "a new bacon-flavored soda," which ends the topic. The joke would be slightly less funny if the most important information in the topic came at the beginning, like this:

> "A new bacon-flavored soda was just introduced by a company in Seattle. So if you love the taste of bacon and you love the taste of soda, you're about to realize how much you love them separately."

■ JOKE MAXIMIZER #4: Make everything clear.

Every part of the joke must be easy to understand. That means your words and sentence structure have to be simple, your meaning has to be unambiguous, and your logic has to be easy to follow. If the audience can't immediately figure out what you're trying to say, they'll be thinking instead of laughing. To see what I mean, take this joke from *LNWJF*:

> "Disney just signed a deal to build a Disneyland theme park in Shanghai. It's just like ours, only in China, Goofy and Pluto are items at the concession stand."

That joke is clear. But what if we took one word out of the punch line so it read, "It's just like ours, only in China, Goofy and Pluto are at the concession stand." Does that mean that employees in Goofy and Pluto costumes work at the concession stand? Does it mean that the concession stand serves dog meat? In general, shorter is better, but that shorter punch line would confuse the audience and they wouldn't laugh as hard.

Another reason a joke might be unclear is that the audience isn't familiar with something referred to in the joke—a "reference." Always keep in mind your audience, and what they probably know, when choosing your references. For example, *Late Night with Jimmy Fallon* tended to attract younger viewers so they might have gotten a reference to, say, a new app for the iPhone that viewers of *Late Show with David Letterman* might not get.

■ JOKE MAXIMIZER #5: Don't telegraph the punch line.

That is, don't use words in the topic and angle of the joke that might suggest to the audience what the punch line is. Telegraphing the punch line will weaken the surprise and, therefore, the laugh. Take this joke from *Conan* about a certain reality TV star:

> "Kim Kardashian, who is five months pregnant, reportedly wants to give birth by C-section. In other words, even in childbirth, Kim is determined to avoid any kind of labor."

That joke works. Now consider this version:

> "Kim Kardashian, who is five months pregnant, reportedly wants to give birth by C-section. That makes sense. She doesn't like to work so of course she'd want to avoid labor."

The wordplay punch line—"labor"—is telegraphed by the word "work" in the angle, so the resulting laugh wouldn't be as big. If you think you might be telegraphing the punch line just reword the joke.

■ JOKE MAXIMIZER #6: Make the punch line parallel.

Sometimes your punch line will be a variation of a word or phrase that appears in the topic or angle. In that case, make sure your punch line copies the structure of that word or phrase as closely as possible. This parallelism will make the punch line more surprising—Hey, it sounds like that other part of the joke!—and therefore funnier. For instance, here's a joke from *LNWJF*:

> "In an effort to compete with Amazon, Walmart is letting customers buy a product online and then pick it up in the store. The company says it's all the convenience of shopping online without any of the convenience of shopping online."

The phrase "any of the convenience of shopping online" in the punch line is parallel to the phrase "all the convenience of shopping online" in the angle; the two phrases share most of the same words in the same order. The joke wouldn't be quite as funny without the parallelism, say if it were worded like this:

> "In an effort to compete with Amazon, Walmart is letting customers buy a product online and then pick it up in the store. The company says it's all the convenience of shopping online without actually being convenient."

Even though the reworded version is a little shorter, which is usually better, adding the extra words to create the parallelism in the longer version is worth it.

■ JOKE MAXIMIZER #7: Use stop consonants, alliteration, and assonance.

If a punch line has any or all of those three features it will be a little funnier, so choose each individual word carefully. Here's a closer look at each feature:

Stop Consonants—A stop, or "hard," consonant is a consonant in which the flow of air through your vocal cords stops completely. Stop consonants include B, D, G, K, P, and T. Of those, K is traditionally regarded as the funniest consonant. I don't know why; it just is.

A few examples: Stop consonants make it slightly funnier for a "guy" to come into a bar with a "duck" than for a "man" to come into a bar with a "hen." In a "Top Ten List" on *LSWDL*, "The Buick is not all the way in the garage" was a funnier entry than "The Chevy is not all the way in the garage" would have been. And in that joke from *LNWCO* that I mentioned earlier in this chapter, "the Corrales-Castillo fight" is funnier than "the Ramos-Lopez fight" would have been.

Maybe K and other stop consonants help induce laughter because they create tiny surprises within a word. Air is flowing through your vocal cords when the stop consonant suddenly shuts it off, breaking the pattern. Or the stop consonant suddenly, surprisingly, starts the air flowing with a little burst. Just a theory.

Alliteration—Alliteration is the repetition of consonant sounds, usually beginning consonant sounds, in nearby words. For example, a sketch on *LNWCO* was named "Pierre Bernard's Recliner of Rage," repeating the R sound. "Pierre Bernard's Recliner of Fury" wouldn't have been quite as funny.

Assonance—Assonance is the repetition of similar vowel sounds in nearby words. For example, *LNWCO* aired a sketch featuring a character named Preparation H Raymond. Repeating the long A sound of "Preparation" and "H" in "Raymond" makes the character's name slightly funnier than, say, Preparation H Richard (since "Richard" doesn't have the long A sound).

Why do alliteration and assonance seem to boost the comedy? It could be because in everyday conversation nearby words aren't usually connected by alliteration or assonance. So when a joke, especially a punch line, does contain words that are unexpectedly connected that way, that extra little surprise gooses the laughter.

Here's an example from *LNWJF* of all three linguistic features in action in the same punch line:

> "A man from California was arrested for trying to smuggle piranhas into the country. And you thought it was scary hiding heroin in your rectum."

"Hiding heroin" contains the alliteration of the repeated H. "Scary," "heroin," and "rectum" repeat the R and have the assonance of the initial short E sound. "Rectum" includes the stop consonant T and both "rectum" and "scary" share the stop consonant K. Now that's precision word selection for maximum impact. See how much power is drained out of that punch line if we strip away most of those linguistic comedy helpers like this: "And you thought it was a challenge stashing heroin up your rear end."

■ JOKE MAXIMIZER #8: Wildly exaggerate.

Ridiculously overstating some element of a punch line can make the punch line more surprising and therefore funnier. Even if the audience has some idea of where the joke is going, an unexpectedly over-the-top exaggeration at the end will help get a bigger laugh out of them. Wild exaggeration can also strengthen a joke by making the point of the punch line perfectly and immediately clear. For example, here's a joke from *Conan*:

> "Costco will no longer sell Apple products in their stores. Apparently nobody wants a hundred-and-twenty-four-pack of iPads."

The wild exaggeration is, of course, the idea that Costco would be selling one hundred and twenty four iPads in one package. Note that the exaggeration has to be excessive to be effective. That joke wouldn't work as well if the exaggeration in the punch line were slighter, like this:

> "Costco will no longer sell Apple products in their stores. Apparently nobody wants a twelve-pack of iPads."

It's true that the appeal of a twelve-pack of iPads would be limited but the audience would have to do some thinking to figure that out; maybe a small business would buy a dozen. The wild exaggeration of the hundred-and-twenty-four-pack makes the punch line instantly clear, and, as Joke Maximizer #4 reminds us, a joke has to be completely clear to work.

■ JOKE MAXIMIZER #9: Get specific.

That is, use specific words in your punch line instead of general ones. Specific words help paint a detailed picture in the audience's minds when they get to the punch line. This makes the punch line funnier because the unexpected vividness of the picture is surprising, like a slap to the brain. For example, take this joke from *LNWJF*:

> "Rihanna revealed this week that she texts Lady Gaga before major events to make sure they don't wear the same outfit. Can you imagine that conversation? It's like, 'Hey, Gaga. Are you wearing the blue satin dress tonight or are you gonna wear the cold-cut platter from Blimpie?'"

(You may remember that pop singer Lady Gaga once appeared on an awards show wearing a dress made of raw meat.) The specificity of "cold-cut platter from Blimpie" is startling and therefore funny. (The phrase is made even funnier by that barrage of stop consonants—K, D, T, P, and B.) The punch line would be much weaker if it ended with more general words, like this:

> "Rihanna revealed this week that she texts Lady Gaga before major events to make sure they don't wear the same outfit. Can you imagine that conversation? It's like, 'Hey, Gaga. Are you wearing the blue satin dress tonight or are you gonna wear some meat from the deli?'"

■ JOKE MAXIMIZER #10: Use the Rule of Three.

The Rule of Three states that you can often make a punch line funnier by constructing it as a list of exactly three items, with the third item being the laugh trigger. The comic triple—unfunny item, unfunny item, funny item—is as old as time, almost a cliché. But comedy writers routinely use it because it helps build surprise into a punch line.

How does it do that? The first two items in the list get the audience thinking in a specific direction, the same way that two points determine a line. The audience expects that the joke will continue along in the same direction until the third item, which contains the laugh trigger, suddenly and surprisingly breaks the pattern.

Why couldn't the list consist of four or more items? Because only three items are needed to establish and then break a pattern. Any additional items are unnecessary so you should omit them to keep the joke as short as possible (per Joke Maximizer #1).

Here's an example from *LNWCO* of the Rule of Three in action:

> "The man who invented LSD is celebrating his hundredth birthday tomorrow. The man plans to spend his birthday surrounded by friends, family, and a nine-foot-tall unicorn."

The joke would be slightly less funny with a fourth item tacked onto the list, like this:

> "The man who invented LSD is celebrating his hundredth birthday tomorrow. The man plans to spend his birthday surrounded by friends, family, neighbors, and a nine-foot-tall unicorn."

Note that the Rule of Three applies not just to Monologue jokes but also to a series of items ending any other kind of joke. For example, when I cover multiple-choice Text Quizzes in Chapter 7 you'll see that the ideal number of possible answers in a quiz question joke is three, the third being the punch line.

■ JOKE MAXIMIZER #11: Don't be too on-the-nose.

A joke that's too "on-the-nose" is one in which the punch line is stated too directly. If a punch line is stated too directly it can seem a little obvious and therefore a little unsurprising to the audience. Rewriting an on-the-nose punch line to make it more indirect can make a joke funnier without actually changing its meaning. For example, take this joke:

> "The NFL fined Titans defensive coordinator Chuck Cecil forty thousand dollars for flipping officials off on Sunday. When Cecil was asked to comment on the fine, he said, 'I flipped off the NFL, too.'"

Something seems a little soft about the joke, right? That's because the punch line is too on-the-nose. But you could rewrite the punch line and get the version that actually aired on *LNWJF*:

> "The NFL fined Titans defensive coordinator Chuck Cecil forty thousand dollars for flipping officials off on Sunday. When Cecil was asked to comment on the fine, he said, 'Well, let's just say it's up to eighty thousand dollars.'"

It's basically the same joke as before, just less on-the-nose and therefore funnier.

■ JOKE MAXIMIZER #12: Consider an act-out.

An act-out punch line consists of dialogue supposedly being said by somebody referred to in the topic or angle of the joke. In other words, the host delivers the act-out punch line as a character mentioned earlier in the joke. For instance, the Lady Gaga joke I used as an example of Joke Maximizer #9 has an act-out punch line; Jay delivers the line as if he were pop singer Rihanna.

Writing the punch line as an act-out can give it a little more impact because hearing the host pretend to be a completely different person is a fun surprise. Here's another example, from *TSWJL*:

> "University of Chicago researchers have found that sleeping more can help you lose weight. How many guys are going to jump on this one? 'Honey, I'm not sitting on the couch all weekend, I'm dieting.'"

The angle of the joke mentions "guys" and the punch line has Jay pretending to be one of those guys. Note that this act-out punch line could easily be replaced with one that isn't acted out, like this:

> "University of Chicago researchers have found that sleeping more can help you lose weight. How many guys are going to jump on this one? Now they can sit on the couch all weekend and tell their wives they're dieting."

The joke still works but doesn't have quite the same impact.

So those are the twelve Joke Maximizers, the word handling skills you need to help you sink a joke in an audience member's brain and score a laugh. Before you consider a joke finished, apply as many Joke Maximizers to it as you can. Focus on these editing techniques and practice using them over and over as you craft your jokes. Soon they'll become instinctive.

FIVE QUALITY TESTS FOR COMEDY

Now that you've written the rough draft of a joke and polished it into a sparkling gem it's ready to be presented to the world, right? Not quite yet. First, subject your joke to some Comedy Quality Tests to make sure you really want to attach your name to it. You should run these tests not just on Monologue jokes but on any piece of comedy you write for public consumption.

Here are the five tests:

■ COMEDY QUALITY TEST #1: Read the joke out loud.

Reading a joke aloud, the way you're asking a host to, is a very effective way to reveal any flaws. Test drive your joke with your mouth the way autoworkers test drive a new car before it leaves the factory. Does your tongue trip over an awkward word or phrase? Rewrite it. Is a word repeated in the joke unnecessarily? Replace the word with a synonym so the audience doesn't get distracted. Does a sentence run on too long? Shorten it or split it into two sentences.

■ COMEDY QUALITY TEST #2: Imagine the host delivering the joke.

Does it sound like the kind of joke the host would deliver, worded the way he would prefer to say it? That is, is the joke in character for the host? If the joke somehow seems wrong for him, revise it or drop it.

■ COMEDY QUALITY TEST #3: Imagine the audience hearing the joke.

Is there a chance the joke might offend a lot of audience members or strike them as unfair or too harsh? Even though celebrities make excellent targets for comedy you don't want to make fun of them for things they can't help. If it's a political joke, does it take sides in a way that's likely to alienate a large segment of your audience? Revise or eliminate any questionable joke to keep the audience (including your readers) on your side.

Even professional writers sometimes find it difficult to predict audience reaction. An article by Ramsey Ess on the Splitsider website describes how staff writer Louis C. K. convinced Conan O'Brien to perform a questionable joke for the *LNWCO* Desk Piece "Actual Items." The joke described some antique coins as being "so old you can buy slaves with them." The audience booed Conan for that one.

■ COMEDY QUALITY TEST #4: Try the joke out on other people.

Professional comedy writers often read jokes to each other and ask, "Is this funny?" so why shouldn't you? Ask some friends whose opinions you trust what they think of your joke.

Even some hosts test their jokes before performing them on national television. Jay Leno often tried out Monologue jokes on members of the *Tonight* show staff and crew. And an article by Rachael Mason on the Splitsider website describes how Jimmy Fallon, before every taping of *LNWJF*, rehearsed his Monologue in front of a small group of tourists brought into the studio, to see which jokes worked best.

■ COMEDY QUALITY TEST #5: Ask yourself if the joke seems familiar.

If your joke feels similar to a lot of other jokes you've heard, it could be perceived as too easy or too "hacky" (that is, written by a hack). Don't submit that joke. You don't want to get a reputation as a lazy writer who regurgitates stale comedy. Aim for fresh topics, unexpected angles on those topics, and punch lines that don't rely on predictable combinations of associations.

What if you're not sure whether your joke will seem hacky? Apply the other Comedy Quality Tests to it and then use your judgment. You may think the audience is sick of jokes about, say, how many heart attacks former Vice President Dick Cheney has had. But then you'll see the host you're writing for deliver yet another joke along those lines. In that case, if you really want to, you can probably take a chance and submit your own Dick Cheney heart attack joke.

Subject your jokes to those five Comedy Quality Tests and you'll have done all you can to make sure your material is worthy of appearing on a late-night television show.

MOVING BEYOND MONOLOGUE JOKES

Now you know how to write a joke for the topical Monologue on a comedy/talk show. Start with a rough draft, polish it, and then test it. The process I've described may seem formulaic but these joke-writing techniques and guidelines work. They're used every day—consciously or subconsciously—by professional writers. To prove it to yourself, write down some jokes you hear in a late-night Monologue, or find them online by searching on "late night jokes." Dissect those jokes like the little frogs they are. Examine their topics, angles, and punch lines, and you'll see the principles I've discussed in action.

Not only are these techniques valuable for writing Monologue jokes, they'll also help you write virtually every other type of comedy piece there is on a comedy/talk show. That's why I'll be referring back to these Monologue joke techniques again and again in the chapters to come.

Before I move on to another type of comedy piece, the Desk Piece, I want to discuss a variation on the traditional Monologue joke. It lands somewhere between a purely verbal joke and the more produced joke that you'll find in most Desk Pieces so it's a good example of the versatility of Monologue joke techniques. I'm talking about a Monologue joke with a visual punch line.

MONOLOGUE JOKES WITH VISUAL PUNCH LINES

A visual punch line consists of something the audience sees, like a custom-made prop, a short video clip, or a doctored photo. (A doctored photo is one that has been altered from the original, say by using Photoshop.) Some hosts like to add variety to their Monologues by including an occasional joke with a visual punch line. Jay Leno and his staff called these jokes "drop-ins."

For instance, during one Monologue on *TSWJL* Jay described a press conference that President Obama held after a political meeting. Jay said you could tell the meeting hadn't gone well from the President's subtle body language at the press conference. Then the audience was shown a video clip of President Obama leaving the press conference. The President angrily kicks open the door of the room (thanks to an editing trick) and storms out. The visual punch line of the normally unflappable

President of the United States booting a door open was a big surprise and got a big laugh.

Note that even though that punch line is visual it was written using one of the same techniques used to write verbal punch lines, Punch Line Maker #1. The topic of President Obama's press conference about the frustrating meeting has two handles: "press conference" and "frustrated." The first handle has the association "leaving the press conference" and the second handle has the association "kick something." The visual punch line of the President kicking open the exit door links those two associations. And the angle about how you could tell the meeting hadn't gone well from the President's body language points from the topic to that visual punch line.

SUMMARY

To make your jokes as funny as possible, edit them using the twelve Joke Maximizers:

- Joke Maximizer #1: Shorten as much as possible.
- Joke Maximizer #2: End on the laugh trigger.
- Joke Maximizer #3: Backload the topic.
- Joke Maximizer #4: Make everything clear.
- Joke Maximizer #5: Don't telegraph the punch line.
- Joke Maximizer #6: Make the punch line parallel.
- Joke Maximizer #7: Use stop consonants, alliteration, and assonance.
- Joke Maximizer #8: Wildly exaggerate.
- Joke Maximizer #9: Get specific.
- Joke Maximizer #10: Use the Rule of Three.
- Joke Maximizer #11: Don't be too on-the-nose.
- Joke Maximizer #12: Consider an act-out.

After you've polished your joke with those Joke Maximizers, subject it to these five Comedy Quality Tests to make sure it's ready for public consumption:

- Comedy Quality Test #1: Read the joke out loud.
- Comedy Quality Test #2: Imagine the host delivering the joke.
- Comedy Quality Test #3: Imagine the audience hearing the joke.
- Comedy Quality Test #4: Try the joke out on other people.
- Comedy Quality Test #5: Ask yourself if the joke seems familiar.

The tools that I've given you in this and the previous chapter for writing topical Monologue jokes are very versatile. They can also be used to write Monologue jokes with visual punch lines and, as you'll see, most of the other comedy on a comedy/talk show.

Now I'll teach you how to write that other comedy. I'll start with Desk Pieces, which often feature jokes that have visual punch lines.

7

DESK PIECES

O N MOST COMEDY/TALK shows, after the host performs his Monologue the band "plays him over" to homebase. The show's director cuts to a lively shot of the band playing instead of holding on a dull shot of the host walking over to his desk. (In TV and film a shot of a performer doing nothing but walking somewhere is called "shoe leather" and is generally avoided because it's a boring waste of time.)

Once the host is seated at his desk he'll usually present the Main Comedy Piece. The reason for doing more comedy right then instead of bringing out the first guest is that comedy tends to hold onto viewers better than most guests. The comedy is fresh, whereas most guests have made many other comedy/talk show appearances. Plus, let's face it: most comedy pieces are more entertaining than most guests.

The Main Comedy Piece could be a prerecorded video, a live piece like an Audience Game, or some other written piece, but frequently it's a Desk Piece.

WHAT'S A DESK PIECE?

I define a Desk Piece (or "Desk Bit") as a segment of fully-scripted comedy that the host performs by himself while sitting at his desk. Let's take a closer look at that definition by breaking it into three parts:

- **A Desk Piece is a segment of fully-scripted comedy.** Consider a *LSWDL* piece like "How Many Santas Can Fit in a Coffee Shop?" The piece consists of Dave ad-libbing jokes as he watches a live camera shot (or "live feed") of staff members dressed as Santa Claus filing into a coffee shop across the street from the studio. It isn't a Desk Piece because even though Dave performs it by himself while sitting at his desk and the premise is scripted, most of the jokes are unscripted. I think of that piece as a Live Semi-Scripted Piece; I'll discuss those in detail in Chapter 12.

- **The host performs a Desk Piece by himself.** That means I wouldn't classify "Staring Contest," on *LNWCO*, as a Desk Piece. In that piece, sidekick Andy Richter tries to win a staring contest with Conan as Andy is distracted by silly, scripted activities taking place behind Conan. Even though Conan performs the piece at his desk I'd call it a sketch because Andy, sitting nearby, performs it with him. I'll cover Joke Basket Sketches like that in detail in Chapter 9.

- **The host performs a Desk Piece while sitting at his desk.** Take a prerecorded piece like "Dave at Taco Bell," on *LSWDL*. It shows Dave joking with customers at the drive-thru window of a Taco Bell. It's not a Desk Piece because even though Dave introduces ("sets up") this video piece while sitting at his desk, he performs all the comedy at the Taco Bell location. I consider "Dave at Taco Bell" to be a Location-Dependent Field Piece. I'll cover those in Chapter 13.

WHY SORT COMEDY PIECES INTO CATEGORIES?

At this point you might be thinking that I'm splitting hairs and wasting time attaching such specific labels to comedy pieces. Why do I think it's important to categorize a comedy piece as a Desk Piece, or a Live Semi-Scripted Piece, or a Joke Basket Sketch, or a Location-Dependent Field Piece? I believe that sorting comedy pieces into categories helps a writer in two ways:

Sorting comedy pieces into categories helps a writer generate ideas for new pieces.

Writers on comedy/talk shows are constantly asked to come up with ideas for new comedy pieces. That task becomes much more manageable if you cut it down to size using comedy categories.

Consider this analogy. Let's say you're hungry some evening. Isn't it easier to figure out exactly what you're going to eat if you first decide whether you're going to a restaurant, ordering food to be delivered to your home, or cooking for yourself? In the same way, if you want to create a new comedy piece you can make the task easier by first deciding on a general type of comedy piece. It's much easier to create, say, an Audience Game than it is to create "something funny." That's because once you've decided what type of comedy piece you're aiming for you can use brainstorming techniques that are specific to creating that type of piece. I'll teach you those specific brainstorming techniques in the chapters to follow.

Knowing what type of comedy piece you want to create also lets you use existing comedy pieces of that type to spark your creativity. For example, one time on *TSWJL* I wanted to create a simple comedy piece based on the fact that Los Angeles had just been hit by a minor earthquake. I started by deciding to create a Desk Piece. Inspired by the "Top

Ten List" Desk Piece on *LSWDL*, I created the piece "What the Richter Scale Means," which listed various Richter scale measurements and their implications. Sample joke: "A 5.0 means that cracks appear in Mitt Romney's hair." (Actually it was the hair of some other celebrity well-known at the time for having a stiff coiffure.)

Here's the second way that sorting comedy pieces into categories helps a writer:

Knowing what category a new piece belongs to helps a writer write that piece.

Each type of piece has certain writing techniques associated with it. If you know those techniques you can write any comedy piece in that category more easily. For example, once you know how to write the Graphic/Prop Piece "New Books" you'll have no trouble writing a similar piece like "New Magazines." And after you learn the ideal structure of a Story Sketch you can make any Story Sketch more entertaining. This book will teach you the techniques for writing each type of comedy piece.

Now that you understand why it's helpful to sort comedy pieces into categories I'll continue my in-depth analysis of one of those categories—Desk Pieces.

CHARACTERISTICS OF A DESK PIECE

Beyond the characteristics that define it, a Desk Piece has three other key characteristics:

Desk Pieces are joke baskets. That is, a Desk Piece consists of a theme—think of it as a basket—and about ten jokes that fit into that basket because they share the same theme. If the theme for a Desk Piece is "New Office Supplies," for instance, the jokes will be fake office supplies that the writers dreamed up and the prop department constructed. (A joke basket is also sometimes called a "joke bucket.")

The jokes in a Desk Piece (or in any other joke basket piece) are independent of one another. They aren't connected by any story element as they would be in some types of sketches. That means jokes can be substituted for each other and the order of the jokes can be changed but the piece will still work just about as well.

Desk Pieces tend to be reliable laugh-getters. Because the jokes in the piece are independent of one another, the entire writing staff can contribute jokes to the piece without having to spend time collaborating on a story line. This means that lots of jokes tend to get written for Desk Pieces, so the jokes that make it onto the show are usually strong.

Desk Pieces tend to be repeatable. If a Desk Piece has an evergreen (that is, non-topical) theme it can be performed again in the future. Because it's a joke basket, all that the writers would have to do is refill it with new jokes. For example, *LSWDL* used to air the Desk Piece "New Father's Day Cards" every year. Some Desk Pieces, like "Thank You Notes" on *LNWJF*, aired every week. And *LSWDL* airs its "Top Ten List" Desk Piece almost every night.

Every head writer loves refillable, repeatable pieces because they really help "feed the beast," that is, fill those empty comedy slots that stretch out indefinitely into the future. Serving up totally new comedy pieces every night is the ideal but coming up with new themes takes a lot of work. Time-tested, repeatable pieces lighten the load considerably. For this reason—plus the fact that they usually play well with audiences—Desk Pieces feature prominently on many comedy/talk shows.

THE SEVEN TYPES OF DESK PIECES

For the same reasons that it's useful to sort comedy pieces into categories it's useful to sort Desk Pieces into seven basic types. I'll go over each type in detail in this chapter but here are brief descriptions:

- **Text Pieces**, in which the jokes consist primarily of words displayed on the screen. The "Top Ten List" on *LSWDL* is an example.

- **Illustrated Monologues**, in which each joke is delivered orally but is accompanied by an undoctored (unaltered) photograph illustrating some aspect of the joke. "Thank You Notes" on *LNWJF* is one example.

- **Text/Photo Pieces**, where a photo illustrates the topic of the joke while the joke itself appears as text on the screen. An example is "Celebrity Survey" on *LNWCO*.

- **Audio Pieces**, in which the jokes consist of brief audio recordings. One example is "Questions" on *LNWJF*.

- **Art Card Pieces**, where the jokes take the form of custom-made artwork that the host displays. An example is "New State Quarters" on *LNWCO*.

- **Graphic/Prop Pieces**, in which jokes based on graphics (that is, text or artwork) are added to otherwise undoctored props. One example of this type of piece is "New Books" on *LSWDL*.

- **Prop Pieces**, where the jokes consist of props constructed by the show's prop department. An example is "New Olympic Souvenirs" on *LSWDL*.

PRODUCING DESK PIECES

The main reason for sorting Desk Pieces into these types is, as I suggested above, that it helps you write the pieces. But there's another reason that has less to do with writing the comedy than with producing it.

Each type of Desk Piece places different demands on various production departments of a comedy/talk show—mainly the graphics, prop, and wardrobe departments. That's why a head writer should consider what types of comedy pieces he's putting into production. If he doesn't, he may inadvertently overburden one of the departments, annoying the people who work there and maybe not getting a finished comedy piece that he was counting on.

For example, an Art Card Piece and a Graphic/Prop Piece would both be produced by the graphics department so a good head writer shouldn't expect them both to get done at the same time. And if the show has just aired a Prop Piece, a savvy head writer might assign the writing staff to write another Prop Piece in a couple of weeks. The idea would be to keep the prop department busy but not too busy and in that way take full advantage of its capabilities.

Each type of Desk Piece also takes a different amount of time to produce. The seven types of Desk Pieces above are listed roughly in order of how long it takes to produce them, from less time to more time. A Text Piece like a "Top Ten List" can be produced in as little as half an hour, since it only involves typing the jokes into a machine. However, an Art Card Piece takes a week or two to get ready, and a Prop Piece takes two to three weeks. A head writer who isn't fully aware of the lead times required for the various types of Desk Pieces runs the risk of not having a piece ready when he needs it.

In many ways a comedy/talk show is like a little factory, turning out episodes instead of products like cars. Just like managing a car factory well, managing a show well means keeping the assembly line moving, maintaining an even workflow, keeping product quality high, and making sure the workforce is happy and fully utilized. Never forget that show business is a business.

Now I'll cover each type of Desk Piece in detail.

TEXT PIECES

Text Pieces are easy to produce. The writing staff churns out a whole bunch of jokes, the head writer and host pick their favorites, and a crew member types the selected jokes into a character generator. When the host performs the piece, the crew member presses buttons and the jokes appear on the screen. (Sometimes text superimposed on the screen is referred to as a "Chyron," after the Chyron Corporation, which manufactures character generators. That's why a Text Piece is sometimes called a "Chyron Piece.")

Because Text Pieces can be produced fast they're often used to fill in at the last minute for a piece that was yanked from the show's rundown for some reason. Text Pieces can also be very topical. A show's staff can write and produce a Text Piece about an event that occurred that very afternoon.

But Text Pieces don't take full advantage of the fact that television is a visual medium. They'd be almost as entertaining if they were written in a book or read on the radio. For this reason Text Pieces should be used as Main Comedy Pieces as seldom as possible. If too many episodes of a show rely on Text Pieces for their comedy the audience will feel somehow shortchanged.

Even though Text Pieces aren't very visual they can be very successful. The most popular Text Piece in the history of late-night television is the "Top Ten List." It only consists of words on the screen and yet it has appeared on thousands of episodes of television hosted by Dave Letterman.

THE "TOP TEN LIST"

I was a writer on *LNWDL* when our amazing head writer, Steve O'Donnell, created the "Top Ten List." Steve told me he got the idea from the ridiculously subjective Top Ten lists that appeared regularly in various publications. He sold Dave on the piece by showing him *Cosmopolitan*'s list of "Ten Most Eligible Bachelors," a list that included, absurdly, eighty-three-year-old CBS executive William Paley.

It took a few "Top Ten Lists" before we figured out how to write them. The first "Top Ten List" ever aired had the topic "Top Ten Words That Almost Rhyme With 'Peas.'" Numbers 10 through 1 were as follows: "Heats," "Rice," "Moss," "Ties," "Needs," "Lens," "Ice," "Nurse," "Leaks," and "Meats." The list was weirdly funny but its style of humor was very conceptual and would have been hard to sustain on a regular basis.

But soon the writers discovered a way of looking at the "Top Ten List" that would allow it to be easily refilled with more conventional jokes and therefore repeated indefinitely. They decided this: a "Top Ten List" is a joke with ten punch lines.

That is, writing a "Top Ten List" is like writing ten Monologue jokes, all of which share the same topic and angle but have different punch lines. For example, the list "Top Ten Rejected Life Savers Flavors" might have as one entry "Disembowelmint." You could reassemble those elements into a self-contained Monologue joke this way: "Life Savers Candy just announced some new flavors. Here's one that didn't make the list: Disembowelmint."

Remember I told you that learning to write topical Monologue jokes would help you write other comedy pieces? The "Top Ten List" is a perfect example. Since a "Top Ten List" is a joke with ten punch lines, you write the list using the same techniques I covered in the chapters on writing Monologue jokes, with some minor variations. Specifically, here's how to do it:

The Six Steps in Writing a "Top Ten List"

1. Pick a topic.

The topic of a "Top Ten List" is like the topic of a Monologue joke. It's the news item or pop culture phenomenon that the list is based on. And it can be either *topical* or *evergreen*.

A topical topic is a current event. Here are some examples:

- The Yankees won the World Series.
- Actress Lindsay Lohan was arrested today.
- The President is visiting China.

An evergreen topic is not a current event but instead a lasting pop culture phenomenon that will be just as fresh months from now as it is today. Examples include:

- Life Savers flavors
- the Easter Bunny
- bad beaches

Picking a topic for a "Top Ten List" is a lot like picking one for a Monologue joke. Look for a news item or pop culture entity that has these three characteristics:

a) It sparks a lot of people's interest, including your own.
Most people have heard about it, relate to it, and care about it.

b) It's something that the audience and host will allow you to make jokes about. Avoid topics that are tragic, disturbing, or offensive, no matter how big the story is. On days when the news is all bad, consider an evergreen topic for your list.

c) It suggests a lot of associations. This characteristic isn't particularly important for Monologue joke topics but it is for "Top Ten List" topics because a "Top Ten List" is a joke with ten punch lines. As you saw in Chapter 5, the punch line of a joke frequently springs from associations suggested by the topic, so a topic needs to suggest a lot of associations if it's going to give birth to ten different punch lines. It must be fertile.

For example, the Easter Bunny has a lot of associations: Easter eggs, hopping, candy, frequent sexual intercourse, Santa Claus, Peter Rabbit, and so on. That's why the Easter Bunny works well as the topic of a "Top Ten List."

What's an example of a "Top Ten List" topic that doesn't have a lot of associations? How about Lamar Alexander dropping out of the race for the Republican Presidential nomination in 1996? The day of that news event I assigned the writing staff of *LSWDL* the task of generating "Top Ten Excuses of Lamar Alexander." It turned out that Lamar Alexander called to mind only a few associations. I only remember one: his trademark plaid flannel shirt. Nevertheless, the writers valiantly cobbled the list together. When it aired, it bombed. I felt like such an idiot. In retrospect I should have assigned an evergreen topic instead of holding out for a current events topic on a slow news day.

Once you've chosen a promising topic for your "Top Ten List" the next step is to:

2. Add an angle.

Like a Monologue joke, every "Top Ten List" has an angle. Remember, the angle is the particular direction a joke takes in getting from the topic to the punch line. In the case of a "Top Ten List," the same angle connects the topic to each of the ten punch lines.

As you saw in Chapter 5, when you write a Monologue joke the punch line often comes to you before the angle and then you create an angle that leads to that punch line. Writing angles for "Top Ten Lists" is different because the angle always precedes the punch lines in your thought process. In fact, before the writing staff of *LSWDL* starts working on that day's "Top Ten List" they are assigned both the topic and the angle for the list. (A note on terminology: What *LSWDL* writers call a "Top Ten topic," like "Top Ten Excuses of Lamar Alexander," I consider to be both a topic—Lamar Alexander dropping out—and an angle, his excuses.)

If the angle always precedes the punch lines in a "Top Ten List," where does it come from? Sometimes the angle is suggested naturally by the topic. For instance, if the topic is "Thanksgiving" one obvious angle might be "things to be thankful for," leading to the list "Top Ten Things We as Americans Can Be Thankful For."

But most of the time the angle is taken from an unofficial list. On that list are a couple of dozen angles that account for about eighty percent of the "Top Ten Lists" ever aired. These angles are used so often because over the years the writers have found them to be very helpful when it comes to generating punch lines.

The main reason these angles are so helpful is that they themselves have a lot of associations. For example, the angle "pickup lines" suggests many actual pickup lines like "Do you come here often?", "Are you a model?", and "Can I buy you a drink?" Each of those familiar pickup lines—associations of the angle—could lead to a punch line when linked to one of the many associations of the topic. For example, "Top Ten Pickup Lines of the Easter Bunny" would be easy to write.

So what are the fertile, time-tested angles on this informal list? In the spirit of the "Top Ten List," here are ten of them. If you're writing your own "Top Ten List" I'd advise you to do what the *LSWDL* writers very often do and pick an angle from this list. After all, why reinvent the wheel?

Top Ten Most Popular "Top Ten List" Angles

10. Least Popular [people, places, or things]. E.g., "Top Ten Least Popular Mall Stores."
9. Good Things about [something you wouldn't normally think has advantages]. E.g., "Top Ten Good Things about Global Warming."
8. Things Overheard at [a place]. E.g., "Top Ten Things Overheard at the Academy Awards."
7. Rejected [things]. E.g., "Top Ten Rejected Names for the New Batman Sequel."
6. Complaints of or Pet Peeves of [a real or imaginary being]. E.g., "Top Ten Santa Claus Pet Peeves."
5. Excuses of [an individual or group of individuals who failed at something]. E.g., "Top Ten Excuses of Lamar Alexander."
4. Questions Asked [about something or by someone]. E.g., "Top Ten Questions Asked on the White House Tour."

3. Reasons that [something is true]. E.g., "Top Ten Reasons Golf is Better than Sex."

2. Ways [that someone could do something]. E.g., "Top Ten Ways the U.S. Postal Service Can Turn Things Around."

1. Signs that [something is true]. E.g., "Top Ten Signs Your Gym Teacher is Nuts."

And here are a half-dozen runner-up angles for "Top Ten Lists":

11. Perks of [a position or accomplishment]. E.g., "Top Ten Perks of Winning a Nobel Prize."

12. Pickup Lines of [a real or imaginary being]. E.g., "Top Ten Pickup Lines of the Easter Bunny."

13. Things You Don't Want to Hear [from a particular person or in a particular place]. E.g., "Top Ten Things You Don't Want to Hear from Your Weather Forecaster."

14. New Slogans for [a person, place, or thing]. E.g., "Top Ten Slogans for Cher's New Perfume."

15. Little-Known or Surprising Facts about [a person, place, or thing]. E.g., "Top Ten Surprising Facts about Curling."

16. [Someone's] Tips for [doing something]. E.g., "Top Ten Summer Fun Tips from the Unabomber."

Note that any given topic can usually be paired with more than one angle to produce different "Top Ten Lists." For example, the topic "Santa Claus" has led to *LSWDL* "Top Ten Lists" entitled "Top Ten Santa Pet Peeves," "Top Ten Things Overheard in Santa's Workshop," and "Top Ten Signs Santa Doesn't Like Your Kid."

Once you've selected a topic and added an angle that seems promising, the next step is to write rough drafts of the "Top Ten List" entries themselves.

3. Write the entries.

Because a "Top Ten List" is a joke with ten punch lines, you write "Top Ten List" entries pretty much the same way you write the punch lines to Monologue jokes. Follow these three steps:

- Brainstorm associations of the topic and possibly also the angle.
- Think about what's going on in pop culture that everybody's talking about.
- Use the results of those first two steps as you try each of the Punch Line Makers in turn. Just to remind you, here they are again:
  Punch Line Maker #1: Link two associations of the topic.
  Punch Line Maker #2: Link the topic to pop culture.
  Punch Line Maker #3: Ask a question about the topic.
  Punch Line Maker #4: Find a play on words in the topic.
  Punch Line Maker #5: Visualize the topic.
  Punch Line Maker #6: State the obvious about the topic.

Let me show you how this process works by analyzing a typical "Top Ten List." The topic is "a bad beach" and the angle is "signs you're at..."

Top Ten Signs You're at a Bad Beach

10. Naked fat guys playing volleyball.
9. You dive into the waves and get a splinter.
8. Cuban on raft lands, looks around, then paddles back out to sea.
7. You have to lie face down to tan so sea gulls don't peck your eyes out.
6. Sign for rest rooms points to the ocean.
5. Hard to hear the lifeguard blowing his whistle inside his biohazard suit.

4. That giant oil slick caused by an offshore Snooki.

3. Five minutes after you finish your sand castle it has cockroaches.

2. Those aren't seashells. They're toenails.

1. It's Bring-Your-Own-Sand.

Here are the techniques that the writer (me) used to create each of those entries:

10. Used Punch Line Maker #3 and answered the question "What would be bad to see at the beach?" by combining the "beach" association "volleyball" and the "bad" association "overweight."

9. Used Punch Line Maker #3 and answered the question "What would make swimming really bad?" by blending the "beach" association "waves" and the "bad" association "trash."

8. Used Punch Line Maker #2 and linked the "beach" association "raft" to the pop culture phenomenon of illegal aliens trying to sneak into the U.S. by water.

7. Used Punch Line Maker #5, visualized the "beach" associations "sunbathing" and "seagulls," and exaggerated what seagulls do.

6. Used Punch Line Maker #1 and linked the "beach" association "rest rooms" and the "bad" association "peeing in the water."

5. Used Punch Line Maker #1 and linked the "beach" association "lifeguard" and the "bad" association "pollution."

4. Used Punch Line Maker #2 and linked the "beach" association "oil slick" to the pop culture personality Snooki, the self-styled "Guidette" from MTV's reality show *Jersey Shore*.

3. Used Punch Line Maker #1 and blended the "beach" association "sand castle" and the "bad" association "vermin."

2. Used Punch Line Maker #5, visualized the "beach" association "seashells," and imagined disgusting things that seashells look like.

1. Used Punch Line Maker #1 and combined the "beach" association "sand" with the "bad" association "Bring Your Own Beer."

So that's an example of how to generate the entries in a "Top Ten List" using the Punch Line Makers.

The *LSWDL* writing staff, as a group, turns in well over a hundred possible entries for each "Top Ten List." If you're writing your own list, ideally you've come up with rough drafts of at least a couple of dozen entries. If you haven't, you probably haven't pushed yourself hard enough to explore all possible areas for jokes. So brainstorm more associations and pop culture references and combine them into more punch lines. If thinking of a lot of associations is difficult, consider switching to a more fertile topic. The idea is to have a large and varied assortment of great jokes to choose from when you put your final list together.

Once you have more than enough rough drafts of entries for your list, it's time to polish them.

4. Edit the entries.

Use the same Joke Maximizers that you learned in Chapter 6 for editing Monologue jokes to edit the entries in your "Top Ten List." The most useful Joke Maximizers for editing "Top Ten Lists" are probably these five:

- **Joke Maximizer #1: Shorten as much as possible.** For example, in "Top Ten Signs You're at a Bad Beach" all unnecessary words and letters were pruned away from "You can see naked fat guys playing volleyball" to get the final version.

- **Joke Maximizer #2: End on the laugh trigger.** I didn't write, "You get a splinter when you dive into the waves" because the laugh trigger is "splinter."

- **Joke Maximizer #7: Use stop consonants, alliteration, and assonance.** Notice the "k" sounds in "peck," "Snooki," and "cockroaches."

- **Joke Maximizer #8: Wildly exaggerate.** Those sea gulls won't just scratch your face; they'll peck your eyes out.

- **Joke Maximizer #9: Get specific.** That sand castle doesn't just have vermin; it has cockroaches.

Now that you've polished each of your two dozen or so possible entries into its final form, it's time to discard a few.

5. Test the entries for quality.

I covered five quality control tests for Monologue jokes in Chapter 6. Subject the possible entries on your "Top Ten List" to those same tests. To review, the tests are these:

- **Comedy Quality Test #1**: Read the joke out loud.
- **Comedy Quality Test #2**: Imagine the host delivering the joke.
- **Comedy Quality Test #3**: Imagine the audience hearing the joke.
- **Comedy Quality Test #4**: Try the joke out on other people.
- **Comedy Quality Test #5**: Ask yourself if the joke seems familiar.

Rewrite or eliminate any entries that don't pass all of those tests.

6. Assemble the "Top Ten List."

Do you still have more than enough polished, high-quality entries to fill the list? If you don't, write more. If you do, follow these steps to assemble your "Top Ten List":

a) Pick the ten entries you think are the funniest.

b) If you've picked two or more entries that rely on the same association, eliminate all but one of them. The main reason for this is to keep the list surprising In the sample "Top Ten List" above you'd only want one entry involving a lifeguard, for example. If you had two, the second lifeguard entry would seem a little familiar and, therefore, less funny. Better to give its slot to a completely fresh entry.

Another reason for not including two entries based on the same association is that they might be logically inconsistent, which would distract the audience. For example, if you've already said that the lifeguard is wearing a biohazard suit the audience would be a little confused if you also told them that he is using mayonnaise as suntan lotion. Sidetracked by their confusion, the audience wouldn't laugh as hard.

After you've eliminated any redundant entries, add runner-up entries from your stockpile to bring the total back up to ten.

c) Put the ten entries you selected in an effective order. Follow these guidelines:

- The first two entries on the list—#10 and #9, since the list counts down—should be surefire punch lines that are virtually guaranteed to get the audience laughing and to get the list off to a solid start.

- Slot a particularly strong joke into position #6, to give the list a boost of energy at its midway point. (In the sample "Top Ten List" above, it's hard to beat that pee joke.)

- Try to alternate longer entries and shorter entries. Varying the pace will help keep the momentum up and the list surprising.

- Put any entries that are particularly weird or conceptual later in the list. (What the heck is "an offshore Snooki" anyway?) Those offbeat jokes will help keep the audience surprised and engaged at a point when their attention might be drifting.

- Entry #1 should ideally have a quality of summation and finality to it. If the "Top Ten List" were a speech, Entry #1 would be what comes after the statement "But if I had to say only one thing about this topic it would be..." Note that the sample "Top Ten List" above wouldn't end quite as strongly if the #1 were the long, very specific "Five minutes after you finish your sand castle it has cockroaches" rather than the punchier, more damning "It's Bring-Your-Own-Sand."

And that's how to write a "Top Ten List."

MORE TEXT PIECES

The "Top Ten List" is probably the best-known Text Piece that appears on comedy/talk shows but you'll occasionally see these other types, too.

Text Quizzes

A Text Quiz typically consists of a question superimposed on the screen followed by three possible answers. Each possible answer appears only when the host reads it aloud and not before, so the audience won't get ahead of the joke.

For example, here's a joke from a "Spring in New York City Quiz" on *LNWDL*:

"This time of year, street fairs are a great place to pick up
    a) shirts from the fifties

b) jackets from the sixties

c) body lice from total strangers"

How to Write a Text Quiz

Here's what you do:

1. Pick a theme for the Text Quiz the same way you'd pick a topic for a "Top Ten List." That is, pick a quiz theme that suggests a lot of associations and that the audience is likely to find acceptable and relatable. For instance, the quiz theme "Spring in New York City" meets those criteria and is especially relatable to Dave's New York City studio audience.

2. Generate possible topics for individual jokes by brainstorming associations of the quiz theme. For example, to arrive at the topic of the joke above, the writer associated "Spring in New York City" with street fairs.

3. For each possible joke topic, use the Punch Line Makers to create a "c" answer. That is, using associations of the joke topic, brainstorm punch lines using the same techniques that I covered in Chapter 5 for Monologue jokes. Note that the punch line of each joke will be the "c" answer because, according to Joke Maximizer #2, the laugh trigger should be at the very end of the joke.

In the case of the sample joke above, the writer used Punch Line Maker #3 and asked about the topic, "What can you get at a street fair?" The answer to the question—the punch line, "c"—was based on an association of street fairs, which is "unclean people."

4. Use the Joke Maximizers to perfect the wording of the "c." In other words, use the editing techniques you learned in Chapter 6 to craft the punch line first, because the wording of the punch line will guide the wording of the rest of the joke. The writer of the sample joke used Joke

Maximizer #9 when he wrote the punch line "body lice from total strangers" instead of the more general, and less funny, "a disease from a passerby."

5. Write the topic and angle of the joke, that is, the quiz question itself. Write the question so that it fits smoothly with the "c" when you read them together as one sentence. For example, the resulting sentence from the joke above would read, "This time of year, street fairs are a great place to pick up body lice from total strangers."

6. Write the "a" and "b." The "a" and "b" should each be plausible, unfunny answers to the quiz question. That is, they should both be straight, to maximize the surprise—and laughter—produced by the abrupt turn taken by the "c." In the sample joke, "shirts from the fifties" and "jackets from the sixties" are both blandly reasonable answers to the quiz question.

7. Apply the Joke Maximizers to the joke as a whole. These three techniques in particular from Chapter 6 are useful when writing Text Quiz jokes:

- **Joke Maximizer #10.** Use the Rule of Three, limiting the possible answers to three.

- **Joke Maximizer #6.** Make the punch line, the "c," parallel the "a" and "b" when possible. For example, in the sample joke above, the "a," "b," and "c" are all of the form "[plural noun] from [plural noun]." Parallelism gives the angle more forward momentum and therefore makes the abrupt turn of the punch line more surprising. To show you what parallelism adds to the sample joke, I'll reword the joke to take it out:

  > "This time of year, street fairs are a great place to pick up
  >   a) vintage shirts
  >   b) a sixties-style jacket
  >   c) body lice from total strangers"

Not as funny, is it?

- **Joke Maximizer #1.** Shorten the joke as much as possible. Here's a trick that might help: move any words that are duplicated in the "a," "b," and "c" up into the question that starts off the joke. For example, your first draft of that sample joke might have been this:

> "This time of year, street fairs are a great place to:
> a) pick up shirts from the fifties
> b) pick up jackets from the sixties
> c) pick up body lice from total strangers"

Even though the "a," "b," and "c" are parallel, including the words "pick up" in all three answers slows down the joke and makes it a little less funny. So you'd move "pick up" up into the question.

Text Comparison Pieces

A Text Comparison Piece compares two subjects, that is, two people, two places, or two things. Each joke is displayed as text on the screen and consists of a pair of related phrases—a straight, unfunny phrase describing the first subject and a punch line phrase describing the second subject.

Here's a joke from a Text Comparison Piece on *TSWJL* called "Christmas in New England vs. Los Angeles," to give you an example:

> "New England Christmas:
> Sleigh riding with other family members
>
> Los Angeles Christmas:
> Joyriding with other gang members"

How to Write a Text Comparison Piece

Follow these steps:

1. Pick a topic for the comparison the same way you'd pick a topic for a "Top Ten List." That is, pick a topic that's likely to be relatable and acceptable to the audience and that has a lot of associations. In the above example, "Christmas," "New England," and "Los Angeles" each have many associations, so generating punch lines for a dozen solid jokes wasn't a problem.

2. Decide which of the two comparison subjects is going to be the butt of the jokes. In the example the writers decided to make fun of Los Angeles. The choice was easy because Los Angeles—"La-La Land"— is generally perceived to be crazier than New England.

But sometimes the choice of which subject to ridicule isn't so obvious. Let's say your assignment was to write a Text Comparison Piece comparing Americans to the French. You'd have to decide whether the punch lines would be about Americans (uncultured and overweight compared to the French) or about the French (smelly and cowardly compared to Americans). How would you choose which of the two subjects to target with your jokes? You'd have to decide which subject would yield more punch lines that the audience would accept as true. In the case of Americans versus the French, you'd have to judge whether more viewers would be likely to think Americans are superior, in general, to the French, or vice versa.

Why couldn't you alternate between the two in the punch lines, sometimes bashing Americans and sometimes bashing the French? Because the constantly shifting point of view would distract the viewer. Each joke would force the viewer to mentally pause and ask, "Who am I supposed to be laughing at now?" To avoid confusion, it's better to pick one subject to make fun of and stick with it.

3. Use the Punch Line Makers and associations of the topic to brainstorm punch lines. The punch line of each joke will, of course, be about whichever subject you've targeted for mockery and will come second in the comparison. In our example, the writer used Punch Line Maker #4 and wordplay to link the "New England Christmas" associations "sleigh riding" and "family members" with the "Los Angeles" associations "joyriding" and "gang members."

4. Use the Joke Maximizers to polish the wording of each joke. Pay special attention to Joke Maximizer #6—make the punch line parallel—just as you would for a Text Quiz. In the above example, "Sleigh riding with other family members" is parallel to "Joyriding with other gang members" because they share the same structure; almost the same number of syllables; and the words "riding," "with other," and "members."

How to Create a New Text Piece

Let's say you're looking for a new, easy-to-produce piece that's also refillable. You decide that a Text Piece would fill the bill. You know how you'd write the jokes for such a piece: you'd use the same Punch Line Makers and Joke Maximizers that you'd use to write a Text Quiz or Text Comparison Piece. But how do you come up with the idea for the piece itself?

One way is to think of the kinds of lists that frequently appear in text-oriented media like newspapers, magazines, and many websites. Such lists can often be adapted into Text Pieces just by substituting jokes for typical entries that might appear in the lists.

Don't just limit yourself to simple lists of people, places and things, like *Cosmopolitan* magazine's "8 Weird Aphrodisiac Tricks From Around the World." Think of more involved lists where each entry consists of two or more parts. Here are a few examples:

■ The Scholastic Aptitude Test (SAT) used to have a section devoted to analogies. That inspired the writers at *LNWCO* to come up with a refillable Text Piece entitled "SAT Analogies." Here's a sample joke:

> "Sunrise : milk them cows ::
> 10 minutes ago : write these jokes"
>
> [Conan read it this way: "'Sunrise' is to 'milk them cows' as 'Ten minutes ago' is to 'write these jokes.'"]

■ Often a magazine article about some subject will include a list of pros and cons. That's what gave the writers of *LNWJF* the idea for their regular segment "Pros and Cons." Here's a sample joke from their "Pros and Cons of Returning to College":

> "PRO: You're a senior!
> CON: For the third year in a row"

■ Lists of dos and don'ts frequently appear in print, too, and at least one late-night show has done the comedy version. Here's a sample joke from "Houseguest Dos and Don'ts" on *LNWDL*:

> "DO: Laugh politely at your host's anecdotes.
> DON'T: Laugh loudly at your host's hairpiece."

ILLUSTRATED MONOLOGUES

Another relatively easy-to-produce type of Desk Piece is what I call an Illustrated Monologue. It consists of a series of verbal jokes that are loosely related by a topic and are each illustrated by an undoctored photograph displayed on-screen. In most cases getting the joke doesn't depend on seeing the photo. The photos merely add visual interest to the piece, turning what would otherwise be just a Monologue into a more-produced Desk Piece.

"Thank You Notes," a regular segment on *LNWJF*, is a good example of an Illustrated Monologue. Here's a sample joke: a photo of a woman's ponytail is displayed as Jimmy says, "Thank you, ponytails, for turning the backs of girls' heads into horses' butts."

How to Create a New Illustrated Monologue

Follow these steps:

1. Think of a topic for a joke basket in which the jokes are purely verbal. That is, think of a topic that could gather together a bunch of interchangeable jokes that consist solely of words. The broader the topic, the more likely it is that the piece will be refillable and repeatable.

For example, the jokes in "Thank You Notes" are purely verbal: all Jimmy has to do is read them aloud to get a laugh. And the topic—things Jimmy is thankful for—is very broad, which makes the piece endlessly repeatable. Another example of an Illustrated Monologue with a broad topic is "Why I Love America" on *TSWJL*. A sample joke: "I love America because here you can run free...[Show photo of Border Patrol officer and illegal alien]...especially if you can outrun the Border Patrol." Jay performed the piece only once, right before the Fourth of July, but we could have repeated it because the topic covered a lot of territory.

2. Write jokes for the piece using the Punch Line Makers and Joke Maximizers. Brainstorm associations of the topic and of pop culture phenomena and link them in surprising ways to say something true. For example, to come up with the Border Patrol joke the writer started with an association of "why people love America"—"here you can run free." Then the writer used Punch Line Maker #2 and linked that association to something in pop culture—illegal aliens running from the Border Patrol.

3. Add an undoctored photo to each joke. Choose a photo that reinforces the punch line, as in the case of the punch line about the Border Patrol officer and the illegal alien. If the punch line can't be illustrated with a photo—say if the punch line is too conceptual—then pick a photo that sums up the angle and guides the audience toward the punch line. To illustrate the "Thank You Note" about ponytails, for example, a photo was used of a woman's ponytailed head that somewhat resembled a horse's rear end.

4. Consider livening up the piece with physical business or staging. If you do you'll elevate the piece even more above a simple recitation of funny lines. During "Thank You Notes," for instance, Jimmy pretends to write out a thank you note as he tells each joke. And Jay performed "Why I Love America" while sitting on a stool in a dramatic pool of light, with an instrumental version of "Yankee Doodle" gradually swelling behind him.

TEXT/PHOTO PIECES

Only slightly harder to produce than an Illustrated Monologue is what I call a Text/Photo Piece. (A Text/Photo Piece is sometimes called a Chyron/ADDA Piece, since a still store machine made by the ADDA Corporation was often used to display photos.) Like an Illustrated Monologue, a Text/Photo Piece consists of a series of jokes related by a general topic. But in a Text/Photo Piece the jokes are superimposed on the screen as text in addition to being illustrated by undoctored photos.

For example, *LNWJF* did a Text/Photo Piece called "Don't Quote Me," which displays photos of famous people along with text of their real and fake quotations. One sample joke shows photos of Franklin Delano Roosevelt with his real quote, "The only thing we have to fear is fear itself," followed by his fake quote, "And two-headed sharks. They're out there; we just don't know it yet."

How to Create a New Text/Photo Piece

Text/Photo Pieces tend to fall into one of two categories: pieces where the topic is a pop culture phenomenon and pieces where the topic is a location or event. "Don't Quote Me" belongs in the first category because the topic is the pop culture phenomenon of people posting inspirational quotations on Facebook. Here's how to come up with ideas for new pieces in each category:

1. The topic is a pop culture phenomenon. Pick as your topic a phenomenon that's a part of many people's lives, like Christmas. Then add an angle to that topic that will let you write punch lines about celebrities. For example, one celebrity-oriented angle on Christmas would be "what celebrities want for Christmas." "What Celebrities Want for Christmas" was actually performed on *LNWDL*, along with other Text/Photo Pieces like "Celebrity New Year's Resolutions" and "Celebrity Summer Plans."

Here's a sample joke from "Celebrity Summer Plans." Dave announces, "Bill Gates," as a photo of Bill Gates fills the screen. Then Dave reads the punch line while it appears on-screen as text: "Two-week yachting trip in his backyard pool." The piece continues with other celebrities and their supposed summer plans.

2. The topic is a location or event. For your topic, choose a location or event that's rich in associations, particularly associations with celebrities. Then add an angle that leads to punch lines about what's happening at that location or event. A timeline angle seems to work well in these pieces. For example, these Text/Photo Pieces were performed on *LSWDL*: "A Day in the Life of the Presidential Campaign," "A Day in the Life of CNN," "Olympics Timeline," and "Academy Awards Timeline."

One sample joke in the "Academy Awards Timeline" piece was this: "4:30 p.m.—Workers apply a final coat of spackle to Joan Rivers's face." Jokes about other celebrities at the star-studded event followed.

Of course there's no reason to be limited by those two categories when you're creating a new Text/Photo Piece. The writers of *LNWCO* tweaked the traditional Text/Photo Piece formats by using the Rule of Three to create "Celebrity Survey." Each joke in that piece consists of three celebrities supposedly completing a sentence. The first two celebrities provide plausible, unfunny responses, while the third celebrity supplies the punch line response. Here's a sample joke in which three celebrities completed the sentence, "I hate being recognized in...": Jeff Goldblum wrote, "Restaurants." Paul Rudd wrote, "Public bathrooms." And Nicholas Cage wrote, "Any recent film I've made." [Nic was supposedly commenting on all the bad movies he's been in.]

Once you have the idea for a new Text/Photo Piece, write jokes for it using the Punch Line Makers and Joke Maximizers.

AUDIO PIECES

In an Audio Piece the jokes consist of audio clips grouped under a general topic. Even though Audio Pieces are fairly easy to produce they're rare on comedy/talk shows, probably because they're visually uninteresting.

Here are a couple of examples.

"New Dial-It Services" [*LNWDL*]—The jokes are funny versions of those premium-rate telephone numbers that proliferated in the 1980s, like psychic hotlines and adult chat lines. Sample joke: Dave says that it's "Dial-a-One-Armed-Man-Hanging-From-a-Cliff." He dials a number on his desk phone and we hear the man who answers say, "Hello?" and then scream as he apparently plummets to his death.

"Questions" [*LNWJF*]—We hear the unspoken musings of Questlove, drummer for the show's band, the Roots, as we see him gazing into the distance. Sample joke: "Is there anything more embarrassing than when you go in to kiss a girl and she turns away...and starts dialing nine-one-one?"

How to Create a New Audio Piece

Follow these steps:

1. For a topic, think of a category of things that exist mainly in audio form. Categories like that include sound effects, songs, subway announcements, and GPS navigation voice prompts. Try to think of a category with lots of real-world examples you can use as angles. On *LLSWCF* Craig did an Audio Piece where the topic was funny messages that have supposedly been left on his voice mail.

2. Brainstorm real items that could fall into your chosen category. For example, continuing with the topic of Craig's voice mail, think of real voice mail messages that a typical person like you might get. A message from your plumber? Your doctor? A police officer? Those are all angles off the topic that might be used to create punch lines.

147

3. Write jokes for the piece using the Punch Line Makers and Joke Maximizers. Start with the topic and the angles you came up with in the previous step. Say you're writing a voice mail message to Craig from the police. You would brainstorm associations of "Craig Ferguson" and "police." Then you might use Punch Line Maker #1 and try linking two of the associations. You might come up with a punch line like this: "Mr. Ferguson, this is the police. We've received a complaint that you were standing on your front lawn exposing your bagpipes."

ART CARD PIECES

An Art Card Piece consists of jokes on a topic that are illustrated with artwork created specifically for the jokes. Because this type of Desk Piece requires custom-made artwork it takes longer to produce than the other pieces I've talked about.

The artwork can be mounted on pieces of cardboard ("art cards") that the host holds up. Alternatively, the artwork can be stored electronically and displayed on-screen when the director cues the still store operator. Some hosts prefer to handle the physical artwork because it gives them precise control over when to reveal the punch line. Instead of relying on the control room, the host himself can make sure that the audience both sees and hears the punch line at the same time, which maximizes its impact.

One example of an Art Card Piece is "Rejected Commercial Characters" on *LNWDL*. It comprises a collection of fake characters that were supposedly rejected for use in advertising. Here's a sample joke: "I think Quaker Oats made a wise decision when they stuck with Cap'n Crunch instead of...[Dave holds up an art card showing a box of Cap'n Crunch cereal with the name 'Lieutenant Crunch' and a picture of Cap'n Crunch holding his hat, ashamed]...Lieutenant Crunch Who

Was Demoted after a Videotape Surfaced of Him Having Sex with Paris Hilton."

Here are other examples of Art Card Pieces:

"New State Quarters" [*LNWCO*]—Artwork depicts fake new quarters issued to commemorate the various states. Sample joke: "New Jersey...Number One in chemical refineries." The illustration shows a quarter engraved with the words "New Jersey, #1 in chemical refineries" and a drawing of a boastful man with four arms, each arm held up to display its index finger.

"Actual Items" [*LNWCO*]—Conan shows print advertisements that have been altered to add jokes. Sample joke: An ad for a sporting goods store shows three aluminum baseball bats, each with its model name printed along its length. The bats are labeled, "Black Magic," "Reflex," and "Rent Collector." (Notice the Rule of Three in action here.)

"Airbrushing the News" [*LNWJF*]—Jimmy shows retouched news photographs. Sample joke: A photo shows First Lady Michelle Obama with her hand on the back of Queen Elizabeth. A second photo has been retouched to show that Mrs. Obama has stuck a sign on the Queen's back reading, "Kick Me."

"TV Show Mashups" [*LNWJF*]—Jimmy shows photos from two TV shows, then a third photo which combines the first two in a weird way. Sample joke: The first photo is of Miley Cyrus as Hannah Montana. The second shows conservative talk show host Sean Hannity. The third photo blends Hannah Montana with Hannity and depicts "Hannity Montana," who looks like Sean Hannity wearing a Hannah Montana wig and lipstick.

How to Create a New Art Card Piece

Do it this way:

1. For a topic, think of a collection of things that primarily exist in the form of pictures. That is, think of a real-world category of illustrations, photographs, or artwork— a category like print ads, news photos, charts, stamps, children's drawings, maps, billboards, place mats, publicity stills, and so on. Pick a category that includes many varied real-world examples to give you plenty of possible angles when you're writing jokes. Say, for example, that your topic is commercial characters.

2. Make a list of real items in your chosen category. Put together a list of several dozen real items by browsing in a store, leafing through a catalog, surfing the Internet, or assembling a stack of magazine clippings. In the case of commercial characters, real items in the category include Chef Boyardee, Mr. Peanut, Betty Crocker, Cap'n Crunch, and also companies like Facebook that don't have a commercial character but could. Those real items are all possible angles for jokes.

3. Write jokes for the piece using the Punch Line Makers and Joke Maximizers. Link associations of the topic and of the angles—the real items you listed—with each other and with pop culture phenomena. In the example above, the writer started with the angle "Cap'n Crunch" and then used Punch Line Maker #2 on the association "Lieutenant Crunch." "Lieutenant Crunch" implied that he had been demoted, perhaps for conduct unbecoming an officer, which suggested the sex-tape celebrity Paris Hilton. Rewording the angle so it pointed to that punch line yielded the joke, "I think Quaker Oats made a wise decision when they stuck with Cap'n Crunch instead of Lieutenant Crunch Who Was Demoted After a Videotape Surfaced of Him Having Sex with Paris Hilton."

4. Add a description of the artwork required. Tell the artist briefly what you think the artwork should look like to best reinforce the punch line. In the Cap'n Crunch example it was enough to write, "The artwork shows a box of Cap'n Crunch cereal with the name 'Lieutenant Crunch' and a picture of Cap'n Crunch holding his hat, ashamed." That's how little ol' Cap'n Crunch might look if he were caught in such a disgraceful position, isn't it?

GRAPHIC/PROP PIECES

A Graphic/Prop Piece is a collection of physical items in a particular category. Each punch line consists of text or other graphics, created specifically for the piece, that has been printed on an item. The host displays each item as he reads the punch line.

Here are some examples of Graphic/Prop Pieces:

New Books

The host holds up a series of books with fake, funny covers. This piece has been performed regularly in various forms on *LNWDL* (as "Bookmobile"), on *LSWDL* (as "Summer Reading"), on *TSWJL* (as "New Books" and "Rejected Kids' Books"), and on *Conan* (as "Coffee Table Books That Didn't Sell").

Here's a sample New Books joke from *LNWDL*: "Here's the perfect gift for photography buffs. It's 'Ansel Adams, The Lens-Cap-On Years.'" The cover of the book is printed with the author and title but is otherwise solid black. And an example of a New Book from *Conan* is: "The Big Book of Filled-In Crossword Puzzles."

New Magazines

The host holds up a collection of fake magazines, catalogs, pamphlets, or other similar publications. Here are some pieces that fall into this category:

"New Magazines" [*LNWDL*]—Sample joke: "Here's a nature magazine that celebrates diversity. It's 'Nearsighted Bird-Watcher.'" The cover shows an out-of-focus photograph of a black bird. The cover line reads, "Blackbird or Starling?"

"Pay-Per-View Events" [*TSWJL*]—Jay holds up a cable TV guide and shows the fake ads inside. Sample joke: "Here's the Baja Off-Road 500. No, it's not a car race. Don't miss the action as five hundred illegal aliens try to sneak across the U.S. border at the same time." The ad features a photo of a southwestern desert and the title "Baja Off-Road 500."

"Christmas Catalogs" [*TSWJL*]—Sample joke: "People who are a little short of cash for the holidays might want to get something from this catalog. It's 'Mr. Pickpocket's Catalog of Stolen Credit Cards.'" The cover shows a wide assortment of credit cards.

New Greeting Cards

Dave Letterman has performed this piece many times in various forms such as "New Father's Day Cards," "New Mother's Day Cards," and "New Valentines." He holds up fake greeting cards with the jokes printed on them. A sample joke: "Happy Valentine's Day to the Tailor Who Measured My Inseam."

Product Labels

This piece consists of real products with funny labels or notations added to them. The host shows the product and then the camera gets a close-up of the punch line printed on it.

A version of this piece on *LSWDL* is "Warning Labels." Sample joke: the warning label on a plastic container of Tic Tac mints reads, "Caution: May contain ticks and/or tacks." *TSWJL* did a similar piece called "The Fine Print." Sample joke: a canned ham reads "Cooked Ham, Water Added" but the fine print on it states, "Actually Cooked Water, Ham Added."

How to Create a New Graphic/Prop Piece

Follow these steps:

1. For a topic, think of a category of everyday objects that typically have words printed on them. For instance, in addition to books and the other categories mentioned above, Graphic/Prop Pieces have also been written about travel brochures and junk mail.

2. Make a list of real items in your chosen category. To write jokes for a "New Books" piece for example, start by making a list (mental or written) of various types of real books. Those types of real books are angles off the topic and you'll use them to write punch lines. Such a list could include biographies, cookbooks, celebrity memoirs, Curious George books, puzzle books, encyclopedias, pop-up books, atlases, children's books, books by Stephen King, and photography books.

3. Write jokes for the piece using the Punch Line Makers and Joke Maximizers. Start with the possible angles, the real items you listed in the previous step. If your topic is books, say, you might start with the angle "photography book" and use Punch Line Maker #1. "Photography" has the associations "Ansel Adams" and "forgetting to take the lens cap off your camera." Linking those two associations results in the punch line "Ansel Adams, The Lens-Cap-On Years."

Another example is that "Warning Label" for Tic Tac mints. The writer used Punch Line Maker #4 on two associations of the angle, "Tic" and "Tac." He realized that "Tic" and "Tac" sound like other, startlingly unexpected, words and used a double dose of wordplay in the punch line to get "Caution: May contain ticks and/or tacks."

4. Add a description of the graphics work required. This is especially important if the graphics are an important part of the punch line. For example, the solid black cover on the book "Ansel Adams, The Lens-Cap-On Years" makes the punch line instantly and vividly clear.

PROP PIECES

Like a Graphic/Prop Piece, a Prop Piece is a collection of physical items—props—in a particular category. But while the jokes in a Graphic/Prop Piece consist mainly of text or other graphics, the jokes in a Prop Piece are the props themselves, which are constructed specifically for the piece.

The host often displays the props on his desk so this is one of those occasions when a desk comes in handy. If the props are too big for the desk he can present them in the production area of the studio, maybe on wheeled tables. In that case the Prop Piece wouldn't technically be a Desk Piece but the joke-writing techniques would be exactly the same.

Prop Pieces tend to be particularly reliable laugh-getters. I think that's because the audience is surprised that somebody went to all the trouble and expense of constructing such silly objects. That additional element of the unexpected—I can't believe they actually made that!—adds to the comedy of the jokes themselves.

Here are some examples of Prop Pieces:

New Products

The host displays fake items that people can supposedly buy somewhere. New Products Pieces have appeared under many names on several late-night shows. For example, *LNWDL* and *LSWDL* aired "New Gift Ideas" (dubbed "Wacky Props" by the writers); "Dave's Toy Shop" (including not "Silly Putty" but "Sensible Putty," perfect for caulking windows); "New Military Items" (featuring the "Remote Control Canteen," which scooted around the floor); "New Medical Aids"; and "New Office Supplies." *TSWJL* presented New Products Pieces with the titles "Summer Products," "Back to School Products," "New Fitness Products," and "The Duller Image Catalogue."

Here's a joke I wrote for a "New Gift Items" segment on *LNWDL*: Dave says, "Heavy sleepers will have no trouble waking up when they use this handy device licensed by a popular television show. It's '*The A-Team* Stunt Alarm.'" The audience sees a man sleeping in a bed. On a nightstand next to the bed are a clock radio and a beer bottle. The clock radio alarm activates, blaring the rousing theme song from *The A-Team* as a pivoting bar attached to the radio smashes the bottle on the sleeping man's head.

Remember when I said in Chapter 3 that the writer of a comedy piece on a late-night show usually produces it? For "*The A-Team* Stunt Alarm" I had to put on my producer's hat to avoid getting my skull fractured. The day the joke was to appear on *LNWDL* I went down to rehearsal to look it over. The prop department had done an impressive job constructing the clock but, to ensure that it would work reliably on the show, had made the pivoting bar holding the bottle out of steel. And the nightstand on which the clock and bottle rested was not fixed at a certain distance from the bed. This meant, as I pointed out to the prop people, that it was possible that the hapless loser in the bed would be hit not just by a harmless breakaway bottle but also by a bulky, steel hinge studded with bolts.

The prop department responded to my concerns by firmly attaching all the props to a rolling platform. Excellent. But that didn't eliminate the danger because the sleeper's head wouldn't be attached to the bed; if he moved after he was positioned backstage he risked serious injury. Since I had written the crazy joke, I volunteered to be the sleeper. During the show, "*The A-Team* Stunt Alarm" activated, the steel bar whooshed over and thudded onto the pillow, and the bottle shattered on my head, the lethal hinge just inches away. Did the joke get a laugh? I was so relieved I didn't notice.

Museums

A Prop Piece can also consist of fake exhibits from a real or imaginary museum. On *LNWDL*, for example, we aired "Museum of Television," "Rock and Roll Museum," and "Museum of Transportation." Among the jokes in that last piece was one I wrote: Dave says, "The museum gift shop is where you'll find this delightful memento of one of the worst ecological disasters of all time. It's the 'Exxon Valdez Oil Globe.'" Dave shows a snow-type globe containing a small tanker ship sitting in a pool of black oil alongside a miniature stretch of Alaskan coastline. Then he shakes the globe, dispersing hundreds of little blobs of oil throughout the clear liquid inside.

I wasn't kidding when I mentioned the trouble and expense of constructing such silly objects. A model maker was hired to make two identical "Exxon Valdez Oil-Globes," one to use during the show and one to rehearse with, since the globs of oil wouldn't have time to settle out before the taping. The prop department told me later that each prop cost $1,000, so that meant $2,000 for that one laugh. At least there was a laugh.

Souvenirs

A Souvenirs Piece is a collection of fake mementos from some particular location or event. For example, *TSWJL* did "Las Vegas Souvenirs." For *The Chevy Chase Show* I created "Items from the Los Angeles Coroner's Office Gift Shop," which included the "Human Rib Cage CD Holder."

And the *LSWDL* piece "Winter Olympics Souvenirs" contained this joke of mine: Dave says, "This souvenir is sure to be snapped up by fans of figure skating and home repair alike. It's from Black and Decker...the 'Tara Lipinski Drill Bit.'" Dave then produces a handheld power drill with a drill bit that resembles figure skater Tara Lipinski balancing on the tip of one skate. Dave uses the rapidly spinning skater to drill a hole into a piece of pine.

How to Create a New Prop Piece

Follow these steps:

1. For a topic, think of a category of physical objects that have something in common. Maybe they're all usually found in the same location (e.g., a toy store) or used for the same general purpose (e.g., medical care) or by the same type of people (e.g., fitness buffs).

If you want the piece to be repeatable, choose a topic with plenty of real items in it, that is, plenty of angles; the more angles a topic has, the easier it will be to write jokes for it. At one extreme, a topic like "New Gift Items" has a virtually unlimited number of angles—basically any real product sold at retail. That's one of the reasons "New Gift Items" has appeared so many times on *LNWDL* and *LSWDL*.

At the other extreme, "Items from the Los Angeles Coroner's Office Gift Shop" on *The Chevy Chase Show* had enough angles to support one installment but not enough that the piece could be repeated (even if the show had stayed on the air). We thought it was worth doing the piece anyway because the topic was fresh and had the virtue of topicality since the real Los Angeles Coroner's Office Gift Shop had just opened.

2. Think of real people, places, and things associated with your chosen category. Those are all possible angles for jokes. For a Winter Olympics Souvenirs piece, for instance, you'd make a mental or written list of all of the sports, the athletes, the rivalries, the equipment, the mascots, the controversies, the host nation, the typical souvenirs, and so on.

Whenever I was trying to come up with angles for the wide-open Prop Piece "New Gift Items" I found it helpful to leaf through the catalogues of quirky merchandise mailed out by Lillian Vernon, Spencer's, The

Sharper Image, and Hammacher Schlommer; nowadays you could browse through those companies' websites. Many of the oddball items for sale could easily be angles that lead to funny variations. For example, the Lillian Vernon "Sink Caddy" holds a sponge, but what other crazily inappropriate item might a caddy hold?

3. Write jokes for the piece using the Punch Line Makers. Start with the topic and the angles—the real people, places, and things—that you thought of in the previous step. For example, when I was writing jokes for a "Museum of Transportation" piece I tried Punch Line Maker #1 on the two handles of the topic: "museum" and "transportation." One association of "museum" was "gift shop snow globe." One association of "transportation" was "the Exxon Valdez oil spill." Linking those two associations in a surprising way through their shared sub-association "stuff floating in water" produced the punch line "The Exxon Valdez Oil-Globe."

You may have to adapt some of the Punch Line Makers slightly to reflect the physical nature of a Prop Piece. For example, one angle on "Winter Olympics Souvenirs" is "figure skating" and one association of "figure skating" is "spinning very fast on one skate." If you were writing the punch line of a Monologue joke you might use a play on words—Punch Line Maker #4. But to generate a punch line for this Prop Piece joke you could try what I've called a "play on images." That is, you could ask yourself what surprising souvenir item a spinning skater resembles. You would then link your answer, an Olympic sponsor's drill bit, to a well-known Olympic skater to arrive at the punch line "It's from Black and Decker...the 'Tara Lipinski Drill Bit.'" (Notice all the stop consonants in that punch line; Joke Maximizer #7 at work.)

Keep in mind that the most successful Prop Piece punch lines tend to be items that actually do something. Not only do functional props tend to be even more surprising—and therefore funnier—to the audience, the host enjoys playing with them. I think one of the reasons Dave Letterman included a figure skater drill bit in two different "Winter Olympics Souvenirs" Pieces, four years apart, is that he had fun operating the power tool. And any time *LSWDL* does the Prop Piece "Rejected FDA Products" the writers are sure to create a disgusting item that Dave can eat or drink, like "Hellmann's Frozen Mayonnaise Bars" that look like Popsicles made of mayonnaise but really aren't.

4. Put your jokes into words using the Joke Maximizers. Write down what the host says to introduce each prop—the angle—and a concise description of what each prop looks like and what it does, if anything. You want your reader to be able to visualize clearly how each joke would play out. For example:

> "Hellmann's is a trusted name in mayonnaise but they misjudged when they tried to enter the frozen dessert market with 'Frozen Mayonnaise Bars.'" [The package looks like a box of Popsicles but reads, "Hellmann's Popsicles. Made With 100% Real Hellmann's." Dave takes out a Popsicle and eats it.]

HOW TO ORDER THE JOKES IN A DESK PIECE

A typical Desk Piece consists of about ten jokes. What order should you put them in to maximize the entertainment value of the piece? The answer goes back to story structure. Since so much of comedy involves telling a story I'd like to take a moment here to discuss story structure a little more.

In most cases, first-rate scripted entertainment goes hand in hand with first-rate storytelling. If you want to captivate an audience with your opera or your sitcom or your graphic novel or your puppet show, tell them a great story. What makes a great story? As I mentioned in Chapter 5, Aristotle said that it must have three acts: the hero wants something, the hero tries hard to get what he wants, and the hero either succeeds or fails.

But another way of looking at those three acts is stated nicely by an impresario in an obscure corner of present-day show business—car auctions. An article by Fernanda Santos in *The New York Times* says this about the president of a company that auctions collectible cars: "The way Steve Davis sees it, arranging collectible cars for display at auction is like writing the script for a good action movie: 'You've got to have a beginning that gets you excited, a middle that grips you and an end that delivers.'"

Have a beginning that gets you excited, a middle that grips you and an end that delivers—that same basic story structure also applies to many comedy pieces on comedy/talk shows. As I suggested in Chapter 5, it shows up in the topic, angle, and punch line of a Monologue joke. You'll notice that it also underlies the guidelines I gave you earlier in this chapter for ordering a "Top Ten List." And that same story structure should shape Desk Pieces, too. Here's how it translates into guidelines for ordering the jokes in a Desk Piece:

- The first couple of jokes should be clear examples of how the piece works and surefire laugh-getters. You want to minimize audience confusion and establish a momentum for the piece.

- The last couple of jokes should be the ones you think are the strongest because you want to end big. In the case of a Prop Piece, you also want to end with the physically biggest jokes since it would be hard to top their visual impact.

- Slot one of your best jokes in the middle of the series, so the energy of the piece doesn't dip.

- Say you have ten jokes and you rate them on a scale of 1 to 5 as follows (5 being the funniest): 1,1,2,2,3,3,4,4,5,5. Arrange the jokes like this when you assemble the piece for performance: 3,3,2,1,4,1,2,4,5,5. This order lets the stronger jokes support the weaker ones and keeps the piece moving.

- Separate any jokes that are similar in angle, physical appearance, subject matter, or any other way so that the piece stays as surprising as possible.

Those guidelines also apply to ordering the jokes in any other comedy piece that consists of a series of unconnected jokes.

SUMMARY

Sorting comedy pieces into categories has two benefits:
- It helps you generate ideas for new comedy pieces by giving you a way to cut that task down to a more manageable size and then use existing comedy pieces as inspiration.
- It allows you to take advantage of writing techniques specific to each category.

One category of comedy piece is the Desk Piece—a segment of fully-scripted comedy that the host performs by himself while sitting at his desk. Desk Pieces have three additional key characteristics:
- They are joke baskets in that they consist of a theme and about ten jokes that share that theme.
- They are dependable laugh-getters.
- They are usually repeatable.

The seven types of Desk Pieces are:
- **Text Pieces**—The jokes are displayed only as text on the screen.

- **Illustrated Monologues**—The jokes are spoken, not displayed on the screen, and are accompanied by undoctored photos.
- **Text/Photo Pieces**—The jokes are displayed as text and are accompanied by undoctored photos.
- **Audio Pieces**—The jokes consist of audio clips.
- **Art Card Pieces**—The jokes are illustrated with custom-made artwork.
- **Graphic/Prop Pieces**—The jokes are physical items that have been altered using custom-made text or other graphics.
- **Prop Pieces**—The jokes are custom-made physical items.

You use slightly different techniques to create each type of Desk Piece but the following five basic steps are typical:

1. Pick one of the above types of Desk Pieces.
2. Pick a topic for your piece that suggests a lot of associations and that your audience is likely to find acceptable and relatable.
3. For possible joke angles, list real items related to your chosen topic.
4. Write jokes for the piece using the Punch Line Makers. Link associations of the topic and of the angles—the real items you listed—with each other and with pop culture phenomena.
5. Polish the jokes using the Joke Maximizers.

Order the jokes in a Desk Piece so that the piece starts with a couple of guaranteed laughs, stays surprising, and ends with a bang. Slot weaker jokes in the middle, flanked by stronger jokes.

Next I'll talk about a type of Desk Piece that spins comedy from things that aren't supposed to be funny. This is the Found Comedy Piece.

8

FOUND COMEDY PIECES

A FOUND COMEDY PIECE is a kind of Desk Piece in which each joke is based on some unaltered object that wasn't originally intended to be funny. That is, the writer finds comedy in an everyday item as it already exists, like a particular newspaper headline. By contrast, each joke in the other Desk Pieces I've discussed is constructed entirely in the writer's mind.

To see the difference, consider one of the Desk Pieces I mentioned in the previous chapter, the Text/Photo Piece "Celebrity Summer Plans." When a writer writes a joke for that piece about, say, Bill Gates, he doesn't need a photo of Bill in front of him. All he needs is the idea of Bill Gates. Some photo of Bill is obtained to accompany the joke only after the joke has been written and is being produced for the show.

But when a writer writes a joke about Bill Gates for a Found Comedy Photo Piece like "What Were They Thinking," the photo comes first. The writer needs to be looking at some actual photo of Bill to be able to write the joke. The joke couldn't exist without the photo because the joke is partly derived from the details in the photo.

To make a sports analogy, writing jokes for the Desk Pieces covered in the previous chapter is like holding a baseball and bat, tossing the baseball into the air, and hitting it; you, the batter, control every step of the process. By contrast, writing jokes for a Found Comedy Piece is like standing at home plate with a bat and hitting a ball that's pitched to you; you have to deal with whatever pitch comes your way. In both cases the batted ball flies out onto the field—meaning the joke is delivered—but the process behind how the ball gets there is different.

Most comedy/talk shows present both totally-scripted comedy pieces and Found Comedy Pieces, the same way that television networks air both totally-scripted shows and semi-scripted "reality" shows. The variety of programming helps keep viewers from getting bored.

THE FIVE TYPES OF FOUND COMEDY PIECES

Found Comedy Pieces fall into five categories:

- **Text Pieces**, where the jokes are based mainly on unaltered words published in print media or online. One example is "Headlines," which was performed every week on *TSWJL*.

- **Photo Pieces**, in which the jokes are derived from unaltered photographs, often news photos. An example of this type of piece is "Barack Obama Facial Expressions" on *LNWJF*.

- **Prop Pieces**, in which the jokes are about unaltered physical objects, usually products offered for sale somewhere. "Supermarket Finds" on *LSWDL* is a piece of this type.

- **Audio Pieces**, where the jokes are written about unaltered audio clips obtained from various sources. An example is "Dave's Record Collection" on *LSWDL*.

- **Video Pieces,** in which the jokes are based on unscripted video clips, possibly of unsuspecting pedestrians. One example is "Amusement Park Quiz" on *LSWDL*.

I'll discuss each of these categories in detail in this chapter. But first let's take a look at the general process for putting a Found Comedy Piece together.

HOW TO CREATE A FOUND COMEDY PIECE

No matter what type of Found Comedy Piece you're creating the process is always roughly the same. It consists of the following steps:

1. For the theme of your piece, pick a category of everyday objects that have a lot of variety. A category composed of a large number of diverse items, like news photos, will give you plenty of potential topics for jokes.

2. Collect a few dozen promising, real items in your chosen category. Because these items will be potential topics, look for promising items the way you'd look for potential topics for Monologue jokes. That is, look for items that attract your attention because they seem weird, offbeat, or interesting in some way. As you collect these items, keep a couple of points in mind:

- To find enough real items to yield a finished comedy piece of about ten jokes you may have to sort through and eliminate dozens of duds. Found Comedy Pieces are a volume operation. They require a lot of raw material since the topics aren't scripted but supplied by the real world. Returning to my baseball analogy, a batter may have to wait out several pitches before he gets one worth taking a swing at.

- Be sure the real items you choose were not originally intended to be funny. Found Comedy Pieces work because of the Superiority Theory of Laughter. So if an amusing headline, say, seems to be a scripted joke instead of a screw-up, the audience won't be able to feel superior to some careless headline writer and won't laugh at your joke about the headline.

3. Write jokes for the piece using the Punch Line Makers and Joke Maximizers. For joke topics, use the real items that you harvested in the previous step. Spread out on the table all those actual headlines, photographs, supermarket purchases, or whatever your piece is about and start brainstorming.

That's the general process. Now let's take a closer look at the different categories of Found Comedy Pieces.

FOUND COMEDY TEXT PIECES

In a Found Comedy Text Piece the jokes are based on words that have been published somewhere. Here are some pieces in this category:

"Police Blotter" [*TSWJL*]—Jay reads clippings about crimes taken from the Police Blotter sections of various newspapers and ad-libs jokes about them. Sample entry: "8:06 p.m.—A woman sped away from a gas station at Hinman and Harvey Avenues with the gas nozzle still in the tank. Police made contact with the woman, who said she had to hurry home for a bowel movement." [Then Jay comments.] "Hey, you don't want to use the bathroom at the gas station, okay?"

"Missed Connections" [*TSWJL*]—Jay reads an ad that actually appeared in the "Missed Connections" section of the website

Craigslist. Then, supposedly to help the person who placed the ad meet the person he's looking for, Jay shows a comedy music video depicting the situation described in the ad.

"Late Night Hashtags" [*LNWJF*]—Jimmy shares actual tweets that his viewers posted on Twitter based on a topic, a hashtag, that he announced on an earlier show. For example, Jimmy announces the hashtag "Worst Car I Ever Had." On a later show he improvises jokes and brief scenes based on his viewers' tweets about their clunkers.

How to Create a Found Comedy Text Piece

I listed the general steps for creating a Found Comedy Piece above. Now let's take a look at how those steps work in the particular case of two pieces derived from newspaper clippings.

1. For the theme of your piece, pick a category of everyday objects that have a lot of variety. Newspaper articles have a lot of variety, which is why Dave Letterman has been able to perform "Small Town News" for years on *LNWDL* and *LSWDL*. For a long time Jay Leno also presented a very similar piece on *TSWJL* called "Headlines."

2. Collect a few dozen promising, real items in your chosen category. Each of those actual news items and headlines is potentially the topic for a joke. The raw material for both "Small Town News" and "Headlines" is assembled in basically the same way. Viewers mail to the shows hundreds of unintentionally humorous headlines, news stories, advertisements, wedding announcements, and other items published in newspapers. (This crowdsourcing saves a huge amount of time. Years ago, writers on *LSWDL* had to find all the offbeat news clippings themselves by personally plowing through the dozens of small-town newspapers that the show subscribed to.)

3. Write jokes for the piece using the Punch Line Makers and Joke Maximizers. Jay ad-libbed any jokes he told about the clippings used in "Headlines" but the process is different for "Small Town News." Before the show, *LSWDL* writers write punch lines for as many clippings as they can. A dozen or so clippings and their accompanying punch lines are chosen from the stack and mounted on cardboard. Finally, Dave displays the mounted clippings on the show and delivers the punch lines.

Here are a few sample jokes from "Small Town News" on *LSWDL*:

> "This is from the *Amarillo Globe-News*, Amarillo, Texas. A wedding announcement..." [Dave shows it.] "Moose-Greaser." [Then Dave delivers the punch line.] "Look out, because that's the sort of thing you get sued for." Using Punch Line Maker #3, the writer asked the question, "What would happen if you greased a moose?" He answered the question, and got his punch line, by using an association of "moose greasing," which is that it sounds very, very wrong.

> "This is from the *American*, Fairland, Oklahoma." [Dave displays a captioned news photo of an elderly man holding up a notebook.] "A raffle winner at the Grand Traveler's Breakfast Club... Jimmy D. Newton won a decorated spiral notebook." [Then Dave comments.] "You know his phone is going to be ringing off the hook with all the town widows calling him." Punch Line Maker #1 was used here. The punch line combines an association of "elderly man" (i.e., "widow") and an association of "raffle winner" (i.e., "becomes popular").

And here are two ads that appeared in "Headlines" on *TSWJL*:

> "This is when you know you're going to a high-class restaurant. It's an ad for Wilson's Barbecue. Look at their slogan: 'U Need

No Teeth to Eat Our Beef.'" [Then Jay comments.] "So if you're dating a meth head, this might be a good place." Jay used Punch Line Maker #3 and asked the question, "Who would appreciate eating at that restaurant?" The answer, and punch line, came from an association of "no teeth," which is "meth addict."

[Jay displays a classified ad.] "Musical Merchandise for Sale: Bedside Commode with toilet riser and grip arms." [Then Jay comments.] "You know, I don't want to go to that concert, okay?" Using Punch Line Maker #1, Jay got his punch line by combining associations of "musical" (i.e., "concert") and "bedside commode" (i.e., "disgusting").

FOUND COMEDY PHOTO PIECES

In a Found Comedy Photo Piece the jokes are based on real, undoctored photographs. Here are some examples:

"Obama Expressions" [LNWJF]—In this piece Jimmy displays a series of news photos of the President. Jimmy tells the audience what the President's facial expression in each photo supposedly means. For example, Jimmy shows a photo of the President laughing and interprets his expression to mean, "Stop tickling me, Biden."

"Animal Thoughts" [LNWJF]—Jimmy shows stock photos of people with animals. He first tells us what the person in the photo is supposedly thinking—the angle of the joke—then the punch line of what the animal is thinking. Both thoughts are superimposed on the photo in comic book-style balloons of text. For example, a photo shows a woman sitting at her desk on an inflatable ball chair as a dog reclines on the floor nearby. The woman is thinking, "I'm sitting on a giant ball." And the dog is thinking, "Sigh. I remember when I had those."

"What Were They Thinking?" [*TSWJL*]—The idea for this piece came from the observation that many people have odd expressions in their driver's license photos. Jay shows the driver's license photos of various people in the studio audience and tells us what each person must have been thinking when the picture was taken.

Here's how that piece was produced. About an hour and a half before the show the writers borrowed over a hundred driver's licenses from audience members waiting to get into the studio. (It still amazes me that people from all over the country would trust us total strangers enough to hand over their driver's licenses. Their trust was not misplaced though; we never lost one.)

Because the piece had to be produced so quickly, some punch lines were written earlier in the day. The writers then found driver's license photos to fit as many of those prewritten punch lines as possible. For example, a photo of some bleary-eyed frat boy would be found to go with the punch line, "Bartender, more Jell-O shots." The writers also pored over the photos and wrote more punch lines on the spot.

Finally, during the show, each selected driver's license photo was displayed as a still. Jay delivered the punch line (which also appeared in a thought balloon on the photo) and we saw the live audience member in the studio, ideally laughing. Another sample joke (for a photo of a smiling, middle-aged guy): "What did I ever do without women's underwear?"

Of course, late-night shows aren't the only places you can find comedy that consists of adding punch lines to photographs. The popular online blog I Can Has Cheezburger? invites people to submit photos of cats or other animals to which funny captions have been added. In fact, the Internet is awash in photographic memes with joke captions, like that picture of a toddler—"Success Kid"—holding up a fistful of sand. And humorous caption contests have been a staple at *The New Yorker* and other publications for years.

How to Create a Found Comedy Photo Piece

Follow these six steps:

1. Pick a theme that involves making jokes about what people or animals are doing. With a theme about people or animals you'll probably have no trouble gathering enough potential topics for jokes, that is, enough real photographs. You'll also have plenty of options when it comes to punch lines because the number of possible things that people or animals could be doing—including things they could be thinking or saying—is infinite.

By contrast, you'd have way fewer options if your theme were about inanimate objects. Inanimate objects don't do anything. And because they don't do anything it's hard to feel superior to them and—according to the Superiority Theory—hard to get an audience to laugh at them. For example, it would be very difficult to write a funny Found Comedy Photo Piece about photographs of rocks.

2. For joke topics, gather promising photographs related to your theme. For instance, if your theme is "Obama Expressions," get lots of photos of the President with various expressions. If your theme is more general, like "A Day in the Life of California," you could harvest raw material by typing "odd news photos" into your favorite Internet search engine. (You'd have to pay for any photos you use on the air, of course.) If you want a dozen jokes in your finished piece, which is a typical number, collect at least a hundred promising photos to start.

What makes a photo promising as a topic for a Found Comedy joke? A promising photo shares three characteristics with a promising topic for a Monologue joke, namely:

> **a) The photo depicts a scene that's somehow out-of-the-ordinary.** In other words, the photo is distinctive, odd, surprising, or attention-getting for some reason. If the photo engages your interest, that's a good sign that it will engage the interest of the audience, too.

> **b) The photo depicts a simple scene.** That's important because what's going on in the photo has to be clear. I don't just mean clear as in "in-focus"; I mean clear as in unambiguous and easy-to-absorb. In most cases, that means the photo shows only one or two people (or animals) performing only one action. If the photo is uncluttered, the audience will all quickly focus on the same handles in the photo, that is, the same key details. That means that the audience will all easily absorb the information from the photo that they need in order to get the joke.

> **c) The photo depicts a scene that is acceptable to joke about.** Before you use a photo for a joke, consider what the photo actually depicts and ask yourself whether anybody might be offended by your using the photo for comedy. Then decide whether the joke is worth the possible fallout.

3. Briefly describe the scene in each promising photograph using its handles. That is, pick out the handles of each scene by (a) identifying the one or two people or things that draw your attention first and (b) naming any action that those people or things are performing. Then use those handles to summarize the scene in a short sentence. Sample descriptive sentences could be "A very unhappy guy is wailing about something" or "A man is holding a meat cleaver to his tongue." This descriptive, topic sentence will bridge the gap between the *visual* topic represented by the photo and a *verbal* punch line.

4. Write a punch line for each photo using the Punch Line Makers and the topic sentence you created in the previous step. For example, say you're

Here's an example of the fall-out that can occur because of a misjudgment about a photo. One time on *TSWJL* Jay showed a photo of the Golden Temple in Amritsar, a site important to the Sikh religion, and claimed that the imposing structure was the summer home of wealthy Presidential hopeful Mitt Romney. The joke earned a big laugh but also the anger of some Sikhs and Indian officials and provoked a minor international incident.

writing "Obama Expressions" and you have a photo that you describe with the topic sentence, "Obama is laughing." You could use Punch Line Maker #3 and ask the question, "Why is Obama laughing?" The two handles of that topic sentence are "Obama," which has the association "Biden," and "laughing," which has the association "getting tickled." Linking those two associations gives you the punch line that aired: "Stop tickling me, Biden."

As another example, say your assignment is to use news photos to write the Found Comedy Photo Piece, "A Day in the Life of California." You describe one photo that grabs your interest with the sentence, "A man holds a bunch of long balloons." You can write a punch line for that photo by adapting Punch Line Maker #2. One handle of the topic sentence is "bunch of long balloons." You can associate long balloons with inflated condoms. Then you can link that bunch of inflated condoms to a pop culture figure who might need them, add an angle, and create this joke: "Valentine's Day means overtime work for Charlie Sheen's personal condom tester."

5. Be sure that each punch line is based on the visual details in the photo but not on the underlying reality of the photo. That is, your punch line shouldn't comment on the scene that's actually depicted in the photo but rather create a new meaning for the scene based on the details in the photo. As Dave Letterman used to tell us writers, "Write to the photo, not about the photo." That's why when I'm brainstorming jokes about a news photo I don't even read the official caption attached to it; I want an unbiased perspective.

For example, if a news photo shows a flabby sumo wrestler your punch line shouldn't be about a sumo wrestler; it should be about, say, an overweight celebrity. Remember the Surprise Theory of Laughter: if you avoid the obvious in your punch line it will be more surprising and, therefore, funnier.

6. Edit each joke using the Joke Maximizers. For instance, be sure the laugh trigger is at the end of each joke. Referring back to the Charlie Sheen joke above, you wouldn't want to bury the laugh trigger "condom tester" and submit this version: "The guy who tests Charlie Sheen's condoms has to put in a lot of overtime on Valentine's Day."

FOUND COMEDY PROP PIECES

A Found Comedy Prop Piece consists of jokes that are based not on two-dimensional images but on three-dimensional objects. The objects aren't custom-built by the prop department, as they would be for a Desk Piece like "New Gift Items," but collected from the real world. They're usually products available for purchase somewhere and, like all Found Comedy fodder, they are inadvertently funny.

Here are some Found Comedy Prop Pieces that have aired in late night:

"Supermarket Finds" [*LSWDL*]—Dave shows an array of quirky items purchased in supermarkets and tells jokes about them. (I can personally attest to the fact that Found Comedy Pieces can be very labor-intensive because I spent many an afternoon tromping around the grocery stores and bodegas of Manhattan trying to find promising products for this piece.) Sample joke: Dave holds up a packaged food item called "Wow, It's Not Chicken!" and comments, "Wow, it's not selling." Note the use of Joke Maximizer #6: make the punch line parallel.

"Do Not Read List" [*LNWJF*]—Jimmy jokes about real books that he holds up and advises his viewers to avoid. Sample joke: Jimmy displays a cookbook with a pot of cheese fondue on its cover and the title "Not Your Mother's Fondue." He comments, "Really? Is it cheese melted in a bucket? Then it *is* my mother's fondue."

"Stuff We Found on eBay" [*TSWJL*]—Jay displays screenshots of unusual items that were listed for sale on the website eBay, like a Dixie cup full of some guy's beard trimmings. After presenting each item and ad-libbing a joke or two Jay invites the studio audience to vote out loud on whether they think the item was "Sold" or "Not Sold." Then Jay reveals the answer. (The "Cup-O-Beard" sold for $1.75.) This added element of audience participation creates a hybrid between a Found Comedy Piece and a Semi-Scripted Audience Piece, freshening up what might have been a routine segment. I'll discuss Audience Pieces in detail in Chapter 12.

How to Create a Found Comedy Prop Piece

The steps are variations of those you'd take to create any Found Comedy Piece:

1. For your theme, pick a category of real physical objects that has a lot of variety. A category like that will give you plenty of items to use as joke topics. Categories consisting of items for sale somewhere, like in a supermarket or on eBay, tend to be fertile for joke writing because of the Superiority Theory of Laughter. We laugh at the lame items because we feel superior to the clueless people who are trying to sell them to us.

2. For raw material, collect two or three dozen promising objects in that category. The most promising objects are the ones that strike you as odd or inappropriate somehow. Those objects—what they look like, what they do, how they're described—are possible topics for your jokes.

3. Write a joke for each object using the Punch Line Makers and Joke Maximizers. As an example, let's look at "Products for a Better You," on *TSWJL*. This Found Comedy Prop Piece features real, if strange, health and beauty aids that are available for purchase online. Sample joke: Jay says, "This is something to help you improve your diet. It's the Peter Petrie Egg Separator." Jay shows a ceramic mug that looks like the head of a man with a bulbous nose. "Now, you all know you're not supposed to eat the yellow part, the yolk. So you break an egg like this... [Jay breaks an egg into the mug.]...hold it up...and the yellow part stays in." The clear part of the egg oozes out of nostril holes in the man's nose, looking like snot. Jay jokes, "See, the real key to this is it makes you lose your appetite so you don't want to eat at all." Jay's punch line was constructed using Punch Line Maker #1. It links an association of the verbal handle "improve your diet" (i.e., "eat less") and an association of the visual handle of dripping snot (i.e., "nauseating").

FOUND COMEDY AUDIO PIECES

In a Found Comedy Audio Piece the jokes are based on unintentionally funny audio clips. You won't find many Found Comedy Audio Pieces on comedy/talk shows, probably because audio pieces don't play to television's strength as a visual medium. But here are a couple of examples:

"Dealing with the Public" [*TSWJL*]—This piece consists mostly of audio recordings of actual calls to 911 operators, with some police videos included for variety. The words of each moronic call are superimposed on the screen to make sure the audience can understand them. Jay ad-libs jokes.

"Dave's Record Collection" [*LNWDL*]—Dave plays and jokes about snippets of audio from offbeat record albums. Sample joke: after listening to ten seconds of the album "Cybill Shepherd Sings Cole Porter," Dave looks worried and remarks, "I think somebody's breaking into my car." Note that that punch line springs from an audio variation of Punch Line Maker #3. The writer asked, "What else does that clip of Cybill singing sound like?" He answered the question by using an association of the singing: "a car alarm."

FOUND COMEDY VIDEO PIECES

A Found Comedy Video Piece consists of, as you can probably guess, jokes based on unintentionally funny video clips. Entire television shows have sprung from this concept of cracking jokes about video footage that isn't supposed to be funny, such as *Mystery Science Theater 3000*, Comedy Central's *Tosh.0*, and truTV's *World's Dumbest* shows (e.g., *World's Dumbest Criminals*, *World's Dumbest Drivers*, and *World's Dumbest Partiers*). The Superiority Theory of Laughter rears its mocking head again: we laugh because we feel superior to the losers caught on camera.

Found Comedy Video Pieces are also popular on comedy/talk shows. Here are some examples:

"Dave's Video Collection" [*LSWDL*]—This segment is the video version of "Dave's Record Collection." Dave shows brief clips from videos available for purchase and tells jokes about the clips. (Each time we did this piece it took forever to put together. Not only did we, the writers, have to find and buy dozens and dozens of off-beat videocassettes, we then had to watch each one in its entirety to find a clip strange enough to mock.) Sample joke: Dave shows a clip of weird, white-haired, German singer Heino crooning among children, then delivers the act-out punch line, "Mommy, I had that nightmare about the creepy singing freak with the white hair again!"

"Elected or Not Elected" [*TSWJL*]—Jay shows a series of political commercials that aired on various TV stations across the U.S., ad-libs humorous comments about them, then asks the audience to shout out whether they think each candidate was "Elected" or "Not Elected." Like "Stuff We Found on eBay," this piece is a good example of how to energize a standard Found Comedy Piece by putting an audience participation twist on it.

"Celebrity Whispers" [*LNWJF*]—The audience sees news footage of celebrities talking to each other on the red carpet at some event. Jimmy uses his own voice to dub in silly things that the celebrities are supposedly whispering to each other. For example, one actress is supposedly explaining to another actress the plot of an episode of the cartoon series "Scooby Doo."

How to Create a Found Comedy Video Piece

The process is similar to creating a Found Comedy Photo Piece. Here are the steps:

1. For a theme, choose a category of real videos that's likely to have a lot of variety. The category should also be one that you think will yield enough clips to serve as joke topics for a full segment. Not all categories qualify. For example, the *LSWDL* staff managed to gather enough strange commercials from CBS-affiliated TV stations to put together a "Small Town Television Commercials" piece, but just barely.

2. Collect raw material related to your theme; then from those videos select several dozen promising clips. Each clip should be about ten or fifteen seconds long. A clip is a promising topic for a joke if it shows a scene that has three characteristics:

- It captures your interest with its peculiarity or inappropriateness.
- It's simple and clear, with not a lot going on in it; it probably features only one or two people performing an activity that's easy to describe.
- The audience and host will consider it an acceptable subject for comedy.

That clip of Heino singing to children that I mentioned above has all three of those characteristics.

3. Briefly describe the scene in each promising video clip using its handles. That is, identify the handles of the scene—the one or two people or things that you notice first and what they are doing. Then use the handles in a short sentence that sums up the scene. This will be the topic sentence that you'll base your verbal punch lines on. For example, the Heino clip can be summarized as "A creepy guy is singing to kids."

4. Write a punch line for each clip using the Punch Line Makers and the topic sentence you created in the previous step. For instance, you could use Punch Line Maker #3 on the Heino clip that you described as "A creepy guy is singing to kids" and ask the "Five Ws and an H" question, "What would a kid say if he saw that creepy guy?" An association of both "creepy guy" and "kid" is "nightmare," leading to the punch line, "Mommy, I had that nightmare about the creepy singing freak with the white hair again!"

For another example of this process in action let's look at the Found Comedy Video Piece "What's On Other Channels," from *LNWDL*. In the piece Dave displays and describes video that viewers could (supposedly) be watching instead of his show; the video clips Dave presents are stock footage, usually old and black-and-white. A sample joke: "Here we have Channel Eleven. I think this might be a commercial." The video clip shows a series of men diving off a building onto a long, fabric chute and sliding swiftly to the ground several stories below. "It's for Ramada Inn's new Express Checkout Service."

How was that joke written? The writer apparently summarized the scene with a sentence like, "Guys leave a building really fast." Then he applied Punch Line Maker #1 to that topic sentence this way: An association of "building" is "hotel" and an association of "leave fast" is "express checkout." Linking those two associations produced the punch line. Finally, Joke Maximizer #9 was used to upgrade the punch line from the general "hotel" to the specific "Ramada Inn."

Just as with the punch lines for a Found Comedy Photo Piece, your punch lines should be "to the footage, not about the footage." In other words, each punch line should spring from the details of the video clip but create surprising new meanings for those details. A weaker punch line for that last joke, one that's "about the footage," would be a punch line that took the scene at face value, like "In this episode of *The Amazing Race*, one team takes a shortcut out of their hotel."

Found Comedy Video Pieces Based on Street Footage

So far I've only talked about Found Comedy Video Pieces that are based on existing footage. But an easier way to gather raw material for such a piece can often be to secretly record footage yourself, say on the street or at a public event. In that case the footage itself isn't "found," since you're creating it. What is "found" is the appearance or unscripted behavior of the unsuspecting people captured by your camera. And you can write comedy about those inadvertently funny people.

Here are some examples of this type of Found Comedy Video Piece:

"What Were They Thinking?" [*TSWJL*]—This is the video version of the Found Comedy Photo Piece I told you about that uses the audience's driver's license photos. In this version Jay shows a series of video clips of unsuspecting pedestrians. For each clip he reads aloud a comic book-style balloon that appears next to the pedestrian's head telling what that person is supposedly thinking. Sample punch line about a young man rolling down the street on a skateboard: "This is the last time I ride Greyhound's Economy Class."

"Pedestrian Theme Songs" [*LSWDL*]—The audience sees candid video clips of individuals on the street. As each video plays, Paul Shaffer and his band perform a short theme song about the individual that they've written with the writers. The lyrics comment in a funny way on some distinctive detail of the person's appearance or behavior. Sample song lyrics for a woman wearing a knee-length coat made of fluffy pink material: "I had no clothes to wear. / It was a horrid situation / until I made a coat out of / my attic's insulation!"

"Arriving at the Oscars" [*TSWJL*]—The audience sees a series of casually-dressed tourists getting off an outdoor escalator. (The show tapes this footage at nearby Universal Studios Hollywood.) Jay announces each individual as if he or she were some celebrity arriving at the Academy Awards. The joke is that the individual actually does kind of resemble the celebrity in an unexpected or unflattering way. Sample joke about an overweight man in a tunic: "Ladies and gentlemen… William Shatner.")

"Amusement Park Quiz" [*LSWDL*]—The host reads quiz questions aloud as viewers watch video clips of scenes in an amusement park. Each clip freezes and three possible answers to the corresponding question are superimposed on the screen. A sample joke about two expressionless men sitting on a park bench: "These men are (a) waiting for their families, (b) enjoying the lovely summer day, or (c) on the least-thrilling ride at the park." This comedy piece is a hybrid of a Found Comedy Video Piece and a Text Quiz.

How to Create a Found Comedy Video Piece Based on Street Footage

Follow these steps:

1. Pick a theme that involves making jokes about who people are or what they are doing. A theme like that will give you plenty of options for generating punch lines.

2. Pick a taping location where there are likely to be many distinctive people, things, and activities. That's important because you'll need lots of video clips, providing a wide variety of potential topics and handles, and you may have a limited amount of time to record them. A downtown street with plenty of pedestrian traffic is usually a good bet, or an event like a parade. Times Square has always been a target-rich environment for *LSWDL* comedy writers, with its mix of kooky locals and vacationing misfits.

3. At your chosen location, record video of sights that grab your attention. Here are some tips for doing that:

- Sound won't be necessary, so you can leave your microphones at home.

- Each shot should be about fifteen to thirty seconds long to give your video editor options.

- You'll probably need at least a hundred different shots to be sure you have enough raw material to write a ten-joke piece because not every shot will yield a solid joke.

- Don't just pick the subjects of your shots at random. Aim to capture scenes with the same characteristics that I listed above for promising clips for Found Comedy Video Pieces. That is, look for scenes that are somehow out-of-the-ordinary and are simple enough that you can summarize them with a brief sentence. That young man on a skateboard? Tape him. That woman in the fluffy pink coat? Tape her, too.

- Be sure your shots of people are candid. The Superiority Theory of Laughter comes into play here: if it's obvious that your subject is aware of the camera, the audience can't feel superior to her and won't laugh as hard. So shoot your unsuspecting subjects from a good distance away to avoid alerting them or maybe use a friend as camouflage, pointing your camera over his shoulder.

4. Have your raw footage edited down into a series of individual shots. Each shot should last about eight seconds and end in a freeze-frame so the video doesn't run out before the host has finished reading the joke. These hundred or more edited video clips are your potential joke topics.

5. For each video clip, write a descriptive topic sentence and use it to create a punch line with the Punch Line Makers. This is the same process I described earlier in this chapter for writing punch lines for Found Comedy Video Pieces.

Take the clip that I described above with the topic sentence "a young man on a skateboard," for example. In this case the writers used Punch Line Maker #2. They associated the handle "skateboard" with "cheap transportation," which suggested the pop culture reference "Greyhound." That yielded the punch line: "This is the last time I ride Greyhound's Economy Class."

6. Polish the joke using the Joke Maximizers. That young man isn't just riding Greyhound, he's riding Greyhound's Economy Class, thanks to Joke Maximizer #8 ("wildly exaggerate").

GETTING RELEASES

One question that might have occurred to you is, "How can a show get away with secretly videotaping people and joking about them on national television?" The answer has to do with releases. A release—or video release form—is a document signed by people after you tape them that gives your show permission to air the clips and possibly make fun of the people. Your show's lawyers provide you with the release forms or you can find them online.

When recording candid footage in a public place, say for a Found Comedy Video Piece, do you need to get releases from every pedestrian that you shoot in order to minimize the chance of your show getting sued? I'm not a lawyer so I can't give you a definitive answer.

What I can tell you is that the lawyers for at least one show I worked on insisted that the staff get a signed release from every identifiable pedestrian our camera operator focused on. One time we shot a Found Comedy Video Piece for that show at a busy intersection in downtown Las Vegas. The crew included four production assistants whose job was to run down and get signed releases from pedestrians. (Me: "The guy in the leather chaps! Get him!")

But another show I worked on didn't really care about getting releases for Found Comedy Video Pieces. The show operated under the principle that individuals in a public place have no "reasonable expectation of privacy" and therefore have no right to expect that they won't appear on national television. To the best of my knowledge that show only faced legal action from disgruntled pedestrians a couple of times even though it had aired dozens of comedy pieces based on street footage over the years.

So whether or not you'll want to bother to get releases from the unsuspecting people you shoot in public places depends on your tolerance (or, more importantly, the tolerance of your show's lawyers) for risk. Of course, if you're shooting people who might reasonably expect privacy, like people in a public bathroom, then you'd better get them to sign releases. And if you're shooting on private property, say inside a store, you'll need a signed release from an authorized representative of the property owner. If you can't get a release that you think is necessary, don't use that person or location in your comedy piece.

And again, I'm not a lawyer. So whatever you do, don't blame me.

SUMMARY

A Found Comedy Piece is a kind of Desk Piece in which the jokes are based on unaltered objects that weren't originally intended to be funny. The five types of Found Comedy Pieces are:

1. **Text Pieces**, based on words published in print media
2. **Photo Pieces**, based on photographs
3. **Prop Pieces**, based on physical objects
4. **Audio Pieces**, based on audio clips
5. **Video Pieces**, based on video clips

Create a Found Comedy Piece by following these four basic steps:

1. **For the theme of your piece, choose a category of real things that has a lot of variety.**

2. **Collect a few dozen promising items in your chosen category.** Look for items that grab your attention. Be sure they weren't originally intended to be funny.

3. **Write jokes for the piece using the Punch Line Makers.** Start with the items that you harvested in the previous step; they are your joke topics. Then, for Found Comedy Pieces other than Text Pieces, identify one or two handles of each item and use those handles in a short topic sentence that describes the item. Finally, use the Punch Line Makers on this descriptive sentence. Make sure that each punch line creates surprising new meanings for the details of the item.

4. **Polish the joke using the Joke Maximizers.**

Until now I've talked mostly about comedy pieces that the host performs by himself. In the next chapter I'll cover pieces in which other performers help the host deliver the jokes—what I call Joke Basket Sketches.

JOKE BASKET SKETCHES

S O FAR I'VE covered Monologues, Desk Pieces, and a particular type of Desk Piece, the Found Comedy Piece. All of those pieces are joke baskets. That is, they're composed of a series of interchangeable jokes gathered together by a single topic or theme, a metaphorical basket. Some of the joke basket topics and themes I've talked about are "Top Ten List" topics, "Thank You Notes," and "Stuff We Found on eBay." Until now the only joke baskets I've discussed are ones performed by the host alone.

Now I'll turn to a different type of joke basket that I call a Joke Basket Sketch. Here are a few of its characteristics:

- A Joke Basket Sketch involves performers in addition to the host. That's why I don't consider a Joke Basket Sketch to be a Desk Piece even if the host is sitting at his desk while he performs in it.

- As with every other joke basket, a Joke Basket Sketch consists of jokes that are interchangeable because they're not strung together in any kind of story line. (If the jokes are tied together by a story line I'd call the piece a Story Sketch. I'll discuss those in the next chapter.)

- There are three types of Joke Basket Sketches: live, taped, and multimedia, which has both live and taped elements.

In this chapter I'll take a close look at those three types of Joke Basket Sketches plus some other sketches you can write using the same techniques. Those other sketches include Cold Openings, Cold Closes, Excursions, Theme Shows, and Joke Basket Characters.

LIVE JOKE BASKET SKETCHES

In a typical Live Joke Basket Sketch, the host introduces the piece at his desk, announcing its topic. Then he delivers a series of jokes on that topic assisted by other performers in the studio, who could be staffers.

Among the categories of Live Joke Basket Sketches you'll see are Costume Sketches, Around the Horns, and Studio Tours. I'll describe each category in turn, including how to come up with ideas for new sketches in each category. Then I'll tell you how to write jokes for those sketches.

Costume Sketches

In a Costume Sketch the punch lines of the jokes are costumes worn by performers. As with many pieces on comedy/talk shows, the jokes may or may not be based on current events. Here are some pieces in this category:

> **"Halloween Costumes"** [*LSWDL*]—Dave stands in a living room set and, each time the doorbell rings, opens the front door to

reveal a youngster in a funny Halloween costume. Sample joke. A trick-or-treater is wearing a large, plastic oblong that reads, "AUX." Dave explains, "It's eerie, it's frightening, it's The Mysterious Button on the Remote Control You Never Use."

"Beachwear Fashion Show" [*TSWJL*]—Jay comments on the new beachwear worn by a succession of male and female models who parade into the studio. Sample joke: Jay says, "Some women will do anything to attract men at the beach. So women who want a little extra edge over their competition will want to wear this TV Sports Bikini. It displays continuous baseball highlights. Men won't be able to take their eyes off you!" A woman strides out wearing a bikini; on each of her breasts is a small TV screen showing baseball highlights.

"Rejected *Star Wars* Characters" [*LNWCO*]—Conan introduces a succession of costumed performers who portray characters supposedly cut out of the latest *Star Wars* movie. Sample joke: Conan says, "George Lucas wanted to make a tougher, meaner version of the robot R2D2 by combining him with a badass TV icon from the 1980s. It didn't quite work, but here he is: R2-Mr. T-2." The R2D2 robot appears onstage with the hairstyle and gold chains of *The A-Team* actor Mr. T. The robot whistles and chirps, which is translated via on-screen text as "I pity the Sith." (Mr. T's catchphrase was "I pity the fool.")

How to Create a New Costume Sketch

For your topic, think of a group of people who are distinguished by their specialized clothing. The clothing should have enough variety to provide plenty of angles for jokes. You can probably create a Costume Sketch out of funny versions of that group's clothing. Examples of groups that fit that description are the ones featured above: trick-or-treaters, beachgoers, and actors in *Star Wars*. What about sports team mascots? Brides? Olympic athletes?

Around the Horns

"Around the horn" is an expression used in baseball. It refers to that little ritual where the infielders throw the ball to each other in turn after their team gets an out (when there are no runners on base). Writers on *LSWDL* also use the term Around the Horn to refer to a comedy piece in which the jokes are delivered by a succession of staff members and other performers positioned around the studio. These are examples of this type of piece:

> **"Shout-Outs"** [*LNWJF*]—Jimmy gives a straight, unfunny shout-out to somebody to start off the piece, after which staff members and other performers in the studio take turns giving their own, funny, shout-outs. Sample joke: band member Kamal gives a shout-out to jalapeño peppers, a food he loves, and shows a bottle of wine he made from them—"Jala-Pinot Grigio."

> **"Staff Show-and-Tell"** [*LSWDL*]—Dave asks the staff if they have anything interesting they'd like to share and a series of staff members delivers the jokes. For example, a camera operator raises his hand but admits he has nothing to share; he only wants permission to take a short break to "water the weasel." Instead of going off to visit the men's room as expected, the camera operator pours water from a pitcher so it appears to be drenching a live weasel in a nearby cage.

> **"Staff Roll Call"** [*LSWDL*]—Dave says it's now about halfway through the show, a good time to take attendance. Dave calls out the names and/or titles of various staffers, real and fake, who deliver jokes throughout the studio. Sample joke: Dave calls for

the "Late Show Town Crier." In response, a performer costumed as a nineteenth-century town crier strolls onto the stage ringing a bell and proclaims, "It's twelve o'clock and the show still sucks."

How to Create a New Around the Horn Sketch

Imagine that the show's staff is some other group of closely connected people. Then, for your topic, brainstorm activities that that other group of people might engage in. There might be an Around the Horn Sketch in having the show's staff perform a funny version of one of those activities.

For example, imagine that the show's staff is an elementary school class. That might have led to the topic "Staff Show-and-Tell." Or what if the staff were a company in the Army? That might have suggested conducting a "Staff Roll Call." And what might a group of coworkers in an office do right before Christmas? They might have a Secret Santa gift exchange, so your show's staff could, too.

Studio Tours

A Studio Tour Sketch is like an Around the Horn Sketch except the jokes are about features of the studio, real or fake. Here are some examples:

> **"What's New for Summer"** [*LNWDL*]—Dave unveils an array of new features that were installed in the studio for the summer. For example, Dave shows a pool of water in front of his desk that contains several nozzles that spurt water in the air when he presses a button. (Dave dubbed the device "The Dancing Waters" and enjoyed operating it so much that he kept it in the studio for several months. He renamed it "The Prancing Fluids" after the Dancing Waters Company objected to the show's use of its name.)

"Tonight Show Internationale" [*TSWJL*]—Jay describes how the show demonstrates respect for the various cultural backgrounds of its staff members. Sample joke: Jay points out that the boom mike operator has ancestors from Poland. The boom mike operator says, "That's right, Jay. And because I love Polish food I'm using my boom mike to make smoked sausage and kielbasa." The camera now reveals that hanging from the long boom mike are a dozen or so large sausages surrounded by clouds of smoke.

"Late Night Budget Cuts" [*LNWCO*]—Conan shows various effects that budget cuts by the network have had on the show. Sample joke: a staffer in the control room sends an instruction to a camera operator via a carrier pigeon.

How to Create a New Studio Tour Sketch

Imagine that the show is a product you might buy in a store. Consider how companies develop, market, and improve those products. Then, for your topic, think about applying one of those practices to the show. For example, clothing companies unveil lines of seasonal fashions, which may have inspired "What's New for Summer" on *LNWDL*. And food companies often modify their products to suit local tastes. That kind of thinking led to the topic "Tonight Show Internationale."

Another technique for creating a new Studio Tour Sketch is to imagine that the studio is a house. Think about what homeowners do to their houses at various times and, for your topic, imagine doing those kinds of things to the studio. For instance, when the economy is bad homeowners save money by cutting back. That observation led to the topic "Late Night Budget Cuts." People also winterize their homes, which is why *LSWDL* did the piece "How We've Winterized the Studio." Homeowners make home improvements, redecorate, and perform tasks on their to-do lists. Any one of those activities could lead to the topic of a new Studio Tour Sketch.

Other Live Joke Basket Sketches

Here's a Live Joke Basket Sketch that doesn't fit into the above three categories:

> **"Jay's Romance Novel"** [*TSWJL*]—Jay and his band leader, Kevin, wear velvet jackets and sit at a writing table in an ornate parlor. They use quill pens to supposedly write their romance novel, delivering a series of jokes. For each joke Kevin recites the angle and Jay delivers the punch line. Sample joke: Kevin says, "He knew she had been around when he slipped his hand up under her dress..." Then Jay adds, "...and wound up shaking another man's hand."

This sketch is a good example of another way to create a Live Joke Basket Sketch: add production value to a Desk Piece. In other words, if you have an idea that could be a Text Piece, an Art Card Piece, or a Prop Piece, ask yourself whether it might work even better if presented by the host with other performers. "Jay's Romance Novel" started out as an idea for a Text Piece but we decided it would be even more entertaining to have Jay and Kevin perform it in costume and ad-lib between jokes. Same idea, different presentation.

Here's another Live Joke Basket Sketch that falls outside the usual categories:

> **"Dave's Party Tricks"** [*LNWDL*]—Band leader Paul pesters Dave to repeat some tricks that Dave supposedly did at a party the previous night. So Dave performs a series of tricks in surprising, funny ways. For example, Dave shows how he can do the mime trick of appearing to "walk into the wind" but he does it

by walking into the real wind produced by a giant fan, six feet in diameter, which also blows litter across the stage.

This example suggests that another way to come up with a new Live Joke Basket Sketch is to think of some group that performs a specialized set of activities. Maybe there's a Live Joke Basket Sketch in showing funny versions of those activities. For example, some partygoers do party tricks, which inspired "Dave's Party Tricks." And stage managers on television shows use specific hand signals to communicate silently. That gave me the idea to do a Live Joke Basket Sketch on *The Chevy Chase Show* called "Studio Hand Signals."

TAPED JOKE BASKET SKETCHES

A Live Joke Basket Sketch is a series of jokes, connected only by a topic, that's performed live in the studio by the host and other performers. A Taped Joke Basket Sketch is the same except all the jokes are, that's right, on tape.

A Taped Joke Basket Sketch is generally presented in one of two ways: as a series of separate tape rolls or as one continuous video. I'll talk about each of those in turn.

Separate Tape Rolls

The host introduces the piece in the studio, announcing the topic, and then sets up each punch line with a sentence or two. Each punch line consists of a brief scene on tape which is "rolled into" (played during) the show. Between tape rolls the host reappears in the studio to set up the next punch line. The effect is similar to a sportscaster in a studio "throwing to" prerecorded video clips as he reports on various stories.

Here are examples of this type of piece:

"Why We Edit" [*LNWDL*]—Dave shows a series of clips, each one supposedly depicting an incident that, for one reason or another, had to be edited out of the show before it was broadcast. Sample joke: Dave sets up the clip with, "Sometimes one of our stage managers gives me a signal and I just don't see it." Then the video clip rolls and the audience sees the show apparently coming back from a commercial break. Dave is sitting sideways at his desk, brushing his teeth. He notices the camera, startled. He spits the toothpaste into a bucket and goes on with the show.

LNWCO has aired a similar piece: "Guests We'll Never Have Back." Sample joke: A magician guest performs the stunt of catching in his teeth a bullet that Conan fires from a handgun. But then Conan accidentally shoots the magician in the chest.

"Satellite TV" [*LNWCO*]—Conan describes the large satellite dish on the roof of his studio building and offers to show the audience some of the many unusual channels the dish supposedly pulls in. Sample joke: Conan sets up the clip with, "Here's one that sounds strange: Kissinger Keep-Away Channel." The clip shows a couple of ruffians on the street tossing Henry Kissinger's briefcase to each other as the former Secretary of State (a look-alike) tries to get it back. On the soundtrack a rock singer repeatedly chants "Kissinger Keep-Away."

(A similar piece has appeared on *LNWDL*: "New Cable Channels." But note that both that piece and "Satellite TV" are different from the Found Comedy Video Piece "What's On Other Channels" that I mentioned in Chapter 8. "What's On Other Channels" is also about fake TV shows but it's based on stock footage, not footage specifically shot for the piece.)

"New iPhone Apps" [*LNWJF*]—Jimmy says he'll show the audience some of the new apps that are supposedly available on the iPhone. The apps appear as short video clips on a monitor next to Jimmy. Sample joke: Jimmy says there's a new app called Sting Confessions, which lets you tap a button and hear rock musician Sting confess something about himself. On the monitor is a still photo of Sting. Jimmy taps his phone and we hear Sting (a sound-alike) sing this to the tune of "Don't Stand So Close to Me": "Sometimes I...get crushes...on cartoon characters."

"Thanksgiving Floats" [*TSWJL*]—Jay and his announcer, Edd Hall, describe the floats that are supposedly passing by in a Thanksgiving Day Parade. Each float has been constructed by the prop department and is seen in a video clip. Sample joke: Jay says, "This year the Santa float is sponsored by the N.R.A., the National Rifle Association." The video clip shows Santa riding in his sleigh and carrying a rifle. Edd adds, "Looks like Santa's bagged himself a magnificent twelve-pointer. And here's a surprise for the kids— it's Rudolph!" Back to the clip, which shows Rudolph strapped to the front of the sleigh, his nose red and Xs on his eyes.

One Continuous Video

In this scenario the host introduces the Taped Joke Basket Sketch in the studio and announces the topic. Then the audience sees one long video that has all the jokes edited together one after the other. The host doesn't reappear in the studio again until the end of the piece. The effect in this case is similar to a reporter on a news show throwing to a tape package that consists of many different scenes.

Here are a few examples of this type of Taped Joke Basket Sketch:

"Dave and Paul Play Golf" [*LSWDL*]—A series of short, wordless scenes show what supposedly happened when Dave and his bandleader, Paul, played a round at a golf course. Sample joke: Dave sinks a putt and reaches into the hole to retrieve his ball. But when he pulls out his hand it's bloody and a vicious (fake) squirrel is chewing on it.

"This Week in Unnecessary Censorship" [*JKL*]—Jimmy introduces his "weekly tribute to the FCC, where we bleep and blur things whether they need it or not." The piece is a series of scenes taken from news and entertainment shows. In each scene, somebody talking—say the President of the United States—has had his dialogue bleeped and his mouth blurred to make it appear as though he is saying something obscene.

"An Insider's Guide to Las Vegas" [*TSWJL*]—The video shows Jay taking the viewer around Las Vegas and performing a series of jokes. Sample joke: Jay stands in front of the immense neon façade of the Flamingo Hilton and says, "You know, the lights on the hotels in Las Vegas literally turn the night into day. But if they're too bright for you, try this. Clap off." Jay claps his hands and the entire neon display goes dark. Jay says "Clap on," clapping again, and it blazes to brilliant life again.

We didn't use special video effects to turn off the thousands of lights on the Flamingo Hilton; we did it for real. A hotel employee just out of camera range gave commands over a walkie-talkie to another employee manning a circuit breaker deep in the bowels of the hotel. The feat was very cool but we didn't have time to stand around marveling at it because Jay had to rush off to "warm" a baby bottle in the fake lava flowing out of the volcano at the Mirage. Hopscotching around Las Vegas to tape that piece made for a busy, surreal night.

"Jay's Bad Cab Ride" [*TSWJL*]—Jay says that when he arrived in New York City he had the worst cab ride ever from the airport to his hotel. The video shows all the unpleasant things that happened during the ride. Sample joke: The cabbie asks Jay, "Do you mind if I play some music?" Jay says, "Go right ahead." The cabbie produces an accordion and uses it to play polka music as he drives. Another shot shows the cab swerving dangerously as it barrels down the street.

I could have died taping that joke for "Jay's Bad Cab Ride." The cab was a prop cab, not intended for serious use, and the latch on the front passenger door was broken. I was crouched down in the cab next to that door monitoring the audio through a headset. I knew the door behind me would pop open if I pushed it but I wasn't bracing myself. As the cab swerved down Ninth Avenue at thirty miles an hour I started to lose my balance. The driver, a professional stunt man with the senses and reflexes of a jungle cat, shot out an arm and grabbed me before I could topple backward out the door. Wherever you are today, sir, bless you.

Remember that Taped Joke Basket Sketches are completely scripted. That fact sets them apart from video pieces like "Conan Visits Ireland" where the host interacts with nonprofessionals in a series of partially improvised scenes. I'll cover pieces like those—I call them Semi-Scripted Field Pieces—in Chapter 13.

Separate Tape Rolls versus One Continuous Video

How do you decide whether to present the jokes in a Taped Joke Basket Sketch as a series of separate tape rolls or as one continuous video? Here's how. In either case, the video clips contain the punch lines of the jokes. But if each punch line requires a different angle to set it up and the angle isn't also contained in the clip, then present the jokes as a series of separate tape rolls. That way the host can deliver the angle for each joke in the studio.

For example, each video clip in the piece "Why We Edit" needs a different angle but the angle isn't built into the clip. So the clips are presented as separate tape rolls. That way Dave in the studio can set up each clip with an angle like (for the clip of him brushing his teeth) "Sometimes one of our stage managers gives me a signal and I just don't see it."

On the other hand, if the angles are all built into the clips together with their punch lines—or if all the jokes have the same angle—then present the jokes as one continuous video. For example, it makes sense to present the jokes in "Dave and Paul Play Golf" as one continuous video because the angles and punch lines are all part of the video. Take the scene where Dave putts his ball into a hole and then gets bitten by the angry squirrel hiding there. It would be redundant to first have Dave, in the studio, set up that clip by saying something like, "Then there was the time I had a little trouble retrieving my ball."

How to Create a New Taped Joke Basket Sketch

Here are three ways to come up with a topic for a new Taped Joke Basket Sketch, whether it consists of separate tape rolls or one continuous video:

1. Think of a category of things that primarily exist in video form. You might be able to create a sketch out of funny videos in that category. For example, outtakes from TV shows, censored scenes from TV shows, and TV shows themselves exist in video form, which suggests sketches like "Why We Edit," "This Week in Unnecessary Censorship," and "Satellite TV." Apps for the iPhone are primarily in video form too, an observation which led to "New iPhone Apps." And how about security camera footage? *LSWDL* did a piece called, "What Our Security Cameras Taped."

2. Think of an activity that has at least a dozen distinct steps. You might build a sketch out of funny versions of those steps. For example, playing a game of golf can be broken down into steps like selecting a club, hitting the ball, driving the golf cart, taking the ball out of the hole, and so on. That's why "Dave and Paul Play Golf" is a good topic. A cab ride involves steps like hailing the cab, putting luggage in the trunk, and dealing with the cabbie's choice of music, so "Jay's Bad Cab Ride" works as a topic. Touring some location is a natural topic because every stop on the tour is a potential angle for a joke; that's the thinking behind "An Insider's Guide to Las Vegas."

(Touring a location is such a reliable source of comedy that whenever a late-night show produces a block of episodes in a different city—referred to as "traveling the show"—it's very likely that one of those episodes will include a video of the host touring that city. City tour videos play particularly strongly because the studio audience in the destination city loves to see the host playing around at landmarks they recognize.)

Some other activities that have distinct steps are: commuting to work, learning a new skill, playing a sport, and having a picnic. Each of those activities has been the topic of a Taped Joke Basket Sketch on a comedy/talk show at one time or another.

3. Think of a Desk Piece that you can upgrade to a video piece. In other words, think of a topic for something like an Art Card Piece or a Prop Piece that you could execute more effectively using video clips instead of artwork or props. For example, "Thanksgiving Floats" could have been an Art Card Piece consisting of an artist's renderings of the floats. But showing video clips of the floats complete with props, actors, and a running commentary by Jay and Edd was much more entertaining.

HOW TO WRITE JOKES FOR A JOKE BASKET SKETCH

Once you've picked a topic for your Live or Taped Joke Basket Sketch, write jokes for it using the Punch Line Makers. You'll have to adjust the Punch Line Makers slightly to reflect the physical nature of some of the jokes in a Joke Basket Sketch the same way you'd adjust them to write jokes for, say, a Prop Piece. But the basic joke-writing techniques are the same. Here are some examples of the process in action:

- If you were writing jokes for "Rejected *Star Wars* Characters" you'd start by listing the most well-known, real *Star Wars* characters. Those real characters are possible angles for jokes. Say you pick R2D2 as your angle and try using Punch Line Maker #2. One association of the D in R2D2 is the similar-sounding letter T. T suggests the pop culture figure Mr. T. Linking Mr. T with R2D2 gives you the punch line "R2-Mr. T-2." Then you expand on that punch line by blending more associations of R2D2 and Mr. T to describe what R2-Mr. T-2 looks and sounds like: It's a robot, but with gold chains; it chirps a *Star Wars* variation of a Mr. T catchphrase; and so on.

- To write jokes for "Why We Edit," start by thinking of real people, places, things, and activities that are typically part of the show; those are all possible angles. Let's say you want to make a joke out of that traditional shot of Dave at homebase as the show comes back from commercial. You could use Punch Line Maker #1 and think of associations of Dave at that point in the show. Among them are "He doesn't know exactly when the break will end" and "He wants to stay well-groomed." Link those two associations and you get the punch line of Dave being startled by the live camera as he brushes his teeth.

- Say you're writing a joke for "An Insider's Guide to Las Vegas." Start by thinking of well-known people, places, things, and activities in Las Vegas. Pick one of those as your angle. Say it's the eye-popping neon façade of the Flamingo Hilton. You could then use Punch Line Maker #3 and ask the "Five Ws and an H" question, "How do you turn the lights off?" One association of "turn lights off" is "The Clapper." That's how you arrive at the punch line where Jay claps the illuminated display off and on.

MULTIMEDIA JOKE BASKET SKETCHES

A Multimedia Joke Basket Sketch mixes live and taped elements. Here are examples of this type of sketch:

"CBS Mailbag" [*LSWDL*]—This is the *LNWDL* sketch "Viewer Mail" under a different name. Dave responds to "actual letters from actual viewers" with jokes, which can be anything from a one-liner (a "snappy") to a wacky prop to a Commercial Parody. The format of the sketch is so flexible that it often provides a home for pieces that don't quite fit elsewhere in the show.

For instance, if a taped Field Piece doesn't turn out to be long enough to fill its own segment of the show, the writers will often find a viewer's letter which could be answered with the taped piece and will incorporate the letter and taped piece into "CBS Mailbag." (And yes, those are actual letters from actual viewers. The raw material for "CBS Mailbag" is crowdsourced, as it is for many Found Comedy Pieces. Several times a week each writer receives a stack of photocopies of letters that viewers mailed in.)

Sample joke from "Viewer Mail": A viewer writes in to demand that Dave mail him a specific type of General Electric bulb to replace one that burned out. Dave angrily responds that even though General Electric recently bought the show's network,

NBC, that's no reason to expect that Dave will be a corporate suck-up and peddle GE's products. Then bandleader Paul opens a cabinet built into the front of his keyboard and, from an extensive display of GE bulbs, picks out the exact one the viewer requested and promises to mail it to him.

"Ask Jay Anything" [*TSWJL*]—Studio audience members take turns at a microphone asking Jay questions that, in reality, have been scripted by the writers ahead of time. Jay answers each question with a joke that may be elaborately produced.

Sample joke: A woman says that her young son, standing next to her, accidentally let go of his red balloon while he was waiting in line outside. Does Jay have a *Tonight* show balloon to replace the one her son lost? Jay responds that, no, he doesn't have any balloons but he'll try to help. He dashes outside and (in a prerecorded video) checks the wind direction, then drives to Disneyland. Once there, Jay (actually a look-alike Disneyland mountain climber) scales the Matterhorn. As the red balloon drifts past the peak, Jay plucks it from the sky. Back in the studio, Jay returns the balloon to the grateful little boy. (A fun perk of writing and directing this joke: I got to see the small-scale basketball court tucked inside the Matterhorn. Photos of it can be found online.)

"Audience Suggestion Box" [*LNWJF*]—Out of a wooden box Jimmy takes suggestions supposedly written by members of that night's studio audience. He responds to each suggestion with a joke or funny activity. Sample joke: An audience member challenges Jimmy to throw a pancake clear over the entire studio audience as if it were a Frisbee. Jimmy accepts the challenge. A chef brings out a stack of pancakes and Jimmy sails them out into the audience as excited audience members try to catch them.

With a broad-enough topic, a Multimedia Joke Basket Sketch like one of the above can accommodate virtually any type of joke. That means that to write jokes for a Multimedia Joke Basket Sketch you might call on the Punch Line Makers, the techniques for writing Joke Basket Sketches that I've covered, or any other comedy writing technique in this book.

COLD OPENINGS, COLD CLOSES, AND EXCURSIONS

Cold Openings, Cold Closes, and Excursions are three other ways the writers can add comedy to a comedy/talk show. These are all self-contained pieces, almost always prerecorded, but they differ in where they appear in the show:

- **A Cold Opening** is at the very beginning of the show, even before the show's opening title sequence.

- **A Cold Close** is at the very end of the show, during or after the show's closing credits.

- **An Excursion** is slotted somewhere in the main body of the show. It's a scene that typically starts with the host announcing that he has to perform some vague or innocuous-sounding task. He leaves the studio, accomplishes the task in a funny way, then returns to the studio and goes on with the show. Frequently an Excursion results in the host behaving inappropriately in a real-world setting.

How to Create Cold Openings, Cold Closes, and Excursions

Cold Openings, Cold Closes, and Excursions stand alone, meaning that they aren't part of larger, multi-joke sketches. Still, a good way to write them is to think of them as single jokes in Joke Basket Sketches that have the following topics:

- For a Cold Opening: "Things That Might Happen Right Before the Show."
- For a Cold Close: "Things That Might Happen Right After the Show."
- For an Excursion: "Things That Might Require the Host to Leave During the Show."

If you think of Cold Openings, Cold Closes, and Excursions this way you can create them using the same techniques I covered for creating jokes for Joke Basket Sketches. Here are some examples of Cold Openings, Cold Closes, and Excursions and how they were conceived:

> **"Schwarzenegger Makeup Chair Cold Opening"** [*LNWDL*]— Before the show, Dave sits in a barbershop-style chair getting his makeup applied. Actor/bodybuilder Arnold Schwarzenegger stands behind Dave with his hands on the chair. Dave chats with Arnold and then gets out of the chair. A wider shot reveals that the chair has no pedestal; Arnold has been using sheer muscle power to hold the chair up with Dave sitting in it. Dave apologizes to Arnold for making him hold up the busted chair. Arnold says it was no problem and casually tosses the bulky chair aside.

I wanted to write a Cold Opening for Arnold when I learned he was going to appear on the show. To come up with the chair idea I used Punch Line Maker #1. I thought of an association of the topic "Things That Might Happen Right Before the Show with Arnold Schwarzenegger"—"Dave sits in a makeup chair." I also thought of an association of "Arnold Schwarzenegger"—"really strong." Linking "Dave sits in a makeup chair" to "really strong" produced the punch line image of Arnold holding up the makeup chair. The final step was to flesh out the sketch with some idle chitchat to set up the surprise reveal.

"Detective Show Cold Close" [*LNWDL*]—This is the Cold Close
I described in Chapter 2. Dave and the members of the band discuss how Dave solved the murder of a guest on that night's show
as if they're suddenly in the epilogue of a 1970s detective show.
They all laugh as the music comes up and the picture freezes.

To create that idea I again used Punch Line Maker #1. I brainstormed on "Things That Might Happen Right After the Show"
and thought of what happens at the end of some detective
shows—"the tie-up-loose-ends epilogue." I linked that association to an association of that night's show—"the guests." That
gave me the punch line idea of an epilogue for a detective show
where one of the guests has been murdered. Once I had that idea
I scripted out the Cold Close as a Parody Sketch. I'll talk about
how to write Parody Sketches in Chapter 11.

"Jimmy and Tom Cruise Zip-Line Excursion" [*JKL*]—Jimmy
and Tom Cruise are in the studio preparing for a cooking demonstration when Tom says he needs fresh eggs. Tom says he saw
a guy across the street selling eggs. Tom takes Jimmy to the roof
of the studio. They zip-line across Hollywood Boulevard and
buy some eggs from staff member Guillermo, who is dressed as a
farmer. This piece combines an Excursion with a Stunt. I'll talk
about how to write Stunt Pieces in Chapter 12.

"O. J. Simpson Chase Excursion" [*TSWJL*]—As Jay concludes
his Monologue he hears a noise in the hallway outside the studio.
He goes out to the wide hallway to investigate and sees, driving
past him, a white Ford Bronco. It's apparently O. J. Simpson, still
fleeing from the police. (This Excursion aired shortly after O. J.'s
infamous low-speed chase through Los Angeles.) The Bronco
rounds a corner and drives away down the hallway inside the studio building chased by two police cars, their sirens whooping and
lights flashing. Jay returns to the studio, his curiosity satisfied.

Punch Line Maker #2—link the topic to pop culture—was useful in writing that idea. I thought of an association of "Things
That Might Require the Host to Leave During the Show"—
"hearing an unusual noise." "Unusual noise" suggested an
enormous news story at the time: "police cars chasing O. J." So
the punch line became Jay leaving the studio and encountering
the pursuit.

The "O. J. Simpson Chase Excursion" is one joke I wrote that could have
killed. Not "killed" in the comedy sense of "gotten a huge laugh" but
literally killed. Just as we were about to tape the Bronco and police cars
speeding down the hallway inside the building I realized that nobody had
secured any of the doors opening onto that same hallway. Some unsuspecting studio worker could have strolled out of an office to go to the
bathroom and gotten run over. Needless to say, we took the proper pre-
cautions to make sure O. J.'s name wouldn't be linked to any more violent
deaths.

"Olympic Torch Excursion" [*LSWDL*]—It's 1996 and runners
are relaying the Olympic torch all over the United States on its
way to the Summer Olympics in Atlanta. Dave tells the audience that he has to go do something (I forget what) and hurries out of the studio. As Dave exits onto Broadway a confused
Olympic runner trots up to him, hands him the torch, and
dashes off. Dave stares at the torch, decides he doesn't want it,
tosses it aside, then hurries away to accomplish whatever his
task is.

I used Punch Line Maker #2 here, too. This punch line connects
an association of "Things That Might Require the Host to Leave
During the Show"—"exit onto Broadway"—with something in
pop culture—"Olympic torch relay through New York City."

The "Olympic Torch Excursion" is another one of my jokes that could have literally killed. This little tango with the Grim Reaper began with a safety feature built into the gas-fueled prop torch: a button that had to be depressed in order for the torch to stay lit. The flame would go out unless Dave maintained continuous pressure on the small button as he received the torch from the runner, which was hard to do. To guarantee that the flame would stay lit during the handoff I, like an idiot, persuaded our prop person to tape the button down in the "on" position. Now the camera is rolling. The Olympic runner carries the torch and its eternal flame up the sidewalk and passes it to Dave, who stares at it as planned, then tosses it aside, inadvertently depositing it under the rear end of a parked Lincoln Town Car.

The torch keeps burning, of course; I've seen to that. And it's just out of reach, directly under the Town Car's gas tank. Dave, the camera operator, and I are all standing only about ten feet away from the ticking car bomb. Another staff member immediately sees the danger. He dashes over and bangs on the driver's window shouting, "Move the car! Move the car!" The startled driver pulls the vehicle ahead, away from the torch, and we all live to shoot Take Two.

So what's the comedy principle you should take away from my experiences with Excursions? Don't literally kill anybody. I'll refer to this principle again in Chapter 12, in the section on Stunt Pieces.

THEME SHOWS

A Theme Show is a special episode in which many key elements of the show have been temporarily modified to reflect a chosen theme. The theme is essentially a joke basket and the show elements become angles for jokes that fit into that basket. Not only will the Monologue and other comedy segments tie into the theme but often the set will be made over, the opening sequence will be changed, and thematically appropriate guests will be booked.

Theme Shows take a lot more work than regular episodes and usually cost more. But a comedy/talk show might do a Theme Show as a play for ratings because Theme Shows are highly promotable. A typical instance of this is when a show travels to a different city for a week of episodes during a ratings sweeps month. Each of those city-themed episodes is saturated with local references.

For example, when *TSWJL* set up camp in New York City for a week the comedy segments included "Jay and Branford Tour New York City," "Jay's Bad Cab Ride," and a piece featuring one of Jay's characters, "Jayro in Manhattan." *TSWJL* and *LNWDL* each did weeks of shows in Las Vegas and each toured the city in a comedy piece. And *LNWCO* once taped a theme episode at a remote location in its home town—on a New York City ferry boat.

A comedy/talk show can also do a Theme Show without traveling to a different location. For example, *LNWDL* once produced an episode in its home studio that was supposedly originating from Japan; even the studio audience was Japanese. Other *LNWDL* Theme Shows included "Christmas with the Lettermans" and "Dave Letterman's Summertime Sunshine Happy Hour." And to help promote the move of *JKL* to an earlier timeslot the show aired the "Jimmy Kimmel Sucks" episode, the theme of which was that actor Matt Damon had hijacked the show to get his revenge on Jimmy.

How to Create a Theme Show

Here are the steps to follow:

1. Pick a promising theme. If a theme is obvious (if, for example, the executive producer of the show announces, "We're doing a week of shows in Chicago") then skip to Step #2. But if you're coming up with your own theme, try generating ideas for one the way you'd generate ideas for a "Top Ten List" topic. That is, consider various pop culture phenomena that could transform the show, like the TV holiday variety specials from the 1970s that inspired "Christmas with the Lettermans." Or look for a theme in something that's really happening on the show. That's how the staff of *JKL* apparently got the idea for their "Jimmy Kimmel Sucks" episode—they were inspired by the show's running gag of Jimmy repeatedly bumping Matt Damon from the show due to lack of time.

Like a promising topic for a "Top Ten List," a promising theme for a Theme Show will do these two things:

a) It will spark a lot of people's interest. You want the Theme Show to attract additional viewers, so you want a theme that's so intriguing that even casual viewers will feel compelled to tune in. The theme for the "Jimmy Kimmel Sucks" episode, for example, is intriguing because (1) Matt Damon is a big movie star; (2) it's fun to see big movie stars misbehave, even if they're just faking it; and (3) the idea of hijacking a show seems fresh.

b) It will suggest a lot of associations. You want a theme with plenty of associations that you can combine with key elements of the show to generate a wide variety of jokes. Continuing with the example of the "Jimmy Kimmel Sucks" episode, here are some associations of the theme "Matt Damon hijacks the show to get his revenge on Jimmy":

- Matt hates Jimmy.
- Matt renders Jimmy helpless.
- Matt insults Jimmy.
- Matt makes Jimmy look bad.
- Matt shows he's a better host than Jimmy.

What are some examples of themes that don't have a lot of associations? How about Flag Day? Needlepoint? The host's Aunt Katie? Writers would be hard pressed to create an engaging Theme Show around one of those.

2. Combine associations of the theme with key elements of the show to generate joke ideas. That is, first brainstorm associations of the theme. Then take each association in turn and ask yourself how it could lead to changing each key element of the show.

Here's how the writers of the "Jimmy Kimmel Sucks" episode apparently combined associations of the theme with key elements of the show (shown in italics) to generate joke ideas:

Association of the theme: Matt hates Jimmy.

Joke ideas: In a *Cold Opening*, Matt explains that he hijacked the show because of Jimmy's abuse. A new *show logo*, "Jimmy Kimmel Sucks," is substituted everywhere for the old logo, "Jimmy Kimmel Live." Images of Jimmy in the *opening title sequence* are defaced.

Association of the theme: Matt renders Jimmy helpless.

Joke idea: Jimmy is duct-taped to an office chair and gagged with, apparently, *Jimmy's own necktie.*

Association of the theme: Matt insults Jimmy.

Joke ideas: Matt's *Monologue* is packed with anti-Jimmy jokes. Matt and all his *guests*, including Jimmy's ex-girlfriend Sarah Silverman, badmouth Jimmy throughout the show.

Association of the theme: Matt makes Jimmy look bad.

Joke ideas: To finish his *Monologue*, Matt brings out a comedian he says is much funnier than Jimmy—Robin Williams. *Camera shots* show Jimmy in the background throughout the show, trussed-up and humiliated. Matt presents a *comedy piece* that shows Jimmy lamely auditioning for movie roles that Matt eventually won.

Association of the theme: Matt shows he's a better host than Jimmy.

Joke ideas: For his *sidekick*, Matt swaps out Guillermo for actor Andy Garcia. For his *bandleader*, Matt trades up to singer Sheryl Crow. Actor Ben Affleck holds *cue cards*. Matt has an easy time packing the show with *celebrity guests*, including stars like Nicole Kidman and Demi Moore who never agreed to be on the show when Jimmy was hosting. In their *interviews*, the guests compliment Matt on his hosting ability. Matt gets Nicole Kidman to really open up to him during her *interview* and confess that she's a kleptomaniac. In prerecorded *bumpers*, celebrities say nice things about Matt and nasty things about Jimmy.

3. Script out your joke ideas the way you would write jokes for a Joke Basket Sketch. The entire Theme Show is a Joke Basket Sketch but within the show there may be other Joke Basket Sketches with separate topics. For example, Matt introduces his new sidekick, bandleader, and cue card guy in an Around the Horn Joke Basket Sketch. And the comedy piece about Jimmy's movie auditions was a Taped Joke Basket Sketch presented as one continuous video.

JOKE BASKET CHARACTERS

Another type of Joke Basket Sketch is one where a comic character delivers the jokes. The character may be played by the host himself, by a staff member, or by a performer from outside the show. As in any Joke Basket Sketch, the jokes delivered by a Joke Basket Character aren't connected by a story line.

When Johnny Carson hosted the *Tonight* show he regularly performed Joke Basket Characters such as Aunt Blabby, Floyd R. Turbo, and Carnac the Magnificent. Carnac was a psychic in an oversized turban who would announce the answer to a question in a sealed envelope, then open the envelope and read the question. The punch lines were almost always plays on words. A sample Carnac joke: The answer is "Camelot." The question is: "Where do Arabians park their camels?"

Here are other examples of Joke Basket Characters:

"Mr. Brain" [*TSWJL*]—Jay plays Mr. Brain, the smartest man in the universe. Jay wears a lab coat and eyeglasses and a video effect makes his forehead look enormous. His bandleader, Branford, sits next to him and asks scripted questions, which Mr. Brain answers in a very condescending way, his voice echoing with reverb. Sample joke: Branford asks, "Is the smallest visible object in the universe (a) a quark or (b) a positron?" Mr. Brain snaps, "Neither! The answer is c. The smallest visible object in the universe is a steak at Denny's. You idiots!" (See Appendix B for the story of how Mr. Brain was created.)

"Clutch Cargo Interview" [*LNWCO*]—A video effect inserts the live-action lips of an impersonator backstage into a photo of a celebrity's face on a monitor. (This crude animation technique was used in 1959 in a cartoon series called *Clutch Cargo*.) Conan interviews the talking photo as if it were the real celebrity. The interviews consist of a series of mostly unconnected jokes delivered by the faux celebrity. Here's a sample joke from when Conan interviewed "President George W. Bush" about his acceptance speech at the Republican National Convention. Conan remarks, "The crowd certainly loved your speech." The President replies, "You're tellin' me. I spoke for an hour, but it wasn't enough for them. They kept yelling 'four more years.' I'm good but even I can't talk that long."

"The Rather Late Programme with Prince Charles" [*LLSWCF*]—Craig is costumed and made up as Prince Charles. He delivers jokes as if he's the Prince hosting a late-night comedy/talk show in England. Sample Monologue joke: "Hey, it's tax season in America, which is great because the last time I was there I slept with my wife, Camilla, and the good news is I can write it off as a charitable contribution."

How to Create and Write for a New Joke Basket Character

Not every host is willing to do characters. Performing as a character requires that the host not take himself too seriously. For example, whenever Jay portrayed his Joke Basket Character Beyondo he had to stand in full view of the studio audience wearing a skintight green body suit. (The green suit made it possible for Beyondo to appear on television as a floating, disembodied head.) But if you are writing for a host or other performer who's willing to transform himself for a comedy piece, here are some tips for creating a new Joke Basket Character:

Think of a character with two or three exaggerated traits. For example, Mr. Brain is brilliant, egotistical, and sarcastic. The "Clutch Cargo" version of President George W. Bush is cocky, idiotic, and Texan. Craig's Prince Charles is childish, English, and a playboy. "Triumph, the Insult Comic Dog" on *LNWCO* is crude, insulting, and a dog.

Give the character an outlandish look to reflect his exaggerated personality. Mr. Brain has a bulbous head. The "Clutch Cargo"

President Bush has those weirdly animated lips. Craig's Prince Charles wears a royal robe and has enormous ears, horrible teeth, and a grotesque comb-over. Triumph is a hand puppet dog smoking a cigar.

Decide how the character will get laughs. That is, figure out the mechanics of delivering the jokes through the character. For example, Mr. Brain delivered punch lines in the form of answers to scripted questions that were asked by Branford but were supposedly submitted by members of the studio audience. A "Clutch Cargo" piece has the mock celebrity delivering jokes in the course of an interview. As Prince Charles, Craig performs a short Monologue and simple Desk (or actually, "Throne") Pieces. Triumph insults people.

Write jokes for the character using whatever techniques apply. You'd write jokes for Mr. Brain as if you were writing a Text Quiz, which I discussed in Chapter 7. You'd write a "Clutch Cargo Interview" with President Bush the way you'd write a Taped Joke Basket Sketch. You'd write Monologue jokes and Desk Pieces for Craig's Prince Charles the way you'd write the same material for any other host. And in Chapter 13 I'll tell you how to write a Location-Dependent Field Piece like the ones featuring Triumph.

Be sure that any jokes you write for a Joke Basket Character reflect the traits you've chosen for that character. This principle, of course, also applies to any dialogue you write for any character in any medium.

SUMMARY

A Joke Basket Sketch is a series of interchangeable jokes, united by a single topic, that involve performers in addition to the host. The three types of Joke Basket Sketches are live, taped, and multimedia.

Live Joke Basket Sketches include these:

- **Costume Sketches,** where the punch lines are costumes worn by performers. For a topic, think of a group of people who are distinguished by their specialized clothing.
- **Around the Horns,** where the jokes are delivered by performers positioned around the studio. To come up with a topic, brainstorm activities that some other group of closely connected people might engage in.
- **Studio Tours,** where the jokes are real or fake features of the studio. Start thinking of a topic by imagining that the show is a product you might buy in a store. What do companies do with their products? Or imagine that the studio is a house. What do homeowners do to their houses?

Taped Joke Basket Sketches can either be presented as separate tape rolls ("Why We Edit") or as one continuous video ("Dave and Paul Play Golf"). Go with separate tape rolls if each video clip needs to be set up with a different angle and the angle isn't part of the clip. Show the sketch as one continuous video if all the jokes have the same angle or if all the angles are built into the clips together with their punch lines.

Here are three ways to generate a topic for a Taped Joke Basket Sketch:

- Think of a category of things that exist primarily in video form.
- Think of an activity that has at least a dozen distinct steps.
- Think of a Desk Piece that you can upgrade to a video piece.

Write jokes for a Joke Basket Sketch using the same basic steps as you would for a Desk Piece:

1. Pick one of the above types of Joke Basket Sketches.
2. Pick a topic for your piece that suggests a lot of associations and that your audience is likely to find acceptable and relatable.

3. For possible joke angles, list real items related to your chosen topic.

4. Write jokes for the piece using the Punch Line Makers and Joke Maximizers.

Multimedia Joke Basket Sketches mix live and taped elements.

A Cold Opening is at the very beginning of the show. Create one by starting with the topic "Things That Might Happen Right Before the Show."

A Cold Close is at the very end of the show. It's a joke with the topic "Things That Might Happen Right After the Show."

An Excursion falls somewhere in the main body of the show. It has the topic "Things That Might Require the Host to Leave During the Show."

A Theme Show is a special episode in which many key elements of the show have been temporarily modified to reflect a chosen theme. To write a Theme Show, follow these steps:

1. Pick a promising theme, that is, a theme that will spark a lot of people's interest and suggest a lot of associations.

2. Combine associations of the theme with key elements of the show to generate joke ideas.

3. Script out your joke ideas the way you would write jokes for a Joke Basket Sketch.

A Joke Basket Character is a comic character who delivers a series of interchangeable jokes. To create and write for a Joke Basket Character, do this:

1. Think of a character with two or three exaggerated traits.

2. Give the character an outlandish look to reflect his exaggerated personality.

3. Decide how the character will get laughs.
4. Write jokes for the character using whatever techniques apply.

Next I'll cover a type of comedy piece in which the jokes are embedded in a story—what I call a Story Sketch.

10

STORY SKETCHES

I N A JOKE Basket Sketch the jokes are performed by the host and various actors and there's little or no story line tying them together. The jokes are interchangeable; they can be swapped out and moved around. By contrast, what I call a Story Sketch is also performed by the host and others but the jokes aren't interchangeable because they're woven into a story line. So a Story Sketch is more like what you probably think of when you hear the word "sketch"—a short, funny story performed by actors.

Story sketches have existed for a long time on television outside of comedy/talk shows, of course. *Saturday Night Live* consists in large part of Story Sketches. So did *MADtv*, *Monty Python's Flying Circus*, and *In Living Color*, a show I wrote for. And Comedy Central has shows like *Key & Peele* and *Inside Amy Schumer* that feature Story Sketches. The techniques I'll be teaching you in this chapter apply to writing Story Sketches not only for shows like those, but also for comedy/talk shows. All good Story Sketches are written using the same principles no matter where they appear.

But the Story Sketches on comedy/talk shows tend to be much less varied than the Story Sketches on shows that consist mostly of sketches. Most of the Story Sketches on comedy/talk shows have the same basic storyline: the host plays straight man in a scene where a comic character disrupts the show for some reason.

The comic character is frequently played by a staff member. That's because on some comedy/talk shows, like *Conan*, many of the writers are also experienced performers. It's also because sketches are often written at the last minute—as is a lot of the comedy on these shows—which leaves the staff little time to cast actors from outside the show.

Here are some examples of Story Sketches:

I myself performed on *LNWDL* in many minor roles such as cop, security guard, Secret Service agent, Canadian Mountie, and Russian general. I was cast because (1) being on staff, I was available; and (2) my jacket size was 40 Regular so I fit into most of the uniforms on hand in the show's wardrobe department. Acting was fun but I always felt a little guilty about taking work away from outside performers with actual talent.

"The Guy Under the Seats" [*LNWDL*]—Writer/performer Chris Elliott plays a guy who interrupts the show by climbing up through a trap door in the studio audience.

"Flashback Master Ron Dempsey" [*LNWJF*]—A guy in the audience interrupts the show and challenges Jimmy to a duel to see who can do better flashbacks.

"Gustavo, the European Guy" [*LNWCO*]—An arrogant audience member tries to convince Conan that Europe is superior to the United States.

"Rude Audience Member" [*LNWCO*]—Conan is exasperated by an audience member who, Conan is convinced, is trying to steal attention away from him by using various video and audio effects.

AN EXAMPLE OF A STORY SKETCH

Before I discuss how to create a new Story Sketch, take a look at the following full-length example from *LNWCO*. I'll be analyzing it in detail. It's a mid-show Second Comedy Piece written by Dan Goor and entitled "SFX Burglar"; as you may know, "SFX" is an abbreviation for "sound effects." (To save room I've single-spaced the dialogue in the script, which is double-spaced in the original.)

ACT 3/SFX BURGLAR – Conan/Brian Stack

(With VT and Pretape)

(OPEN ON: BUMPER)

(DISS. TO: CONAN)

(MUSIC: LIVE BAND)

(OPEN ON: CONAN AT HOMEBASE)

(CONAN TEASE)

> CONAN:
> Our next guest is a great actor. You
> know him from such movies as...

(SFX: PHONE RINGS)

(CONAN PICKS UP THE PHONE)

> CONAN:
> Hello?

> BOB:
> (HUSHED) Hey, Conan, this is Bob Tway
> from the Sound Effects department.

> CONAN:
> What's going on Bob? We're sort of in
> the middle of a show here.

> BOB:
> Sorry, it's just...I think there's been
> a break in. I think there's someone in
> the sound effects room with me.

(SFX: CRASH)

> CONAN:
> What was that? Are you okay?

> **BOB:**
> Yeah, sorry, that was my fault. I just
> hit the crash button.

(SFX: CRASH)

> **BOB:**
> See?

> **CONAN:**
> Oh, phew, I thought...

(SFX: DIFFERENT CRASH)

> **CONAN:**
> We get it, Bob.

> **BOB:**
> No, no, that was him.

> **CONAN:**
> Oh. Are you okay? Can you see him?

> **BOB:**
> He's getting closer.

(SFX: FOOTSTEPS GET CLOSER)

> **BOB:**
> And closer.

(SFX: FOOTSTEPS GET EVEN CLOSER)

> **BOB:**
> And even closer!

(SFX: FOOTSTEPS RUN AWAY)

> **CONAN:**
> Sounds like he took off.

> **BOB:**
> No, he just leaned on the "footsteps
> run away button." He's right on top of
> me.

(MUSIC: SUPER DRAMATIC MUSIC STING)

> **CONAN:**
> You don't need to play a dramatic music sting.

> **BOB:**
> That was him. He has a boombox, and a GUN!

(SFX: GUN COCKS)

> **BOB:**
> I'm gonna lunge for him.

(SFX: STRUGGLE SOUNDS, FOLLOWED BY LOTS OF CRASHING)

> **BOB:**
> I knocked him over.

> **CONAN:**
> Good, now get out of there.

(SFX: POLICE SIREN)

> **CONAN:**
> Phew, the cops are there.

> **BOB:**
> No, he's got me pinned up against the machine. He's pressing my face into the buttons.

(SFX: HORSE NEIGHING)

(SFX: CAR BRAKING)

(SFX: WOMAN SIGHING)

(SFX: GUN SHOT)

> **CONAN:**
> Was that a real gunshot?

> **BOB:**
> No, a sound effect.

(SFX: GUN SHOT)

> **BOB:**
> But that one was real.

(SFX: GUN SHOT)

                    BOB:
     Not that one.

(SFX: GUN SHOT)

                    BOB:
     Real.

(SFX: GUN SHOT)

                    BOB:
     Sound effect.

(SFX: GUN SHOT)

                    BOB:
     Sound effect again.

(SFX: GUN SHOT)

                    BOB:
     That was real.

(SFX: ELEPHANT ROARS)

                    BOB:
     Elephant sound effect.

(SFX: GUN SHOT)

                    BOB:
     Real gun shot.

(SFX: GUN SHOT)

                    BOB:
     Sound effect gun shot.

(SFX: ELEPHANT ROARS)

                    BOB:
     Real elephant.

(SFX: GUN SHOT)

                    BOB:
     Real elephant firing real gun.

>   CONAN:
> BOB! Wait a minute. You're alone in
> there aren't you?

>   BOB:
> Uh...No?

>   CONAN:
> Bob. Those were all effects, weren't
> they?

>   BOB:
> Maybe.

>   CONAN:
> You're a sad man, Bob.

>   BOB:
> That hurts, Conan.

(SFX: DIAL TONE)

>   CONAN:
> You're still on the phone aren't
> you?

>   BOB:
> Yes.

>   CONAN:
> Get a life, Bob. (AD LIB OUT)

(BUMPER: OUT)

(MUSIC: LIVE BAND)

(INTO: COMMERCIAL #3)

THE NINE STEPS TO CREATING A STORY SKETCH

A Story Sketch is like any other story so it should have the same basic structure that our collectible car auctioneer laid out: "a beginning that gets you excited, a middle that grips you and an end that delivers." Elaborating on that basic structure I've developed a list of steps you should follow when you're creating a new Story Sketch. These steps are only guidelines but I believe that the more closely your sketch follows them the more entertaining it will be.

Here are the nine steps, as illustrated by the above sketch, "SFX Burglar," from *LNWCO*:

1. Think of a comic character with two or three exaggerated traits.

You may remember this technique from the previous chapter where I recommended it for creating a new Joke Basket Character. Imagine a character with two or three extreme and distinct ways of thinking or behaving. Two or three diverse traits will be enough to define the character sufficiently and exaggerating those traits will make the character funny; in fact, you should apply Joke Maximizer #8 here and wildly exaggerate the traits.

For an example of a comic character, take a close look at the one in "SFX Burglar." What are Bob's three distinct traits? He is (a) a sound effects technician, (b) a liar, and (c) an attention hog. And here's how those traits are exaggerated:

a) Not only is Bob a sound effects technician, he can expertly use sound effects to manipulate people.

b) Not only is Bob a liar, he lies constantly and outrageously, even to the most important person on the show, Conan.

c) Not only is Bob an attention hog, he interrupts a nationally-televised show and takes it over.

When you're brainstorming possible traits for your comic character you may get inspiration from one of these sources:

- Real people, places, and things on the show, like the sound effects technician who grew into "SFX Burglar" or the open space under the audience seating that gave rise to "The Guy Under the Seats"

- Real people you know, like the disruptive show-offs who probably inspired "Rude Audience Member"

- People, places, and things in pop culture, like the snooty Europeans who morphed into "Gustavo, the European Guy" or the TV and movie flashbacks that sparked "Flashback Master Ron Dempsey"

2. Make your comic character want something.

Be sure your comic character has a specific goal that he wants to achieve during the sketch. This desire will drive the character and, in turn, will drive the sketch; that is, it will propel the action in the sketch forward. A character who enters the studio and just behaves weirdly will quickly lose the interest of the audience. For example, it's not enough to write a sketch where the comic character, a new intern on the show, is a vampire. The Vampire Intern has to want to accomplish something specific during the sketch, like drink the host's blood.

To see why this principle is important, take another look at the world of automobiles. Collectible car auctions have their fans. But which event gets higher television ratings, the biggest collectible car auction in the country or the Indianapolis 500? The race, of course. The main reason is that the cars at a car auction are beautiful to look at but have no drivers. The cars at the Indy 500 are not only beautiful, they're being driven at over two hundred miles an hour by top professionals, all of them risking their lives to cross the finish line first. An Indy car driver is a colorful character who also wants something, and that makes him compelling to watch.

In the case of "SFX Burglar" Bob wants something, too: lots of airtime. Everything Bob does in the sketch he does so that Conan will let him stay on the air for as long as possible. This desire of Bob's drives the sketch, the way the desire of the comic character drives most Story Sketches on comedy/talk shows.

It's possible to write a sketch that's driven by the host instead. For example, you could write a sketch where Conan wants to fire Bob. But in general the host's desire in a Story Sketch is simply to keep doing a good show. This brings me to the next step:

3. Have someone, probably the host, oppose your comic character.

The Indianapolis 500 would be pointless and boring if there were only one driver in the race. Likewise, an entertaining Story Sketch needs someone making it hard for the comic character to get what he wants. On a comedy/talk show this opponent is almost always the host because the host is the person who most wants the show to continue without any disruption. "SFX Burglar" fits this pattern, with Conan as the opponent.

Throughout the sketch Conan tries to minimize the danger Bob is supposedly in and to dismiss him. For example, Conan says: "We're sort of in the middle of a show here." "We get it, Bob." "Sounds like he took off." "You don't need to play a dramatic music sting." "BOB! Wait a minute. You're alone in there aren't you?" "Bob. Those were all effects, weren't they?" "You're a sad man, Bob." "You're still on the phone aren't you?" Conan forces Bob to work very hard to stay on the air.

Another key point: the choices you've made in these first three steps should be obvious very early in the sketch. That is, in the first ten or fifteen seconds of the sketch you should tell the audience who the comic character is, what he wants, and who stands in his way. Spelling out this conflict quickly will help you engage your audience so they'll pay attention to and laugh at what follows. It will give the audience that "beginning that gets you excited" instead of a beginning that confuses or bores them.

In "SFX Burglar" the basic conflict is set up by the first four speeches, starting with Conan answering the phone, "Hello?" and ending with Bob saying, "I think there's someone in the sound effects room with me."

4. Have your comic character take several different steps to get what he wants, each step more radical than the last.

First have your comic character do something fairly reasonable to get what he wants, something that's also consistent with the traits you've given him. This Plan A won't entirely work because if it did work the sketch would be uninvolving and too short. So next have your character do something more radical. When that fails, have your character resort to something even more drastic. This escalating series of actions keeps the sketch surprising and absorbing.

To think of these funny moves by your comic character, free associate on his traits and on the challenge he's facing. Ask yourself what that particular character might do in that particular situation and how he would react when he couldn't achieve his goal.

In "SFX Burglar" Bob first grabs Conan's attention with a statement that could be true, that somebody has broken into the sound effects room; it's a lie but not an obvious one. Bob uses his sound effects expertise to support his claim, which is consistent with his traits. When Conan doesn't totally believe that Bob is in serious trouble, Bob has to work harder and harder to convince Conan not to cut him off. Bob uses his sound effects to tell increasingly outrageous lies:

- The intruder is getting closer and closer.

- The intruder just leaned on the "footsteps run away button" and is actually right on top of him.

- The intruder is pressing Bob's face into the sound effects buttons.

5. Raise the stakes.

Raising the stakes is a valuable, time-honored technique in any form of storytelling. It gives a story an energy boost and takes it to an even more engrossing level. It helps create that "middle that grips you." In the case of a Story Sketch, raising the stakes means magnifying the consequences of the comic character either getting or not getting what he wants.

The writer of "SFX Burglar" raises the stakes with this line: "He has a boombox, and a GUN!" Now if Bob fails to keep Conan talking to him and Conan dismisses him, Bob could get shot and possibly even killed.

6. Have your comic character do something really extreme.

The outrageousness of the action should peak as the comic character gets ever more desperate to achieve his goal. Remember Joke Maximizer #8 and wildly exaggerate the lengths to which your comic character goes. Having the character go completely over the top will help keep the sketch surprising to the end.

Bob takes his actions to an extreme with that long, fast-paced series of "real" and "sound effect" gunshots that culminates in the total absurdity of a real elephant firing a real gun.

7. Have your comic character not get (or get) what he wants.

In other words give your sketch "an end that delivers." If your sketch just stops suddenly and leaves the story you've been telling unresolved, the audience won't be satisfied.

In a Story Sketch on a comedy/talk show the comic character almost always fails to get what he wants. That's because most comic characters want to disrupt the show in some way and a character can't continue to disrupt the show indefinitely. The show must go on the way it always has; the sketch mustn't change that.

In "SFX Burglar" Bob ultimately fails when Conan gets wise to his deception and forces Bob to back off. Bob has to fail at the end of the sketch because if he succeeds he'll be on the phone with Conan forever and Conan won't be able to do his usual show anymore.

8. Throw in a final twist.

The best sketches end with a twist, a particularly surprising final joke, to help make sure they go out on a big laugh. Here are five ways to introduce a twist into the ending of a Story Sketch:

a) Deliver the same type of joke that the sketch has delivered repeatedly but from an unexpected direction. This is the technique used in "SFX Burglar." Throughout the sketch Bob tricks Conan with sound effects. The final twist has Bob trying to trick Conan with a sound effect involving, for the first time, the telephone Conan has been using.

b) Shift the focus of the sketch onto an unexpected character in the sketch. For example, "SFX Burglar" could have ended with an apparently genuine armed burglar entering the studio and asking Conan for directions to the sound effects booth, which Conan would innocently give him.

c) For the first time in the sketch, have the comic character attack the host on a personal level. For example, "SFX Burglar" could have ended with Bob calling Conan a gullible jackass, then claiming that he accidentally leaned on the "gullible jackass" button.

d) Imply that the sketch is about to start all over again in a slightly different context. "SFX Burglar" could have ended with the phone of Conan's bandleader Max ringing.

e) Have the host give the comic character a taste of his own medicine. "SFX Burglar" could have ended with Conan telling Bob to press "the last button in the second row, that one without a label." Bob pushes the button and we hear a recording of Bob's wife having enthusiastic sex with Conan. Conan claims it's not real...just a sound effect.

9. Add the dialogue.

Once you've used those first eight steps to plot out the beats of the story—the skeleton of the sketch—flesh out the sketch by adding the dialogue. The basic rules for writing dialogue are simple—every line you write for each character in the sketch should ideally be these three things:

a) On story, in that the line moves the story ahead along the path you've outlined. Your comic character should say things to help him get what he wants and the host should say things to oppose him. Don't let your dialogue sidetrack your characters. If you do, the momentum of your sketch will slow and the attention of the audience will wander.

b) In character, in that the line reflects the traits of whoever is delivering it. Each line from a character should be something you could imagine that character saying, said the way that character would say it. This applies to the host, to the comic character with his exaggerated traits, and to any other character who has lines in the sketch.

c) As funny as possible, in that the line is worded in a way that maximizes its potential to get a laugh. Most of the comedy in a Story Sketch will come from the story itself, from the unexpected situations you put your characters into and the surprising and ridiculous things those characters do in response. But you should polish the lines of dialogue that convey that story using the Joke Maximizers. Remember especially Joke Maximizer #1 and make sure the dialogue is very economical, with no superfluous words (unless using superfluous words is a trait of one of your characters).

SUMMARY

In a Story Sketch, the jokes are woven into a story which is performed by the host and other performers. Usually the story has the host playing straight man in a scene where a comic character disrupts the show for some reason.

The nine steps to creating a Story Sketch are:
1. Think of a comic character with two or three exaggerated traits.
2. Make your comic character want something.
3. Have someone, probably the host, oppose your comic character.
4. Have your comic character take several different steps to get what he wants, each step more radical than the last.
5. Raise the stakes.
6. Have your comic character do something really extreme.
7. Have your comic character not get (or get) what he wants.
8. Throw in a final twist. Here are five ways to do that:
   - Deliver the same type of joke that the sketch has delivered repeatedly but from an unexpected direction.
   - Shift the focus of the sketch onto an unexpected character in the sketch.
   - For the first time in the sketch, have the comic character attack the host on a personal level.
   - Imply that the sketch is about to start all over again in a slightly different context.
   - Have the host give the comic character a taste of his own medicine.

9. Add the dialogue. Every line of dialogue should be three things:
- on story
- in character
- as funny as possible

Next I'll tell you how to write a particular type of Story Sketch where you don't have to create the story yourself; you take it from a work that already exists. I'm talking about a Parody Sketch.

PARODY SKETCHES

I N THE WORLD of law, the word "parody" has a fairly precise definition that involves the concept of commenting on the original work. But in the world of comedy writing, the definition is usually looser: a parody is considered to be a funny imitation of an artistic work that typically wasn't intended to be funny. In this chapter I'll be focusing on Parody Sketches, which I define as funny imitations of scripted videos that usually weren't supposed to be funny. Parody Sketches frequently appear not only on comedy/talk shows but also on sketch shows like *Saturday Night Live* and on comedy websites like Funny or Die. You'll see Parody Sketches based on the following types of videos:

Movie Scenes and Movie Trailers—For example, *LSWDL* aired a parody of a trailer for the movie *Inglourious Basterds*. In it Dave portrays "Hitler's Irritable Downstairs Neighbor, Gunter," who complains when Hitler repeatedly pounds on a table.

TV Shows and TV Show Promos—Among the many TV show parodies that appeared on *LNWJF* is "Game of Desks," an elaborate send-up of the HBO series *Game of Thrones*. The parody alludes to Seth Meyers taking over from Jimmy as host of *Late Night*.

TV Commercials and Public Service Announcements (PSAs)—As one example, on *LNWJF* Jimmy plays actor Charlie Sheen selling his (fake) new cologne "Winning for Men" in a parody of a Calvin Klein-style fragrance commercial.

News Videos and Documentaries—*JKL* aired a parody of a Ken Burns documentary. Instead of the Civil War, the parody is about "The Late Night War," the war for the *Tonight* show between Jay Leno and Conan O'Brien.

AN EXAMPLE OF A PARODY SKETCH

Before I tell you how to create a Parody Sketch, have a look at the following full-length example that I co-wrote. I'll be exposing the details of its inner workings. It's a parody of a TV commercial, one of the dozens of comedy pieces on *TSWJL* that grew out of the murder trial of O. J. Simpson. (In Appendix B I talk about the role that O. J. trial comedy like this may have played in helping *TSWJL* climb past *LSWDL* in the ratings.) Note that "VTPB" is an abbreviation for "videotape playback."

"OIL OF O. J. COMMERCIAL"

JAY IS AT HOMEBASE

> JAY
> Sometimes it seems as though everybody
> is trying to make a buck off the O. J.
> Simpson trial. I saw a commercial for
> a product today. I couldn't believe
> this. Take a look.

VTPB:

O. J. LOOKS WORN-OUT AT DEFENSE TABLE (NEWS FOOTAGE)

> EDD (V.O.)
> A long trial can be really
> rough...especially on your hands.

O. J.'S SCRAPED AND SWOLLEN HAND ON TABLE RADIATES ANIMATED
HEAT WAVES (PRETAPED FOOTAGE)

> EDD (V.O.)
> Hot television lights and paper cuts
> can make your hands sore and chapped.

JUDGE ITO AT BENCH, REACHES DOWN (NEWS FOOTAGE)

> EDD (V.O.)
> So what's your best defense against
> courtroom skin damage?

JUDGE ITO'S HAND PICKS UP BOTTLE OF OIL OF O. J. (PRETAPED
FOOTAGE)

> EDD (V.O.)
> Experts agree...it's Oil of O. J.

JUDGE ITO'S HANDS APPLY THE LOTION, THEN SET BOTTLE DOWN ON
BENCH (PRETAPED FOOTAGE)

> EDD (V.O.)
> Oil of O. J. will actually help
> preserve your skin's DNA with a
> special...

FACES OF LAWYERS SHAPIRO, COCHRAN, AND BAILEY APPEAR, THEN
FLY INTO MOUTH OF BOTTLE (PRETAPED FOOTAGE)

> EDD (V.O.)
> ..."Dream Team" of moisturizers,
> nutrients, and emollients.

JUDGE ITO RUBS HIS HANDS TOGETHER (NEWS FOOTAGE)

> EDD (V.O.)
> Just rub it in. Oil of O. J. is a
> specially-formulated lotion as rich
> and smooth as Johnnie Cochran.

CHYRON: RICH AND SMOOTH AS JOHNNIE COCHRAN

O. J. GETS UP FROM DEFENSE TABLE AND WALKS TOWARD BENCH
(NEWS FOOTAGE)

> EDD (V.O.)
> Go get some Oil of O. J. for yourself,
> and watch that evidence of skin damage
> disappear.

JUDGE ITO'S HAND APPLIES LOTION TO O. J.'S HANDS, WHICH RUB
IN THE LOTION (PRETAPED FOOTAGE)

> EDD (V.O.)
> The miracle ingredients in Oil of
> O. J. even help ease the symptoms of
> arthritis.

BEAUTY SHOT OF OIL OF O. J. BOTTLE WITH HOURGLASS AND GAVEL
ON JUDGE ITO'S BENCH (PRETAPED FOOTAGE)

> EDD (V.O.)
> Oil of O. J. For hands so soft and
> young-looking, you'll never have to
> wear gloves again.

CHYRON: YOU'LL NEVER HAVE TO WEAR GLOVES AGAIN

END OF VTPB

JAY GOES ON WITH SHOW

THE NINE STEPS TO CREATING A PARODY SKETCH

As I talk about these steps I'll focus mainly on creating parodies of TV commercials because you'll see a lot of those in the various comedy outlets. But the same basic steps also apply to parodies of other scripted videos like movie trailers and TV show promos. Here are the nine steps, as illustrated by the "Oil of O. J. Commercial":

1. For your topic, choose a video that's ripe for parody.

Two characteristics make a video, such as a commercial, ripe for parody:

Most people have seen it.

The audience needs to be already familiar with what you're parodying if they're going to get your jokes. That fact alone makes writing a parody different from writing a Monologue joke. When you write a Monologue joke you can include in your topic all the information that the audience has to have in order to understand the joke. For instance, you can start the joke by telling the audience that "two Oklahoma women were caught shoplifting two thousand dollars' worth of merchandise stuffed in the rolls of their body fat." That's all they need to know for the joke to work.

But when you write a parody of, say, a skin lotion commercial, the audience has to know in advance what a skin lotion commercial looks and sounds like without your having to show them first. You can't start your comedy piece with a real skin lotion commercial and then follow that with your parody because if you did, it would take too long to get to the funny part.

So ask yourself what TV commercials, movies, TV shows, and other scripted videos are well-known at the time you're trying to choose what to parody. Then ask yourself which of those well-known videos also have this second characteristic of a video that's ripe for parody:

Most people have an emotional reaction to it.

If the audience feels a certain way about what you're parodying you can reflect that feeling with your jokes and get bigger laughs.

For example, the "Oil of O. J. Commercial" parodies the type of commercial you might have seen for a popular skin lotion that was called, at the time, Oil of Olay. Most people probably feel that commercials for skin lotions make extravagant claims; the products are, after all, just skin lotions. That's why a parody which mocks the self-importance of that sales pitch will probably resonate with the audience.

So look for possible parody topics the same way you'd look for possible topics for Monologue jokes: pay special attention to high-profile commercials, movies, and other scripted videos that you think are interesting, dumb, surprising, annoying, weird, hypocritical, or disgusting.

2. Add an angle to the video you're parodying.

Once you've chosen the video you're going to parody—your topic—decide what direction you want your parody to take—your angle. Your angle will be the central governing idea of your parody, the main way that your parody will differ from the video it's parodying, your parody's Big Twist.

When you add a parody angle to a topic, keep the angle simple. It should basically amount to changing one association of the topic. The angle should be so simple that you can summarize your parody with a short sentence in this form: "It's this [the topic] but with this one key change [the angle]." For example, you could summarize the "Oil of O. J. Commercial" as "It's an Oil of Olay commercial but the lotion is for use at the O. J. Simpson murder trial." Being able to state the central idea of your parody very clearly and specifically this way will help focus your writing and make it easier to generate jokes for your parody.

Here are four techniques for generating promising parody angles for any given topic video. (Note that these techniques are very similar to the Punch Line Makers I covered in Chapter 5.)

a) Ask a question about the topic and answer it using an association of the topic.

For example, Apple once ran a commercial for its iPod music player that featured an earphone-wearing iPod user dancing enthusiastically in silhouette against a solid-color background. The commercial was familiar and engaging—a great topic for a parody. A writer on a sketch show at the time apparently asked, "What might really happen to someone rocking out to loud music on an iPod?" The writer answered that question by associating the iPod in the topic video with news stories of people getting their iPods stolen. So the central idea of the parody became "It's that Dancing iPod User commercial but the dancer gets his iPod stolen." The parody of the iPod commercial started with an iPod user dancing in silhouette and then had a mugger enter in silhouette and steal the dancer's iPod at gunpoint.

b) Link an association of the topic to something that the association suggests in popular culture.

For instance, a well-known series of Calvin Klein fragrance commercials featured men talking aimlessly to the camera about their lives. Apparently a writer for *LNWJF* linked the random blather in the commercials to the ramblings of actor Charlie Sheen, who was drawing attention at the time for his off-the-wall pronouncements about himself. So the central idea of the parody became "It's a Calvin Klein fragrance commercial but the guy talking weirdly to the camera is Charlie Sheen."

c) Use a play on words to combine associations of the topic or to link the topic to something in popular culture.

This technique was used in a radio commercial parody produced by Jones American Comedy Network. The topic was a commercial for Cottonelle Bathroom Tissue. The writer noticed that changing one vowel sound in Cottonelle Bathroom Tissue yields Kittenelle Bathroom Tissue and used this play on words to link Cottonelle to kittens. The central idea of the parody became "It's a Cottonelle Bathroom Tissue commercial but the toilet paper consists of live kittens."

d) Use a play on images to link the topic to something in popular culture.

We *TSWJL* writers used this technique to come up with the concept for the "Oil of O. J. Commercial." One morning Jay mentioned that he had seen a news clip of Judge Ito at the O. J. Simpson trial rubbing his hands together. Jay thought that Judge Ito looked as if he were rubbing lotion into his hands and suggested that we build a commercial parody around the clip. So the central idea of the parody became "It's an Oil of Olay commercial but the lotion is for use at the O. J. Simpson murder trial."

(You may be surprised to learn that the idea for this parody didn't come from the play on words "Oil of Olay"/"Oil of O. J." In fact, the name for our fake lotion was one of the last punch lines we added to the parody; we just got lucky that the name was so perfect. When you're parodying a real product or service, the more your parody name sounds like the real name, the better. I'll talk more below about keeping the stylistic elements of the parody as close as possible to those of the original.)

Note that unlike short parodies, full-length movie parodies like *Airplane*, *Scary Movie*, and *Spaceballs* almost never have only one angle. That's because it would be too hard to come up with ninety minutes of jokes if the writers could only go in one direction for punch lines. Instead, full-length movie parodies have multiple angles, each one taking off from a different scene or character.

Take *Spaceballs*. When the writers started out to write a parody of science fiction movies like *Star Wars* they didn't say something like, "It's *Star Wars* but everybody is a cat." If they had they would have run out of jokes pretty fast. Instead they just thought of *Spaceballs* as "*Star Wars* but funny." Then they came up with multiple angles like the evil Darth Vader character being a short guy wearing an enormous helmet and a planet getting all of its atmosphere sucked away by a gigantic vacuum cleaner.

3. Study the stylistic elements of the video you're parodying.

Remember how I said in Chapter 5 that the topic of a Monologue joke should be factually true and not intentionally funny? The same general principle applies to Parody Sketches. The stylistic elements of your parody—the particular details of how it looks and sounds—should be true to the video you're parodying and not try to get laughs by themselves. That way the punch lines you write into your parody will be even more surprising and therefore funnier.

This means that if you want to create a parody of, say, a particular TV commercial you have to study the real thing so you can imitate its style. Everything about your parody commercial should closely resemble the real commercial except for the punch lines. Specifically, the parody commercial and the real commercial should be alike in at least these nine ways:

a) Actors, both on-screen and voiceover—are they young, middle-aged, or elderly? Male or female? Model-attractive or next-door-neighbor?

b) Tone of any dialogue—is it formal or folksy? Authoritative or whimsical? Urgent or laid-back?

c) Visuals—are the shots interior or exterior? People shots or product shots? Static shots or action shots? Brightly-lit or moody? Any animation?

d) Pace of the editing—are there many short shots? Fewer but longer shots? Cuts or dissolves?

e) Music—is there any? Rock, classical, or hip hop? Lively or soothing? Brass or strings?

f) On-screen Text—when it is used? What size? What font? Static or moving?

g) Length. The audience knows very well how long a real commercial is. If your parody commercial is much longer than a real commercial you run the risk of losing the audience's interest, just as you would with a Monologue joke that goes on too long.

h) Format. Does the real commercial have a problem-solution format? Does it center on a product demonstration? Does it depict a slice-of-life? Does it use a spokesperson? Does it rely on testimonials?

i) Structure. Given the format you're using, in what order do things happen in the commercial? In other words, how is the story of the commercial constructed?

In the case of the "Oil of O.J Commercial," we writers chose a format that's typical for a real skin lotion commercial, the problem-solution format. This format dictated the following general structure for the parody commercial:

- Identify the problem.
- Introduce the product as a solution to the problem.
- Mention the product frequently.
- Describe the features of the product.
- Tell how the product's features solve the problem.
- Show someone getting the benefits of using the product.
- End with a tag line.

4. Brainstorm associations of the video you're parodying.

Make a list—written-down or in your head—of people, places, and things suggested by your topic video. Let your brainstorming be guided by the format and structure of that video.

For example, to write the "Oil of O. J. Commercial" parody you'd think of associations of a real TV commercial for a skin lotion. Since you've decided that your parody will have a problem-solution format, you'd focus in particular on associations that have to do with skin problems, skin lotion features, the benefits of using skin lotion, and so on. You might come up with a list of associations like this:

Dry skin	Skin cells
Roughness	Rich
Chapped skin	Non-greasy
Soreness	Smooth
Skin damage	Scented
Pain in hands	Rub lotion in
Arthritis	Rejuvenate
Special ingredients	Replenish
Secret formula	Soften
Moisturizers	Jergens Lotion
Nutrients	Oil of Olay
Emollients	Vaseline Intensive Care

5. Brainstorm associations of the angle you added.

Just as you did for the topic of your parody, make a list of people, places, and things that come to mind when you think of the angle you've picked for your parody. This is where it helps to have a simple, specific angle, one that you can state in a short sentence. Having an angle like that makes it easier to generate a comprehensive and detailed list of associations, which will make it easier to write punch lines.

The angle of the "Oil of O. J. Commercial" is that the skin lotion is for use at the O. J. Simpson murder trial. Here are some of the associations you might write down for that angle:

O. J.	TV lights and cameras
Dream Team	Long trial
Defense	Evidence
Lawyers Cochran, Bailey, and Shapiro	DNA

Cochran is polished	Paperwork
Cochran is successful	Exhibits
Bailey is famous	Expert witnesses
Prosecution	Houseguest Kato Kaelin
Lawyers Clark and Darden	Jury
Judge Ito	Trying on the bloody glove
Gavel	O. J.'s arthritis
Courtroom	"If the glove doesn't fit,
Low-speed chase	you must acquit."

6. Create punch lines by linking associations of the topic and of the angle.

This step is similar to Punch Line Maker #1, one of the techniques I showed you in Chapter 5. Take each association on your "topic" list and try to combine it with an association on your "angle" list in a way that makes a surprising but true observation. Not every item on each list will link up with an item on the other list, of course. But every time you can make a clever connection you have a possible verbal or visual punch line for your parody.

Let's look at how associations on the "Skin Lotion Commercial" list and on the "O. J. Simpson Murder Trial" list were linked to create some of the punch lines in the "Oil of O. J. Commercial" parody:

- "Roughness" + "Long trial" = "A long trial can be really rough... especially on your hands."

- ("Chapped skin" + "Soreness") + ("TV lights" + "Paperwork") = "Hot television lights and paper cuts can make your hands sore and chapped."

- "Oil of Olay" + "O. J." = "Oil of O. J."

- ("Moisturizers" + "Nutrients" + "Emollients") + ("Dream Team" + "Cochran" + "Bailey" + "Shapiro") = the verbal punch line "...a special 'Dream Team' of moisturizers, nutrients, and emollients" and the visual punch line of the three lawyers' faces flying into the mouth of the bottle.

- ("Rich" + "Smooth") + ("Cochran is polished" + "Cochran is successful") = "Oil of O. J. is a specially-formulated lotion as rich and smooth as Johnnie Cochran."

- "Special ingredients" + "O. J.'s arthritis" = "The miracle ingredients in Oil of O. J. even help ease the symptoms of arthritis." [A background note: the prosecutors accused O. J. of suspending use of his arthritis medicine so that his hands would swell and not fit into the bloody evidence glove.]

- ("Soften" + "Rejuvenate") + "Trying on the bloody glove" = "For hands so soft and young-looking, you'll never have to wear gloves again."

This process may seem formulaic, especially since I used mathematical symbols to describe it, but that's because it is formulaic in many ways, like so much of show business scriptwriting. Professional writers juggle the formulas in their heads—automatically, instinctively—but that doesn't mean the formulas don't exist.

Try to come up with as many punch lines as you can, many more than you'll need to fill out the parody. You'll be taking out the weaker punch lines later and you'll want plenty of strong punch lines available to take their place.

7. Put your punch lines in an effective order.

Now that you have lots of possible punch lines, assemble your favorites into a rough draft of your parody. As you do, follow these guidelines:

a) Don't worry if your rough draft is unpolished and too long. You'll edit it later, after you have the basic building blocks in place.

b) Use the structure of the video you're parodying as the structure of your parody. For example, we writers of the "Oil of O. J. Commercial" adhered to the problem-solution format structure because that was the structure of the real skin lotion commercials we were parodying. So the parody begins with a punch line identifying the problem—"A long trial can be really rough... especially on your hands." Then the parody introduces the product with a punch line—"Experts agree...it's Oil of O. J." The parody continues with punch lines about the product's features, benefits, and so on until the tag line, which is also a punch line.

c) As early in the script as possible, make it clear what your angle is. Until your angle is obvious to the audience they won't have the information they need to appreciate your punch lines so they'll be confused and their attention will wander.

In the "Oil of O. J. Commercial," the angle is clearly stated by the lines, "So what's your best defense against courtroom skin damage? Experts agree...it's Oil of O. J." Those lines tell the audience, "This is an Oil of Olay commercial for a lotion to be used at the O. J. Simpson murder trial." They're the third and fourth lines of dialogue in the parody and they come where the product would be introduced in a real problem-solution commercial; they can't come any sooner because cutting either the first or second dialogue line, lines which identify the problems that the lotion promises to solve, would hurt the parody.

d) If the structure of your parody allows it, arrange your punch lines so they build throughout the script. That is, as the parody continues the punch lines should get edgier, more exaggerated, more outrageous, and therefore more unexpected. This will help ensure that the parody maintains its forward momentum and keeps the audience engaged.

In the "Oil of O. J. Commercial," the punch lines build from one alluding to DNA evidence to punch lines involving O. J.'s "Dream Team," Johnnie Cochran's slickness, Judge Ito personally applying lotion to O. J.'s hands, and O. J. manipulating his arthritis.

e) End with one of your strongest punch lines. Ideally your final punch line should yank the parody in a surprising direction so it ends on a big laugh. This final punch line will be your tag line if the commercial structure you're using includes one.

The tag line of the "Oil of O. J. Commercial" is "You'll never have to wear gloves again." It takes the parody in a new, edgier, direction, toward the gloves that O. J. was accused of wearing during the murders; one of the most dramatic and controversial moments of the trial was when O.J. tried to put on one of the bloody gloves. For that reason, the tag line is a particularly strong punch line to end on.

f) Write new punch lines as needed. As you're fleshing out the structure of your parody with punch lines you may notice that you need more in a certain area. For example, you may realize you need a funny tag line. If that's the case, go back to your lists of associations, maybe add a few new associations, and then write more punch lines to fill in the gaps.

8. Add visuals that boost the comedy.

What the audience is seeing at any given moment in your parody should reflect what they're hearing. "See it and say it" as the expression goes. Real commercials maximize their impact this way and your parody should, too.

But ideally you should use each visual in your parody not just to reflect the audio but also to enhance the comedy. One way to do that is to create a video image that illustrates a portion of audio in a surprising way. An unexpected video shot can make a line of dialogue that's already funny even funnier. An example of this in the "Oil of O. J. Commercial" is when the announcer talks about a "'Dream Team' of moisturizers, nutrients, and emollients" at the same time the audience is seeing the faces of O. J.'s three lawyers fly into the mouth of the lotion bottle. The flying faces are startling and irreverent and therefore add visual punch to the audio punch line.

A surprising video shot can also add a laugh to audio that isn't funny by itself. For instance, when the announcer in the "Oil of O. J. Commercial" says "Just rub it in," the audience sees news footage of the real Judge Ito rubbing his hands together for an unusually long time, looking exactly as though he's applying hand lotion. The shot is such an unexpectedly perfect illustration of the announcer's straight line that it amounts to a punch line and gets a laugh.

9. Edit the script into its final form.

Take these six steps to edit the rough draft of your parody into final shape:

a) Eliminate weak punch lines. If a punch line doesn't seem as strong as the others in your script, cut it. That way your parody will speed right along from laugh to laugh. The audience won't miss a punch line that they never knew existed.

Here's a punch line that was cut from the "Oil of O. J. Commercial" before it was produced. In the rough draft of the script it came right before the closing beauty shot of the Oil of O. J. bottle.

```
O. J. SHOWS HIS HAND TO THE JURY
(NEWS FOOTAGE)

          EDD (V.O.)
     Just ask a jury of your peers...
     Oil of O. J. lets you put your
     best hand forward.
```

Not a bad punch line but not quite up to the level of the rest. Plus, the next line of dialogue in the script also refers to "hand" and, as you'll see in the following step, that's a problem. So the punch line was cut.

b) Eliminate punch lines that are similar to others in the script. If more than one punch line is based on the same association, consider cutting all but one of them to keep your parody as surprising as possible. In the "Oil of O. J. Commercial" you wouldn't want to include a second Johnnie Cochran punch line, for instance, especially since his face also appears in the flying "Dream Team" shot.

c) Eliminate punch lines that aren't consistent with the format you've chosen. That is, cut punch lines that don't fit into the structure of the commercial you're parodying. For example, this punch line was cut from the very top of the rough draft of the "Oil of O. J. Commercial":

```
WIDE SHOT OF O. J. TRIAL COURTROOM
(NEWS FOOTAGE)


            EDD (V.O.)
    You know the feeling. You're in
    court, and the testimony is taking
    forever.
```

It's a redundant punch line because the next line talks about the "long trial." But more important, keeping that punch line in would lead to the parody taking too long to identify the product, which a real commercial with a problem-solution format wouldn't do. So that first punch line was taken out before the parody was produced.

d) Eliminate even more punch lines until your parody is approximately as long as the video you're parodying. This means that a commercial parody should ideally be no more than a minute long. Most real commercials are thirty seconds long but some are sixty seconds, so a minute-long commercial parody seems plausible. The "Oil of O. J. Commercial," as aired, was just under a minute long. Read your script aloud at the pace you imagine it playing out on-screen to estimate how long the finished video will be.

Sure, comedy/talk shows and sketch shows often air commercial parodies that are way longer than a minute but I'd argue that those parodies would be funnier if they were a more realistic length. Those shows have to fill a lot of time with comedy so sometimes they're tempted to leave a sketch on the long, flabby side rather than tighten it up.

e) Make sure the stylistic elements of your parody match those of the video you're parodying as much as possible. In addition to length, your parody should closely resemble the real video in its tone, its visuals, its use of music and on-screen text, and its other stylistic details. You'll have to use your judgment, though. For example, the "Oil of O. J. Commercial" didn't include a musical underscore, even though many skin lotion commercials do, because we writers felt that music didn't fit with the O. J. murder trial setting.

f) Polish your script using the Joke Maximizers. The following techniques in particular are helpful in punching up parody scripts:

- Shorten as much as possible.
- Put the laugh trigger at the end of each punch line.
- Make sure everything in the script is clear and logical.
- Use stop consonants, alliteration, and assonance.
- Wildly exaggerate in your punch lines.
- Use specific words in your punch lines instead of general ones.
- Use the Rule of Three in any punch line with a list.

Note that even though the focus of the above nine steps is on writing Parody Sketches that are videos, most of the same steps also apply to writing parodies in other media. For example, if you were writing a parody of a particular website you'd want to be sure that the website is

widely viewed, that you study its stylistic elements, that you link associations of the website to associations of your angle to create punch lines,
and so on.

SUMMARY

In the context of a comedy/talk show, a Parody Sketch is a funny imitation of a scripted video that usually wasn't intended to be funny. Parody
Sketches are often based on the following types of videos:

- Movie Scenes and Movie Trailers
- TV Shows and TV Show Promos
- TV Commercials and Public Service Announcements (PSAs)
- News Videos and Documentaries

The nine steps to creating a Parody Sketch are these:

1. For your topic, choose a video that's ripe for parody. That means it
has these two characteristics:

- Most people have seen it.
- Most people have an emotional reaction to it.

2. Add an angle to the video you're parodying. The angle is your parody's Big Twist. It should be simple, the result of changing one association of the video you've chosen as your topic. Here are four ways to come
up with promising parody angles for your topic video:

- Ask a question about the topic and answer it using an association
  of the topic.
- Link an association of the topic to something that the association
  suggests in popular culture.
- Use a play on words to combine associations of the topic or to link
  the topic to something in popular culture.
- Use a play on images to link the topic to something in popular culture.

3. Study the stylistic elements of the video you're parodying. You want your parody to closely resemble your topic video except for the punch lines. Your parody and the original video should be very similar in at least these nine ways:

- actors
- tone
- visuals
- pace of the editing
- music
- on-screen text
- length
- format
- structure

4. Brainstorm associations of the video you're parodying. Be guided by the format and structure of that video.

5. Brainstorm associations of the angle you added.

6. Create punch lines by linking associations of the topic and of the angle. Come up with more punch lines than you need.

7. Put your punch lines in an effective order. Follow these guidelines:

- Don't worry if your rough draft is unpolished and too long.
- Use the structure of the video you're parodying as the structure of your parody.
- As early in the script as possible, make it clear what your angle is.
- If the structure of your parody allows it, arrange your punch lines so they build throughout the script.
- End with one of your strongest punch lines.
- Write new punch lines as needed.

8. Add visuals that boost the comedy.

9. Edit the script into its final form. Here's how:

- Eliminate weak punch lines.
- Eliminate punch lines that are similar to others in the script.
- Eliminate punch lines that aren't consistent with the format you've chosen.
- Eliminate even more punch lines until your parody is approximately as long as the video you're parodying.
- Make sure the stylistic elements of your parody match those of the video you're parodying as much as possible.
- Polish your script using the Joke Maximizers.

Until now the only comedy pieces I've talked about are completely scripted. But in the next two chapters I'll tell you how to write pieces that can't entirely be committed to paper—Semi-Scripted Pieces.

12

LIVE SEMI-SCRIPTED PIECES

Every element of a scripted comedy piece—what happens, when it happens, who says what, and so on—is specified by the writers. Therefore, assuming the performers don't ad-lib and the script is produced as written, the only unpredictable aspect of the piece is how the audience will react to it. But comedy/talk shows also air a different type of piece which I'll cover in this chapter and the next—what I call a Semi-Scripted Piece.

What's a Semi-Scripted Piece?

I define a Semi-Scripted Piece as a comedy piece in which the host or a correspondent follows a scripted outline in order to accomplish a task. Because the piece isn't entirely scripted, the final form it takes isn't totally under the control of the show's staff.

The reason a Semi-Scripted Piece isn't entirely scripted is that it can't be. That's because a lot of the comedy in the piece is expected to come from unpredictable interactions with civilians, like pedestrians, or from performing a stunt. No one knows ahead of time exactly what the civilians will say or exactly what will happen during the stunt.

A Semi-Scripted Piece on a comedy/talk show is similar to a so-called "reality" show on network television. In both cases much of what the audience sees has been written ahead of time, such as what the host says and what situations the civilians are placed in. But the exact way that the finished product unfolds depends to some extent on the unscripted, spontaneous reactions of the civilian participants.

How Semi-Scripted Pieces Get Laughs

Semi-Scripted Pieces get laughs with four different types of jokes:

- **Jokes that are written ahead of time** and delivered as the piece is produced.

- **Jokes that are ad-libbed by the professional on-camera talent** (maybe with the help of writers) as the piece is produced.

- **Funny things that civilian participants spontaneously do or say**, which may be even funnier than the jokes that come from the professionals.

- **Jokes that are added after a piece is recorded, during the editing process** (that is, "in post-production" or "in post"). For example, after the professional on-camera talent performs a lame joke, cutting to a reaction shot of a deadpan civilian spectator will usually get a laugh from the audience. (Of course the civilian may actually have been reacting to something completely different at the time but a cheap laugh is still a laugh.)

As I discuss each type of Semi-Scripted Piece I'll tell you how to write any of the jokes that don't come spontaneously from civilians.

TYPES OF SEMI-SCRIPTED PIECES

Semi-Scripted Pieces can be live or prerecorded. They can be produced completely in the studio, completely outside the studio ("in the field"), or a combination of both.

Live Semi-Scripted Pieces that are produced completely in the studio include these:

- Audience Pieces, where the host interacts with the studio audience
- Phone Call Pieces, where the host interacts with the outside world by telephone
- Some Stunt Pieces, where the host performs an entertaining physical activity

Live Semi-Scripted Pieces that are produced partly inside and partly outside the studio include these:

- Remote Camera Pieces, where the host interacts with the outside world by means of a camera placed in a remote location
- Other Stunt Pieces

Semi-Scripted Field Pieces, which are produced completely outside the studio and are prerecorded, include these:

- Location-Dependent Field Pieces, like Hidden Camera Pranks
- Location-Independent Field Pieces, like Pedestrian Games

In the next chapter I'll talk about that last category, Semi-Scripted Field Pieces. I'll devote the rest of this chapter to the various types of Live Semi-Scripted Pieces, starting with Audience Pieces and moving on to Phone Call Pieces, Remote Camera Pieces, and Stunt Pieces.

AUDIENCE PIECES

In an Audience Piece the host interacts with the studio audience in order to accomplish some task. Not every host does Audience Pieces but they're good for a show to have in its comedy repertoire for a number of reasons:

- They allow the host to show off his skill at improvising and "crowd work."
- They inject some unpredictability into the show and provide a refreshing change of pace from the joke-joke-joke rhythm of completely scripted comedy pieces.
- They can take the host away from his desk, which makes the show a little more visually interesting.
- They can often be produced at the last minute to take the place of another comedy piece that fell out of the show for some reason.
- They are usually refillable and repeatable.

Audience Pieces can be sorted into five basic categories: Audience Stories, Audience Talents, Audience Game, Audience Voting, and Audience Task. I'll discuss each of these in turn.

Audience Stories

In an Audience Stories Piece the host's task is to get audience members to tell anecdotes about themselves on a given topic.

Here are some examples of Audience Stories Pieces:

> **"Brush with Greatness"** [*LNWDL*]—Audience members describe their chance encounters with celebrities. For example, one audience member talks about how he was riding in a hotel elevator when actress Shirley MacLaine got on and behaved strangely.

"Brush with the Law" [*LNWDL*]—Audience members tell about their encounters with the police and minor-league crimes they've committed, like stealing a banana.

"Midnight Confessions" [*TSWJL*]—Audience members confess things that they've never told anyone about before. For example, one woman confesses that she had sex with her husband in a bank after it closed. Jay ad-libs, "Is there a penalty for early withdrawal there?"

"Dates from Hell" [*TSWJL*]—Audience members talk about terrible dates they've been on.

"Idiots for a Day" [*TSWJL*]—Audience members tell stories about stupid and embarrassing things they've done. For instance, one guy said he took off his pants outdoors because ants had crawled up inside them and he wound up dancing around in his underwear in front of twenty children from a local day care center.

How to Produce an Audience Stories Piece

Let's say a show wants to air a piece like "Midnight Confessions." Here's how the staff would typically produce it.

The day the piece is going to be on the show the production staff prints up questionnaires that read something like this: "Have you ever done something that you've never told anybody about? Maybe something you're ashamed to admit? Something you thought might get you in trouble? Write down your secret here and we might pick you to be on the show." The questionnaire also has space for the person's name and hometown.

A couple of hours before the show is taped, staff members start distributing the questionnaires and small "golf" pencils to audience members waiting in line outside the studio. Most audience members write something down. Hard as it may be to believe, the lure of appearing on national television is so strong that plenty of people will volunteer to expose their dark secrets.

An hour or so before the taping, staff members start collecting the questionnaires and delivering them to a handful of writers. The writers divvy up the questionnaires and, as the clock ticks down to show time, hunt for diamonds in the rough—stories worthy of consideration.

The writing team decides which stories are promising enough to make the first cut. The writers split up, track down each chosen audience member in line, and ask him or her to tell their whole story on the spot. This seemingly casual interview is an audition that's intended to answer these questions:

- **Is the story true?** The writers have to play detective to weed out stories concocted by audience members willing to lie to appear on television. The problem is that if a story is phony, the pressure of telling it on the show will make that fact obvious and the story won't be funny. That's because an Audience Stories Piece is a kind of Found Comedy Piece and you may remember from Chapter 8 that if an item in a Found Comedy Piece is intentionally funny the audience can't feel superior and they won't laugh.

- **Does the audience member have an acceptable personality?** The writers know that the story won't be entertaining, and the host will be annoyed, if the storyteller is an obnoxious jerk who won't play along. You want audience members who will tell their stories straight and not try to ask the host questions or crack jokes themselves.

- **Is the audience member reasonably articulate?** The writers don't want a storyteller who has a problem communicating. The story would take too long to hear and the audience would feel uncomfortable instead of superior and not laugh.

- **Is the audience member camera-shy?** One of the last questions I always ask potential participants is, "Would you be okay with telling that story on TV, in front of all those lights and cameras? Are you sure?" I haven't had an audience participant freeze on me yet but there's always a first time.

The four or so audience members with the most entertaining stories who have also passed the writers' audition are asked to appear on the show. The chosen audience members and anybody who came with them are seated in the studio in taped-off seats along one aisle. That way the host will be able to reach them easily with a microphone.

The names of the audience participants, along with one-sentence descriptions of their stories, are typed on file cards. The cards are put in an effective order so the piece will get off to a flying start with a strong story and end with an even stronger story. Then, minutes before the show taping begins, a writer reviews the cards with the host, not to give the host a lot of details about the stories but just to reassure him that he's not walking into a disaster.

Finally the writers heave a sigh of relief. Starting with nothing but a stack of blank questionnaires they've assembled a full comedy piece in less than two hours. They'll heave another sigh of relief when the host works his magic with the piece during the taping and earns big laughs with his ad-libs.

How to Create a New Audience Stories Piece

Creating a new Audience Stories Piece means thinking of a topic. Follow these two steps to come up with a topic that will yield plenty of entertaining tales:

1. Think of a topic that grabs your attention.

Imagine you're drifting through a cocktail party full of total strangers. If you overhear any one of these snatches of conversation you'll probably stop to hear the rest of the story:

- "I never felt so stupid in my life."
- "I got in trouble with the police yesterday."
- "You know who was at the urinal next to me? Harrison Ford."

Any story that you'd be interested in hearing from a random stranger at a cocktail party probably has a topic that could support an Audience Stories Piece like "Idiots for a Day," "Brush with the Law," or "Brush with Greatness."

So think of topics that would get audience members to talk about things people don't usually share with strangers:

- their sex lives
- their misfortunes
- their bad relationships
- their secrets
- their celebrity gossip

It may help to keep in mind the Superiority Theory of Laughter and brainstorm topics that would let the audience feel superior to the storytellers. Also, realize that it doesn't take much to let a person feel superior: *TSWJL* once did an Audience

Stories Piece about the worst Christmas present people ever received.

2. Make sure your topic is highly relatable to the audience.

You want a topic that virtually everybody in the audience will have had some experience with. That's because you want virtually everybody to have a story that might be a candidate for your comedy piece. Like any other Found Comedy Piece, an Audience Stories Piece requires a lot of raw material.

Almost everyone has been on a bad date, for instance, which is one reason that "Dates from Hell" works. By contrast, relatively few people have been on a bad train trip. So the topic "Nightmare on the Rails" would probably not yield enough entertaining audience stories to fill out a piece.

When to Rule Out an Audience Stories Piece

If your studio audience consists of fewer than three hundred people you probably shouldn't try to produce an Audience Stories Piece. An audience that small, even responding to a universally relatable topic like "Midnight Confessions," may not give you the four or so satisfying stories that a full piece needs.

My experience bears this out. The home studios for *TSWJL* and *LSWDL* each seat around four hundred. But Dave's previous home, the *LNWDL* studio in 30 Rockefeller Plaza, only seated around two hundred. Two hundred audience members, we writers on that show discovered, couldn't offer up enough solid stories with a topic like "Brush with Greatness." That's why "Writer's Embellishments" were introduced. "Writer's Embellishments" were a way to ensure that even the dullest story would get a laugh. They were scripted continuations of the stories that were penned by the writers backstage at the last minute and given to the audience participants to read aloud during the taping.

For example, the *LNWDL* writers added to that Shirley MacLaine elevator anecdote a Writer's Embellishment that was inspired by the actress's belief in spiritualism. The audience member told his story and then, as the words "Writer's Embellishment" flashed on-screen, he went on to say that later that night he saw a shimmering image of Miss MacLaine levitating over his bed. He added that he summoned hotel security and they "beat the pixieish entertainer senseless."

Audience Talents

The host's task in an Audience Talents Piece is to get audience members to demonstrate unusual talents they have.

Here are a couple of examples:

"Audience Show and Tell" [*LSWDL*]—Audience members relate entertaining anecdotes about themselves or display unusual objects or skills. For example, one audience member presents a video clip of his brief appearance on some other television show. Another audience member demonstrates his ability to play a harmonica with his nose. Yet another audience member squeezes his entire body through a stringless tennis racket.

"Meal or No Meal" [*TSWJL*]—Three judges onstage (one of whom is usually the show's band leader) watch audience members demonstrate odd talents. After each audience member performs, the judges vote on whether he or she deserves a gift certificate for a meal at a local restaurant. For example, one audience member saws off the entire top of a can of beer with his teeth and another man swallows eight hot dogs whole in thirty seconds.

How to Produce an Audience Talents Piece

It's extremely unlikely that four or so people with impressively weird skills will just happen to show up in any given studio audience. Also, participants in an Audience Talents Piece may need props to perform their tricks or old video clips to tell their stories. For those reasons the participants in an Audience Talents Piece are not cast from that night's studio audience as they are for an Audience Stories Piece. Instead, they've almost certainly been chosen days or even weeks before they actually appear on the show.

So how are the participants in an Audience Talents Piece cast? There are several ways:

- Show staffers can hand out a questionnaire to audience members waiting in line before a taping. The questionnaire asks if they have anything entertaining they're willing to share on the show and lists some examples. Writers or producers interview each promising candidate and ask to see any relevant prop or a demonstration of the talent (maybe on video) as soon as the candidate can provide it. Candidates who make it past that cut are asked to return to the show at a later date ready to perform.

- Instead of handing out a questionnaire, show staffers can ask the audience seated in the studio before the show—during the audience warm-up—whether anyone has a talent they want to demonstrate. Promising candidates are interviewed and possibly videotaped. Those who are selected are invited to appear on a later show.

- A show staffer can spot a video of someone's offbeat talent online, say on YouTube. The staffer can then contact that person and interview him or her.

- Aspiring participants can pitch themselves by contacting the show and sending in videos of themselves demonstrating their talents.

How to Create a New Audience Talents Piece

All Audience Talents Pieces are variations on the basic idea of "audience members show us something that makes them special." "Audience Show and Tell" varies that basic idea by tying it to a children's school activity. "Meal or No Meal" adds to that idea the element of three judges voting, the way judges do in a competition reality show like "America's Got Talent." So the best way to create a new Audience Talents Piece is to put your own twist on that same basic idea.

To come up with a new twist, free associate on the idea of "people showing off things that make them special." For example, one association might be a circus sideshow. So why not do an Audience Talents Piece with the topic "Audience Freak Show"? The band would play calliope music. Each audience participant would introduce himself with a circus freak-style name, like "The Human Can Opener" for the man who bites open beer cans. Each performance would be accompanied by sound effects of a crowd gasping and screaming. It would be the same basic idea as the other Audience Talents Pieces, just with different packaging.

Audience Game

In an Audience Game the host's task is to moderate a game played by members of the studio audience. The host can either go up into the audience to play the game or invite the audience participants down to the stage.

Audience Games have the benefits of any Audience Piece. They get the host away from his desk and allow him to improvise with the audience. But Audience Games have the added benefits of being especially lively and—if a quiz is involved—of giving the home viewers a chance to play along.

On *The Ellen DeGeneres Show* Ellen often features Audience Games like "Blindfolded Musical Chairs." *The Rosie O'Donnell Show* had a lot of Audience Games too, like "Fact or Quacked."

Here are some examples of Audience Games on late-night shows:

"Know Your Current Events" [*LSWDL*]—Dave goes into the audience and asks audience members open-ended quiz questions. The obvious answer is always wrong; the answer that Dave supplies as the correct one is the punch line. Sample joke: "After last weekend's Groundhog Day celebration, Punxsutawney Phil's handlers can expect six weeks of what?" The audience participant guesses, "Winter." But Dave says the correct answer is "Rabies."

"Stump the Band" [*LSWDL*]—This is a version of the game that was played regularly on *The Tonight Show Starring Johnny Carson*. Dave goes into the audience, where each audience participant announces the title of an obscure song that he or she doesn't think the band will know. The band performs its own funny, made-up version of the song, after which the audience participant sings the real song.

"Models and Buckets" [*LNWJF*]—This game is played onstage. A dozen female models each hold a bucket. Two male contestants—audience members—take turns picking buckets. After each bucket is selected, the model holding it dumps its contents on the contestant's head. If the bucket contains a hundred dollars, that contestant wins the game and keeps the cash. But the bucket usually holds something messy like cheese sauce, strawberry jam, or baked beans.

"What's in My Pocket?" [*The Late Show with Ross Shafer*]—This game was played on a late-night show in the 1980s. Ross goes into the audience with small objects, like a garlic press, in his pants pockets. Audience members feel Ross's pockets and try to guess what the hidden objects are.

How to Create a New Audience Game

Here are four techniques you can use:

1. Add a game element to a comedy piece that's not already a game. That's how I came up with the "Know Your Current Events" game one morning on the way to work. I knew we had no Main Comedy Piece approved for that night's show so we needed one that could be produced quickly. I also knew that Dave likes to go into the audience and that Text Quizzes had always been successful on the show so I created a piece that combines those elements.

2. Put a comedic spin on a game that already exists. You could concoct a wacky variation of, say, a board game like Candy Land, a party game like bobbing for apples, or even a TV game show. To keep the concept of your new game easy to explain, try to blow up only one major element of the original game. For example, "Models and Buckets" was inspired by the game show "Deal or No Deal," in which models hold briefcases containing dollar amounts. Simply swap briefcases containing dollar amounts for buckets containing stuff you wouldn't want poured on your head and you have your new idea. And "Stump the Band" is a variation of the old game show "Name That Tune" in which the band does the song guessing instead of the audience participants.

3. Turn a humiliating or uncomfortable experience into a game. The idea here is to exploit the Superiority Theory of Laughter: we laugh when we suddenly feel superior to someone else. Devise a game that results in somebody's humiliation or discomfort and the audience will laugh. The writers of *LNWJF* used this technique often. In addition to "Models and Buckets" the show featured the game "Competitive Spit-Takes," which has audience members spitting in each other's faces. Another game on *LNWJF*, called "Wax On, Wax Off," involves an audience member getting hair ripped off his chest when his friend can't answer difficult trivia questions. In an unusual twist, Ross Shafer's "What's in My Pocket" inflicted the uncomfortable experience—being groped by a stranger—on the host himself.

4. Turn an activity inspired by a current event into a game. Free associate on a person, place, or thing in the news and come up with a related activity that can be translated into an Audience Game. Any game you develop this way may not be repeatable but has the advantage of being topical. For example, I was inspired by an upcoming Super Bowl to create a game for *TSWJL*: Two audience members race through an obstacle course designed to simulate what a typical Super Bowl viewer does at home during a commercial break. The audience contestants negotiate obstacles like grabbing a certain beer can out of an ice-filled tub and finding a particular foil-wrapped sandwich in a packed refrigerator.

Production Tips for an Audience Game

If you're involved in producing a new Audience Game you'll want to follow these guidelines:

1. Be sure the game is safe to play. An over-enthusiastic participant, pumped up by adrenaline and the TV cameras, might get careless and get hurt. So try to anticipate what could go wrong. Before we ran contestants through that Super Bowl Obstacle Course we made sure they were wearing non-skid shoes because we realized that ice water from the beer tub would probably splash all over the floor, which it did.

2. Keep the basic rules simple. The host has to explain the basic rules and the more time that takes, the less time there is for actually playing the game. Plus, if the rules aren't clear, the audience will be puzzling over them instead of enjoying the game.

3. Have other rules on standby for every possible scenario. You want to keep the basic rules of play simple but you also want to know in advance what you'll do in case of a tie, say, or if a contestant wins the game too quickly. You don't want to have to figure that out on the fly while the show is being taped. If a contestant playing "Models and Buckets" wins the hundred dollars too early in the game, for instance, Jimmy already knows what to do: the models get new buckets and the game is played again, this time with both contestants getting dumped on at the same time.

4. Rehearse the game. Run through the game at least once, even if it's only mentally, to be sure the contestants will be able to play it in the time allotted.

5. Make your prizes funny. If you're awarding prizes, consider them to be opportunities for jokes. A prize could be surprisingly random, like the Explod-O-Pop microwave popcorn Dave hands out on "Know Your Current Events." Or the prize could relate to the game's theme in an unexpectedly literal way. For example, the consolation prize for "Models and Buckets" is a *Late Night with Jimmy Fallon* bucket hat.

Audience Voting

The host's task in an Audience Voting Piece is to do something on the show that the studio audience voted to do. A piece like this gives the studio audience some control over a nationally-televised show, power they seem to enjoy.

Here are some examples:

"Pick a New Catchphrase" [*LNWDL*]—This piece was inspired by the frequent use of catchphrases in advertising. Dave wants to launch a new catchphrase into the popular culture. Six actors in costume come onstage and each recites a different silly catchphrase. The audience votes with their applause (measured by an "applause meter") for their favorite; the winning catchphrase in one edition of the piece was "They pelted us with rocks and garbage!" At the end of the piece Dave has the audience chant the winning catch phrase in unison.

"Spread a Rumor" [*LNWDL*]—Dave wants to spread a rumor that has no basis in fact. He reads a number of ridiculous, fabricated rumors and the audience votes for their favorite. Finally, Dave does something to spread the rumor. One time the winning rumor was that a large shipment of wheat that the U.S. had just sold to the Soviet Union would turn the Soviets' urine blue. I had the idea to spread the rumor by phoning the local office of TASS, the Soviet news agency, and Dave did it. (Five years later the Soviet Union collapsed. Maybe that rumor was true after all and the demoralized Soviets just gave up.)

"The Custom-Made Show" [*LNWDL*]—Dave has the audience vote with their applause on what show elements they want to see. Each time the audience is invited to vote on a show element they're given a choice between two options. Thanks to audience voting, one Custom-Made Show dispensed with the usual show opening of musical theme, video montage, and announcer. Instead the show opened with the theme for the old TV western

Bonanza, a video montage of items from the 1968 Sears catalogue, and an announcement delivered by the Lieutenant Governor of New York, Alfred B. DelBello. Then an audience vote had Dave, instead of performing his usual Monologue, using a tennis cannon to fire balls at the door of a studio across the hall where a live TV show was taking place.

How to Create a New Audience Voting Piece

Here are three rules of thumb:

1. Have the audience vote on something meaningful. The audience will participate more enthusiastically if they know their vote will have a significant result. So make sure your piece pays off the voting in some concrete way that affects either the outside world or the world of the show. For example, Dave tries to introduce the winning catchphrase into the popular culture either by having the audience chant it, by phoning it in to newscaster Tom Brokaw, or by displaying it on the huge Spectacolor sign in Times Square. And the audience vote at the beginning of "The Custom-Made Show" actually changes the way the show opens.

2. Make the options entertaining. Think of the options that the audience will be voting on as opportunities for punch lines. For example, in "Pick a New Catchphrase" it's funny to see nerdy twins recite in unison, "They pelted us with rocks and garbage!"; a deadpan tough guy grunt, "Hey, how much for the Buick?"; and an elderly woman purr, "Nicely packed, bag boy."

3. Make the options easy to produce. You have to be prepared to actually do whatever the audience votes for, so make sure the options you offer them don't take a lot of time or money to produce. On "The Custom-Made Show," for example, you wouldn't want the audience voting on whether to replace the opening theme music with either "Satisfaction" by the Rolling Stones (way too expensive) or a rap song containing the names of everybody in the studio audience (way too time-consuming).

Audience Task

In an Audience Task Piece the host's goal is to get one or more audience members to perform some task either inside or outside the studio.

Here are some examples of Audience Task Pieces that take place inside the studio:

> **"A Song for Oprah"** [*JKL*]—To commemorate media giant Oprah Winfrey earning the top spot in the *Forbes* Celebrity 100 list, Jimmy has his studio audience join him in singing the song "All Hail Oprah" to a huge photograph of Oprah. The lyrics include the lines, "All hail Oprah. She keeps us safe and sound. And if we ever doubt her, she'll unleash her evil hounds."

> **"Audience Member Facebook Photo"** [*Conan*]—Conan has an audience member take a new photo with him for the audience member's Facebook page. Conan and the audience participant don scarves and sit together on a motorcycle onstage. Thanks to a green screen video effect and the breeze from an electric fan it appears in the finished photo as if Conan and the audience participant are cruising down a highway.

And these Audience Task Pieces take the participants out of the studio:

> **"Buy Paul a Present"** [*LSWDL*]—It's bandleader Paul's birthday so Dave gives an audience member ten dollars and sends him out into Manhattan to buy Paul a present. The audience member reappears at the end of the show with his gift: a small license plate reading, "Paul."

"Vending Machine Thanksgiving" [*LNWDL*]—On Thanksgiving Day Dave sends two audience members out to vending machines in the hallway. Using rolls of quarters provided by the staff the audience participants buy the rest of the studio audience Thanksgiving dinner from the vending machines. At the end of the show the audience participants pass out the potato chips, cookies, and candy bars they bought to the appreciative audience.

How to Create a New Audience Task Piece

Follow these three steps:

1. Pick a topic for the task that will grab the interest of the audience. Start by coming up with potential task topics the way you'd come up with potential Monologue joke topics. Ask yourself what's going on in the world that the audience cares about, like the increasing popularity of Facebook. Or consider what's happening in the studio that the audience might have an emotional reaction to. For example, as a writer on *LNWDL* I realized that the audience might be slightly conflicted about being cooped up in our studio on Thanksgiving Day.

2. Think of possible Audience Tasks related to that topic. To do that, brainstorm a list of activities associated with the topic and then see if any of those activities suggest possible Audience Tasks. Thinking about the topic of Thanksgiving I realized that the *LNWDL* studio audience would normally be eating their Thanksgiving dinner. That association suggested the task of feeding the audience with the food at hand.

Another activity associated with Thanksgiving is the Macy's Thanksgiving Day Parade, which the studio audience might never have seen up close. So another possible task might have been to have audience participants twist toy balloons into balloon animals during the show and then, near the end of the show, have them parade through the studio holding their inflated creations.

3. Out of all your possible Audience Tasks, choose the most satisfying.
Here are some ways you can tell whether a task will satisfy the audience:

- **The task is surprising and silly.** Throughout the "Vending Machine Thanksgiving" piece it was fun to see camera shots of the two audience participants feeding endless quarters into the vending machines and reaping their junk food harvest.

- **The task has a specific goal.** That is, the task isn't open-ended. The audience will know that the task has been completed because they'll see that the goal has been achieved. Carrying out a task is a story and audiences prefer stories that have definite endings. The audience knew that the Thanksgiving Day task had been completed, for example, when they saw the junk food being handed out.

- **The task can be completed during the show.** That way the audience can have the satisfaction of seeing the ending. If the task will be carried out throughout the show, adjust the timing so it's completed near the end of the show; you want to entice the home viewers to watch the whole show to see how the task turned out instead of going to bed. In the case of "Vending Machine Thanksgiving" we prepared bags full of junk food before the show and secretly gave them to the audience participants towards the end of the show to guarantee that they'd be able to feed the entire audience: a little cheat.

- **The task ends with the audience getting something.** Again, carrying out a task is a story and the end of any good story has to deliver. The audience doesn't need to get something physical like vending machine junk food. They could get to do or see something cool. Even learning the answer to a question could be enough, like finding out what that audience participant bought bandleader Paul Shaffer for his birthday.

PHONE CALL PIECES

In a Phone Call Piece the host carries out a silly, surprising task that requires him to make a semi-scripted phone call from his desk. These calls are particularly entertaining when they involve yanking an unsuspecting civilian out of his everyday life and onto a television show, what I call the Touched by Show Business factor. According to the Superiority Theory of Laughter, audiences feel superior to the bewildered civilian who is being put on the spot by the host, so they laugh.

Here are some Phone Call Pieces I created:

> **"Dave Calls a Pay Phone"** [*LNWDL*]— One day I was staring out my office window, literally looking for inspiration, when I saw a pay phone down on Sixth Avenue. I wondered whether it was physically possible to call it and get it to ring. We found out that it was. So a few days later the audience watched as Dave called that pay phone. It was like fishing for pedestrians. Dave's ad-libs were entertaining but I was sweating: Would a passerby answer the endlessly ringing phone? Or would I be responsible for an unsatisfying comedy piece with no payoff? Finally someone picked up the phone, chatted with Dave, and agreed to be escorted into the studio. There he stood, blinking in the glare of the lights and the applause of the audience.
>
> After that, Dave called pay phones many times, even after he moved from NBC to CBS. Dave called the pay phone outside the Ed Sullivan Theater so often that fans would congregate around

it during tapings on the off chance Dave would call it and they could appear on the show.

"Dave Makes a Hotel Wake-Up Call" [*LNWDL*]—I wanted Dave to make a wake-up call that had been scheduled for a guest staying in a hotel somewhere. So I first had to figure out where in the world English-speaking hotel guests might be getting wake-up calls around the time our show was being taped. The answer was the west coast of Australia. So we made arrangements with a hotel in Perth and Dave, from his desk during the show, woke up a businessman out of a sound sleep. To ensure that the piece would have a definite ending, we assigned Dave an absurd task: to convince the groggy businessman to flush his toilet. The businessman did and luckily the audience found the gurgling of an Australian toilet sufficiently satisfying.

"Dave Plays a Cuban in Tic-Tac-Toe" [*LNWDL*]—In 1984 the Soviet Union and other Communist Bloc countries boycotted the Summer Olympics in Los Angeles. I thought the American viewing public might be disappointed by that and might appreciate watching the United States go head-to-head with a Communist country on a different playing field. Dave would represent the U.S.A., the event would be tic-tac-toe over the phone, but who would be the Red opponent? After considerable research we learned that Dave could direct-dial Cuba without breaking any U.S. laws and found a bilingual journalist on the island who was willing to play along. On the show, Dave and his Communist adversary traded tic-tac-toe moves over the phone and, for a few minutes, the neutered Olympics were forgotten.

The tic-tac-toe piece went over so well that a couple of weeks later we took the competition to a new level. This time the Cuban journalist faced a live tic-tac-toe-playing chicken I had spotted in a coin-operated amusement machine in Manhattan's Chinatown. After that deranged matchup, the Soviet Union never boycotted another Olympics.

"Chevy Picks a Business Card" [*The Chevy Chase Show*]—I got this idea from those goldfish bowls you see at some restaurants in which you leave your business card to try to win a free meal. We brought one of those bowls from a local restaurant onto the show. Chevy drew a business card at random, called the number on it, and told the guy whose card it was that he'd win a meal if he got to the studio by the end of the taping.

How to Create a New Phone Call Piece

Here are a couple of approaches:

1. Insert the host into some task that people commonly use their phones for. In other words, think of a task that people usually accomplish with a phone call, then have the host either make or receive that call. For example, the idea of using a phone for a wake-up call inspired Dave's call to Australia. Many people also call the Butterball Turkey Hotline (a.k.a. "Talk-Line") around Thanksgiving. That gave the writers of *LNWDL* the idea of having a few of those calls rerouted to Dave's desk during the show. Without identifying himself, Dave had fun talking turkey with the unsuspecting civilian callers.

2. Think of possible phone calls related to a topic in the news. This approach is similar to creating an Audience Task Piece. Think of something going on in the world that the audience is probably interested in. Then brainstorm activities associated with that topic and see if any of those activities suggests a possible phone call by the host. That's the thinking that inspired Dave's phone call to Cuba. The Olympics boycott was in the news, which was associated with competition. Competition suggested a game that could be played over the phone: tic-tac-toe. A similar thought process led to Dave phoning one of the coaches of a football team headed for the Super Bowl. Dave's task was to convince the coach to use a ridiculous new "surefire" play—the "Windshield Wiper."

Production Tips for a Phone Call Piece

If you're producing one of these pieces here are a couple of recommendations:

1. If possible, don't tell the person being called what the call is about. When the host makes a call during the show you want to be sure the right person will answer the phone but you also want that person to be surprised. So before the show, arrange the call like this: Tell the person that TV host so-and-so will be calling them at a certain time. Get the person's advance permission to broadcast the call but don't tell the person what the call will be about. This procedure virtually guarantees that the desired person will answer the phone when the host calls but also preserves some element of surprise. And you want that surprise because the more off-balance the target is, the more the audience will feel superior and laugh.

2. If the host's task will take longer than the phone call to complete, try to have the task completed near the end of the show. That way more home viewers might decide to watch the entire show to see what happens. For example, when Chevy phoned the owner of a business card, the audience had to wait to see whether the guy would make it to the studio in time. (He arrived with a few minutes to spare, a little stunned at being Touched by Show Business.)

REMOTE CAMERA PIECES

What I call a Remote Camera Piece is where the host in the studio performs some task by means of a camera placed in some location outside the studio. The host can see the participants at the remote location but the participants rarely see the host; two-way video is a more complicated set-up. In many of these pieces the participants at the remote location only talk with the host via two-way audio. But in some Remote Camera Pieces there isn't any audio involved at all, just a video shot of the location. I'll give examples of both types of piece below.

Remote Camera Pieces are good options for a comedy/talk show to have for these reasons:

- They "open up" the show and break the visual monotony of always seeing the studio interior and the desk-bound host.

- In many cases they can be produced on short notice. All the crew has to do is lay some cable to get a camera outside.

- As any Semi-Scripted Piece does, they inject an intriguing unpredictability into the show and allow the host to show off his skill at improvising.

Remote Camera Pieces with Two-Way Audio

Here are some Remote Camera Pieces where the host in the studio can see and talk with the participants at the remote location but the participants can't see the host:

> **"Give a Pedestrian a Big Entrance"** [*LSWDL*]—Dave chats with random passersby via a camera positioned on Broadway right outside the studio. With input from the audience Dave selects a pedestrian and asks her, "Have you ever had a big entrance?" When the pedestrian says no, Dave gives her one. The camera precedes the bewildered pedestrian into the studio, where she's greeted by a lively song from the band, sweeping spotlights, swirling confetti, and a standing ovation by the audience.

(Note that this piece, like many Remote Camera Pieces, has the same Touched by Show Business factor that some Phone Call Pieces have. The audience enjoys watching the host usher some overwhelmed civilian into the glare of his show.)

"The Hollywood Walk of Fame Game" [*TSWJL*]—Via a camera on Hollywood Boulevard, Jay recruits two pedestrians to play a Hollywood-themed comedy trivia game. The pedestrians use as a game board the inscribed stars of the celebrities embedded in the sidewalk. For example, a contestant gives a correct answer and moves ahead two stars to, say, Groucho Marx. The first contestant to get to Regis Philbin wins.

"Chinese Theater Twister" [*TSWJL*]—Jay chats with tourists via a remote camera in the courtyard of the world-famous Chinese Theater in Hollywood. Jay persuades two tourists to play the game of Twister using the imprints of celebrities' hands and feet in the concrete. Jay spins a spinner in the studio and calls out, say, "Right hand—Charlton Heston" and a tourist places his right hand in the imprint of actor Charlton Heston's right hand. The surprise end to the game comes when Charlton Heston himself makes a (prearranged) appearance and gruffly demands that the tourist stop playing around in his handprint.

Remote Camera Pieces with No Audio

Now here are a couple of Remote Camera Pieces with no audio component. That is, the host doesn't talk with anybody outside the studio; he only watches what's going on at the location and ad-libs jokes.

"How Many Guys in Spider-Man Suits Can Fit into Jamba Juice?" [*LSWDL*]—A camera is trained on a Jamba Juice restaurant across the street from the studio. Dave, at his desk, cues staffers wearing Spider-Man costumes to enter the Jamba Juice, one at a time at first, then in groups. Comic suspense builds as the audience waits to see how many Spider-Men will wind up loitering absurdly behind the plate glass window of the restaurant. The answer: twenty-eight, if you include a handful of staffers wearing different costumes, like ones of Superman and Dracula.

"Can a Guy in a Bear Suit Say Hello on a New York City Pay Phone?" [*LSWDL*]—A camera is aimed at a pay phone down on the street. In the studio, Dave comments as a guy in a bear suit walks up to a civilian talking on the pay phone and, apparently, asks to say hello to the person the civilian is talking to. The audience watches this silly social experiment until, yes, the civilian lets the bear say hello on the phone.

How to Create a New Remote Camera Piece

Here's an approach with two steps:

1. Pick a topic from the local environment. Think of the people, places, and things in the neighborhood around the studio. They are all possible topics, meaning locations for a Remote Camera Piece. Consider possible locations farther away if your show has access to a satellite truck or some other kind of remote camera feed. In the examples above the topics include the Jamba Juice across the street, the pay phone outside, the Hollywood Walk of Fame, and the Chinese Theater.

When I was writing for the *Tonight* show we focused on famous locations like those last two to help set the show apart from its competition. Similar to the way that Dave often takes advantage of Manhattan for *Late Show* comedy pieces, we wanted to use iconic southern California landmarks in the comedy on the *Tonight* show. We wanted viewers to see comedy on Jay's show that they couldn't see anywhere else.

2. Think of surprising activities related to that topic. To do that, brainstorm associations of your chosen topic. Then see if any of those associations suggest an unexpected activity to perform at the location.

For example, an association of the pay phone outside the studio is making a phone call, which suggests interrupting a phone call in some odd way. The inscribed stars on the Hollywood Walk of Fame can be visually associated with the layout of a board game like Trivial Pursuit, which suggests playing a game with pedestrians. And one association of the Chinese Theater is tourists placing their hands and feet into the celebrity imprints, which suggests playing Twister.

STUNT PIECES

In a Stunt Piece the host and/or a guest performs an unusual physical feat. The comedy comes from the surprising nature of the Stunt and from the host's ad-libs. The Stunt may take place inside or outside the studio. If the Stunt takes place outside, it may be partially or completely prerecorded. The longer it takes to prepare the host for the Stunt and the farther away from the studio the Stunt is located the more likely it is that the Stunt will be prerecorded.

Here are some examples of Stunt Pieces.

> **"Stupid Pet Tricks"** [*LNWDL* and *LSWDL*]—Pet owners have their pets perform offbeat tricks in the studio. For example, a dog blows bubbles out her nose in her water dish. *LNWDL* spun off a similar piece, called "Stupid Human Tricks," which features people performing odd stunts. Yet another offshoot on *LSWDL* is "Audience Show and Tell," which I discussed in the section of this chapter on Audience Talents Pieces.

"Conan Competes in a Triathlon" [*TSWCO*]—Conan says he's inspired by the fact that his guest, actress Teri Hatcher, recently competed in a triathlon in Malibu. So Conan challenges Teri and races her in a mock triathlon around the studio building. (As Conan ran to the finish line on stage he slipped, fell backward, and hit his head on the hard floor. He was taken to the hospital with a concussion.)

"Charlie Sheen's Olympic Event" [*TSWJL*]—The Winter Olympics are underway and actor Charlie *Major League* Sheen is going to be on the show. So I have the idea that Charlie will participate in a unique *Tonight* show Olympic event—he'll throw a baseball through the D in the world-famous Hollywood sign.

"Studio on the Highway" [*LNWDL*]—Coming back after a commercial break, Dave sits behind his desk at homebase. But something about the shot looks a little off. Is it the lighting? The camera pulls back to reveal that Dave, his desk, and the section of scenery behind him are all mounted on a flatbed truck speeding down a highway at sixty miles an hour. Behaving as if nothing is out of the ordinary, Dave says that now he'll be doing the Desk Piece "Small Town News" and asks Paul for a little introductory music. Paul, riding with his keyboard in the back of a pickup truck, glides up alongside Dave's flatbed and performs the musical intro. Then Dave delivers

I was a pleasure working with Charlie Sheen on his "Olympic Event." He had only one small request: he said he wanted to be sure he didn't cramp up before hurling the baseball so he asked if we would arrange for a masseuse to accompany us, preferably a blonde. So an attractive blonde in a skintight black catsuit clambered down the hill to the Hollywood sign with us and rubbed Charlie's shoulders. Charlie stayed loose and—yes!—made the impressive uphill throw through the D.

an abbreviated version of "Small Town News," releasing each newspaper clipping into the slipstream as he finishes with it.

"Dropping Stuff Off a Five-Story Tower" [*LNWDL*]—Dave drops a wide assortment of objects off the top of a firefighter training tower in New Rochelle, New York. The objects include a bowling ball, a gumball machine, and a piñata full of baked beans. The laughs come from Dave's mostly ad-lib remarks, the surprising objects, and the satisfying and sometimes unexpected ways the objects behave when slamming into the concrete at the base of the tower.

We had to rehearse the "Studio on the Highway" stunt to make sure that we could get good audio in the strong wind and also, of course, that we wouldn't kill Dave. Since the stunt was my idea I was tapped to ride on the flatbed. This resulted in one of the most thrilling, and most embarrassing, moments of my career. The thrilling part was sitting behind the desk, blasting down the highway, jabbering away to give the audio system a good test. The embarrassing part came later, when I was in Dave's office showing him the test footage. I didn't realize until that moment that while I was talking on the flatbed I had been instinctively imitating Dave. I stopped the tape as soon as I could. If Dave was annoyed by my impersonation he never mentioned it.

"Suit of Velcro" [*LNWDL*]—Dave wears coveralls and gloves to which have been sewn strips of Velcro, the "hook" part. In the studio is a tall wall covered with the other component of Velcro, the "loop" part. After performing a few tricks, such as catching a Velcro-covered basketball on his chest, Dave bounces off a mini-trampoline and sticks chest-first to the Velcro wall, a couple of feet off the floor.

An experience I had while "Dropping Stuff Off a Five-Story Tower" is further proof of the importance of the comedy principle "don't literally kill anybody." In previous editions of the piece Dave had dropped various melons. The smashing pumpkins and other melons looked terrific when seen from above in slow-motion, like fireworks detonating, but I wanted to up the ante. The next logical step seemed to me to be a watermelon filled with napalm.

I happened to own a certain U.S. Army Technical Manual; this was back when you could buy books like that without worrying about being slapped onto a watch list by the Department of Homeland Security. From that manual I got a recipe for gelled gasoline—napalm, essentially. On the roof of the tower I stirred the ingredients together and poured the mixture into a hollowed-out watermelon.

When the time came to tape the shot we perched the watermelon on the edge of the roof. Dave lit the fuse—a rag hanging out of the watermelon—and then waited. He was standing only a few feet from the Molotov Watermelon and I was crouched down out of sight right next to it. As the flame crept up the rag, inching closer to the napalm, I decided I didn't care about messing up the audio track and whispered urgently, "Kick it off! Kick it off!" Finally, at the last possible instant, Dave booted the watermelon off the roof. It erupted into a gratifying explosion of flame on the concrete below. I never did find out why Dave took so long to launch the menacing melon.

That firefighter training tower was torn down less than a year later. I like to think that its foundation had been dangerously weakened by the Molotov Watermelon and the punishing impacts of all those grandfather clocks and frozen turkeys.

My undergraduate degree in engineering helped me make the "Suit of Velcro" work. I got technical spec sheets from Velcro Industries listing the shear strength and pull-apart strength of various types of Velcro. Then I estimated the number of square inches of surface contact that a suit and gloves could provide and concluded that such a suit could conceivably bear Dave's weight. When Dave gave the green light, our costume department had the suit constructed.

Since I was roughly Dave's size I was the first person to test the Suit of Velcro. I'll never forget the moment I pressed my chest into the wall and lifted my feet off the floor. My calculations were correct: it worked! Soon I discovered that if I choreographed my movements correctly I could actually crawl up the Velcro wall like Spider-Man.

A legal footnote: Now there are party supply companies that will rent you a Suit of Velcro and a Velcro wall to let you do what Dave and I did. So how much cash did *LNWDL* rake in from the idea? Zero. Even if it could be proven that manufacturers got the idea from *LNWDL* there's no way the show could collect any money from them. That's because although the Suit of Velcro first appeared on a copyrighted television show, the *idea* for the Suit isn't copyrighted and can therefore be exploited for profit by others. According to the website of the U.S. Copyright Office:

> "Copyright does not protect ideas, concepts, systems, or methods of doing something. You may express your ideas in writing or drawings and claim copyright in your description, but be aware that copyright will not protect the idea itself as revealed in your written or artistic work."

The entertainment industry takes this legal principle very seriously. That's why ideas are stolen in show business all the time.

"Suit of Alka-Seltzer" [*LNWDL*]—Dave puts on coveralls which are completely covered with over three thousand Alka-Seltzer tablets. Cables lower him into a Plexiglas tank about the size of a phone booth that's almost full of water. Bubbles and white foam churn furiously around Dave until he's safely hoisted out.

Have I mentioned the comedy principle "Don't literally kill anybody"? I can't mention it often enough, as the hair-raising tale of the "Suit of Alka-Seltzer" proves. Before the Plexiglas tank was built, our scenic designer brought a small model up to the production offices to show the writers. I happened to be the only writer around so I took a look at it. I asked the designer about the water level and she said it would come up to within about two feet of the top of the tank. I pondered this and then mentioned that I thought dissolving Alka-Seltzer tablets produced carbon dioxide. The designer remarked that that was interesting. I rummaged around some more in my mental storehouse and said that I believed carbon dioxide is heavier than air. The designer didn't see my point. My point was that maybe the carbon dioxide would displace all of the breathable air at the top of the tank. But I didn't press the issue. What did I know? Maybe my memory of high school science was faulty.

It turns out that it wasn't. A staff member tested the suit in rehearsal and, sure enough, as soon as the Alka-Seltzer started bubbling he began to suffocate. An alert stagehand yelled, "Pull him out! Pull him out!" and the staffer was hauled out of the tank and lowered safely to the floor, gasping for breath. A nurse on standby attended to him and he recovered with no ill effects. Sorry, my friend. I should have told you about my theory. Dave got the word, though. When he wore the suit on the show he also wore a small breathing apparatus.

How to Create a New Stunt Piece

Try generating ideas this way:

1. Pick a well-known physical activity as a topic for the Stunt Piece.
For possible topics, focus mainly on activities associated with the show or on visually interesting activities in real life.

2. Once you've picked a topic activity, add an extreme angle. To come up with possible angles, brainstorm associations of the topic activity, then add a big twist to each association. By adding an angle to the activity, you're trying to devise a way to perform an exaggerated, surprising, or cool version of that same basic activity.

For example, here are the topic activities and angles underlying the Stunt Pieces described above:

Topic Activity: Pets performing tricks
Angle: Instead of standard tricks, stupid tricks

Topic Activity: Competing in a triathlon
Angle: Instead of on an official course, around the studio building

Topic Activity: Competing in an Olympic event
Angle: Instead of a serious event, a pointless event at a Hollywood landmark

Topic Activity: The host sitting at his desk
Angle: Instead of in the studio, on a moving flatbed truck

Topic Activity: Accidentally dropping something
Angle: Deliberately dropping something

Topic Activity: Velcro sticking little things together
Angle: Instead of little things, the host and a wall

Topic Activity: Two Alka-Seltzer tablets bubbling in water
Angle: Instead of two tablets, three thousand tablets

3. Be sure there's a way to do the Stunt Piece safely. If you see something potentially hazardous, or think something could be dangerous, say something.

SUMMARY

In a Semi-Scripted Piece, the host or a correspondent follows a scripted outline to accomplish a task that involves interacting with unpredictable civilians or performing a stunt.

Semi-Scripted Pieces get laughs with four different types of jokes:
- Jokes that are written before the piece is produced
- Jokes that are ad-libbed by the professional on-camera talent, maybe with the help of writers
- Funny things that civilian participants spontaneously do or say
- Jokes that are added during the editing process

Live Semi-Scripted Pieces include Audience Pieces, Phone Call Pieces, Remote Camera Pieces, and Stunt Pieces.

Audience Pieces

Audience Pieces have the host interacting with the studio audience in order to accomplish some task and can be sorted into five basic categories:

1. Audience Stories, where the host's task is to get audience members to tell anecdotes about themselves on a given topic. Choose a topic that grabs your attention and is highly relatable to the audience.

2. Audience Talents, where the host's task is to get audience members to demonstrate unusual talents they have. To generate a topic for a new Audience Talents Piece, free associate on the idea of "people showing off things that make them special."

3. Audience Game, where the host's task is to moderate a game played by members of the studio audience. Here are four ways to create a new Audience Game:
- Add a game element to a comedy piece that's not already a game.
- Put a comedic spin on a game that already exists.
- Turn a humiliating or uncomfortable experience into a game.
- Turn an activity inspired by a current event into a game.

4. Audience Voting, where the host's task is to do something on the show that the studio audience voted to do. When creating a new Audience Voting Piece, follow these guidelines:
- Have the audience vote on something meaningful.
- Make the options entertaining.
- Make the options easy to produce.

5. Audience Task, where the host's goal is to get one or more audience members to perform some task. Follow these three steps to create a new Audience Task Piece:
- Pick a topic for the task that will grab the interest of the audience.
- Think of possible Audience Tasks related to that topic.

- Choose the most satisfying of those possible Audience Tasks. A task will be satisfying if it's surprising and silly, it has a specific goal, it can be completed during the show, and it ends with the audience getting some tangible or intangible reward.

Phone Call Pieces

In a Phone Call Piece the host carries out a silly, surprising task that requires him to make a semi-scripted phone call from his desk. Often this call will involve literally or figuratively hauling an unsuspecting civilian into the spotlight, what I call the Touched by Show Business factor.

To create a new Phone Call Piece you can either insert the host into some task that people commonly use their phones for, or have the host make a call that's somehow related to a topic in the news.

Remote Camera Pieces

A Remote Camera Piece has the host in the studio performing a task by means of a camera placed in some location outside the studio. Participants at the remote location may or may not be able to converse with the host, depending on the piece.

Start creating a new Remote Camera Piece by picking as a topic a location outside the studio from which you can get a live video feed. Then brainstorm associations of that topic to see if any suggest a surprising activity to perform at the location.

Stunt Pieces

In a Stunt Piece either the host, a guest, or both perform an unusual physical feat. Create a new Stunt Piece by picking as your topic a well-known physical activity, and then transforming that activity with an extreme angle. And always remember, safety comes first.

So far I've only talked about Semi-Scripted Pieces that are performed live or mostly live; they all take place at the same time as the show they're a part of. Next I'll talk about Semi-Scripted Pieces that are not only shot before the show is taped—sometimes weeks before—they're also shot completely outside the studio. These are Semi-Scripted Field Pieces.

SEMI-SCRIPTED FIELD PIECES

I N A SEMI-SCRIPTED Field Piece, also known as a "Remote" or a "Field Piece," a camera crew records the host or a correspondent performing a task somewhere outside the studio that involves civilians. A staff member, usually a writer, supervises an editor in turning the resulting raw footage into a finished comedy piece.

Why Semi-Scripted Field Pieces Are Good for a Show

Semi-Scripted Field Pieces have all the advantages of any Semi-Scripted Piece. For one thing, the comedy has a refreshingly unpredictable quality because it arises from interactions with non-professionals. In addition, Field Pieces are popular among viewers for two other reasons:

- Because they're taped outside the studio, they break the visual monotony of the show. Viewers appreciate seeing the host out in the real world for a change.

- Because they're produced before the show itself is taped, all the weaker material can be edited out. Therefore, even though

Field Pieces don't have the intriguing spontaneity of Live Semi-Scripted Pieces, they tend to have more laughs per minute.

The Host Needs a Task in a Field Piece

The same way every Monologue joke and comedy piece needs a topic, every Field Piece needs a topic, too. In the case of a Field Piece, the topic is the task. Every time you send your host out on a Field Piece you have to be sure he has a task to perform.

Without a task the host would just wander around with a handheld microphone cracking random jokes. With a task the piece has an engine, a spine, a point. A task also holds the audience's interest with a built-in question: will the host succeed at the task or not? And a task gives the writers a focus for writing jokes for the piece before the host even arrives at the remote location. I'll talk more about pre-writing jokes a little later.

So every Field Piece needs a task. And just as the topic starts a Monologue joke, the task should always be spelled out to the audience at the start of a Field Piece. Sometimes the host explains the task when he's introducing the piece in the studio. But most writers prefer to have the host or correspondent state his task on tape, at the beginning of the finished Field Piece itself. That way the piece is self-contained and can stand on its own even if it's replayed outside of the show, say on a website.

For example, on *The Chevy Chase Show* one Field Piece opened with Chevy on Hollywood Boulevard saying to the camera, "You know, a lot of people think that just because I've been making movies for years and I have my own TV show that I'm rolling in money. It's just not true. I, like so many other folks today, have to work a second job to make ends meet. And that's why I'm here." At that point Chevy motions to the storefront behind him which reads: Wax Museum. This scripted speech tells the viewer what Chevy's task is in the piece: to do his second job at the wax museum. I'll come back to this piece later in this chapter when I discuss Hidden Camera Pranks.

A Correspondent Can Fill In for the Host

Audiences seem to appreciate Field Pieces the most when the host himself is out on location. They enjoy seeing how this character they know so well behaves outside the comfort zone of his usual environment. But participating in a Field Piece can take the host away from his office for a couple of hours to a couple of days, depending on how far away the taping location is. So the host often can't afford the time it takes to shoot as many Field Pieces as he'd like. And sometimes the host just doesn't want to participate in a particular Field Piece. That's why in Field Pieces correspondents frequently substitute for hosts.

Correspondents can be professional comics or, just as often, amateurs plucked from the show's production staff. For example, Dave Letterman has sent out one of his stage managers, Biff Henderson, on dozens of Field Pieces. Jay Leno dispatched an intern, Ross Mathews. Jimmy Kimmel has sent out security guard Guillermo Rodriguez.

If a correspondent is filling in for the host in a Field Piece, the writers will tailor the jokes in the piece to the personality and talents of the correspondent. Except for that difference, the same techniques apply to creating a Field Piece for a correspondent as for the host. For simplicity's sake, as I review those techniques I'll assume the on-camera talent is the host.

Live Versus Taped: How Do You Decide?

Sometimes you'll have an idea for a new Semi-Scripted Piece and it won't be obvious whether it would be better to do the piece live or to tape it as a Field Piece. Doing it live gives it the excitement of unpredictability, the feeling that anything can happen. Taping it gives you the opportunity to "cut to the funny" and minimize dead spots. So how do you decide which way to produce the piece?

Your decision should depend on how important you think it is for the host to complete the task you've assigned him. In general, the more difficult you expect the task to be, and the more you think the audience will want to see the task completed, the more you should lean toward taping the piece.

For example, let's say it's the first day of spring and you want your host to find the first robin of spring. That is, your host's task is to find a civilian named Robin. One way to do this piece would be live, as a Remote Camera Piece. The host, during the show, would chat with pedestrians out on the sidewalk and ask each one whether his or her name is Robin. If that process doesn't produce a Robin, the host could cast a wider net and ask if each pedestrian's name is Robert or Roberta, or if each pedestrian has ever done any robbin'. Eventually the host would declare victory even if the pedestrian merely knows someone named Robin. Since the task of finding a Robin is really just an excuse to let the host goof around with pedestrians, I think this version of the piece would turn out just fine.

But another way to produce the Robin piece would be as a Field Piece. The host and a camera crew would walk around in a park with a lot of foot traffic searching for an actual robin. When they don't succeed, they could shift to looking for a person named Robin. Eventually some pedestrian would probably say she knows someone named Robin. If that Robin lives or works a reasonable distance away, the host and crew could go there. The moment when Robin identifies herself to the host in person would be a nice, triumphal ending for the piece.

So which would be the better way to "Find the First Robin of Spring," live or on tape? Without more information I think it's a toss-up. In real life the decision would probably rest on which version the show needed more: a live piece for that night's show or a taped piece for next week.

The Two Basic Types of Semi-Scripted Field Pieces

Semi-Scripted Field Pieces can be divided into two basic types, which I call *Location-Dependent* and *Location-Independent*.

As the name implies, the comedy in a Location-Dependent Field Piece depends on the piece being shot at a particular location. That is, most of the jokes are based on the people, places, and things at that location.

By contrast, the comedy in a Location-Independent Field Piece depends mainly on the reactions of civilians to things the host says and does. That means that a Location-Independent Field Piece can be shot almost anywhere there are enough civilians for the host to interact with.

Now I'll talk in more detail about each type of Field Piece and give you tips on how to write them.

LOCATION-DEPENDENT FIELD PIECES

Let's start by looking at some examples of Location-Dependent Field Pieces. In each case the host's or correspondent's main task is to extract comedy from that particular location.

> **"Comedian Andy Kindler at Yankees Spring Training"** [*LSWDL*]—Sample scenes are: Andy jokes with the players, brushes his teeth with a souvenir toothbrush in the gift shop, and licks a hot dog as he works at a concession stand.

"Stage Manager Biff Henderson at Super Bowl XLV" [*LSWDL*]—Scenes include: Biff apparently changes the channel on the world's largest high-definition television, asks singer Christina Aguilera who she thinks is going to win the game, and has members of the winning Green Bay Packers rub his bald head.

"Jay Gets Las Vegas Hotel Guests to Try on Showgirl and Showboy Costumes" [*TSWJL*]—Jay goes room-to-room with racks of skimpy, flamboyant outfits and has hotel guests try them on. Then he convinces a pudgy guy in a showboy outfit to walk through the lobby.

"Ross the Intern Goes to Pit Crew School" [*TSWJL*]—Sample scenes are: Ross races to unscrew the nuts from a tire, jokes with NASCAR drivers, and holds the pit flag during a race.

"Jake Byrd Attends Sarah Palin's Movie Premiere in Iowa" [*JKL*]—Scenes include: Jake (a character played by Tony Barbieri) interrupts as the film's director is giving an interview, leads a chant for Sarah Palin, and gets Palin to autograph his box of Milk Duds candy.

"Security Guard Guillermo Goes to the NBA Finals" [*JKL*]—Sample scenes are: Guillermo asks Miami Heat player Chris Bosh who his favorite player is; asks Miami Heat player Mike Miller who the better dunker is, Mike or Teen Wolf; and asks Mavericks player Shawn Marion if he's "in it to win it."

And now I'll take a close look at a successful Location-Dependent Field Piece from *LNWCO*. This piece is vivid proof of the Superiority Theory of Laughter, the theory that explains the audience appeal of many Semi-Scripted Pieces. I'll describe the piece in detail and then use it as an example of how to create a new Location-Dependent Field Piece. The piece shows Triumph the Insult Comic Dog interacting with fans waiting in line to see the premiere of *Star Wars: Episode II—Attack of the Clones*. (Triumph is a hand puppet dog manipulated and given voice by one of the writer/performers on *LNWCO*.)

Here are punch lines from "Triumph at the *Attack of the Clones* Premiere":

- Triumph asks an overweight fan in an unidentifiable costume if he's dressed as a "huge nerd."

- Triumph tells a fan playing the board game Stratego on the sidewalk that the fan is "getting away from the drudgery of your normal, mundane life...spent playing Stratego at home."

- Triumph tells one of the only young females he found among the crowd of males, "You can choose from all kinds of guys who have no idea how to please you."

- Triumph talks about how much time these guys are spending in line and asks a man how he explains that to his imaginary girlfriend.

- Triumph asks a little girl dressed in costume, "What parent forced you to do this?"

- Triumph tells a pregnant woman that she has a "little future nerd" inside her. Triumph asks when the baby is due and then remarks, "That's the last time he'll ever see female genitalia."

- Triumph asks a guy dressed as a wizard, "Seriously, have you ever talked to a woman without having to give your credit card number?"

- Referring to the movie's plot, a young male fan says that he's not allowed to talk about spoilers. Triumph replies, "Here's a spoiler. You will die alone."

- Triumph inspects control buttons on a fan's Darth Vader costume and asks, "Which of these buttons calls your parents to pick you up?"

- Witnessing "an actual *Star Wars* Nerd Wedding," Triumph asks a spectator a question about the couple: "Where are they spending their honeymoon...which arcade?" Moments later, Triumph notes, "The groom has kissed the bride...after years of practicing on his sister."

How to Create a New Location-Dependent Field Piece

Like any so-called "reality" or "unscripted" show on television, Field Pieces are to a large degree written. The host doesn't just hop into a van with a camera crew, drive around until he sees something interesting, then get out and start chatting with people. Someone, usually a writer, picks the location ahead of time.

Once the host is at the location he ad-libs jokes but he also has a writer or two just out of camera range suggesting more funny things he can say or do. The writers ad-lib some of those jokes themselves on the spot but also pitch jokes that they wrote before they even arrived at the location. The more material the writers create ahead of time, the less pressure there is on them and the host once the camera starts rolling in what could be a chaotic environment out in the field.

So Field Pieces are largely written. How? Here are the steps that writers typically take to create a new Location-Dependent Field Piece:

1. Pick a location with a lot of associations.

A completed Location-Dependent Field Piece should be at least four minutes long; any shorter than that and the piece probably couldn't fill its own comedy segment on the show. But Location-Dependent Field Pieces can also run considerably longer than four minutes. The Triumph *Star Wars* piece clocks in at over ten minutes, uninterrupted. (Sometimes if a Field Piece contains a lot of worthwhile material the piece will be divided into "pods" of three or four minutes each, which are then run in several spots throughout one show.) Four to ten minutes is a long time for a comedy piece to sustain itself without any interruption by the host in the studio. So to be successful a Location-Dependent Field Piece must contain a lot of solid jokes.

Since the jokes in a Location-Dependent Field Piece arise from the location, your chosen location has to have a lot of distinctive people, places, and things associated with it; you'll need plenty of associations to construct all the jokes you need. In the case of the Triumph piece, the crowd outside a *Star Wars* movie premiere in New York City certainly promises a lot of associations: *Star Wars* costumes, *Star Wars*-themed activities, and nerdy fans, to name a few. That's what made it a fertile location for a Location-Dependent Field Piece.

Of course, sometimes the writers for a comedy/talk show don't get to choose the location for their next Location-Dependent Field Piece; the location is assigned to them. For example, to help out a local affiliate the network may ask the host to pay a comedic visit to the Mall of America in Bloomington, Minnesota. In a case like that, the writers just make the best of it. The process of writing the piece stays the same.

2. Research the location ahead of time.

Find out as much about the location as you can before the day of the shoot. You're looking for specific and detailed associations of the place: Who's there? What's distinctive about those people? What is there? What do those things look like? What do they do? Can the host do anything with them? If you have plenty of information about the location you can write a lot of jokes in the comfort of your office which, as I've said, will reduce everybody's stress level during the shoot itself.

One time another *LNWDL* writer and I were helping Dave tape a comedic tour of the Toy Fair in New York City. We writers hadn't done any joke writing in advance. I forget why; maybe we'd been assigned to the piece at the last minute, maybe we were overconfident, or maybe we were just too lazy to take the subway all the way downtown to do advance research. So while Dave was taping a funny exchange at one exhibitor's booth we writers were barely one step ahead of him. We were literally running from booth to booth, frantically scanning racks of toys and novelties for our next joke to pitch to Dave so he wouldn't have to stand around waiting in the crowd. I learned my lesson then: research the location ahead of time.

You can research your chosen location in advance in several ways:

- **Scout the location.** That means visiting the location ahead of time, making notes, and jotting down jokes based on what you find.

- **Draw on your knowledge of similar locations or events.** For example, if you've ever seen any news reports about *Star Wars* fans or Comic Con you know the sort of characters and activities you're likely to encounter at a *Star Wars* movie premiere.

- **Go online.** For example, the Mall of America website is chock-full of fun facts, information about the stores, photographs, and other details I needed to write jokes in advance for a Field Piece on *The Caroline Rhea Show*.

- **Phone a contact at the location.** Your show's production staff will usually get permission ahead of time to shoot the Field Piece at the location, particularly if it's on private property. Whoever their contact is will be happy to answer any questions you have.

Once you've done your research it's time to use it to write some punch lines. Whether you write them ahead of time or at the location, only moments before the host delivers them, the techniques are the same. They're similar to those you'd use to write a Found Comedy Video Piece, which I covered in Chapter 8. Here's how to do it.

3. List a lot of associations of the location.

The location will be the topic of all your jokes, so review your research about it. Then brainstorm a list of people, places, things, phrases, descriptions, activities, and so on that come to mind when you think about the location. You'll use those associations to create punch lines.

For the location "a crowd of *Star Wars* fans" you'd list associations like *Attack of the Clones*, the names of the other *Star Wars* movies, Darth Vader, Jar Jar Binks, and "May the Force be with you." You'd also list "nerd" and all of its many sub-associations like "no social life," "probably male," "doesn't date," "sexually inexperienced," "loves video games," "dresses weirdly," "lives with his parents," and so on.

When you actually arrive at the location, make another list of associations consisting of the particular people, places, things, and activities you see there. Describe the sights with a short phrase, translating each sight into verbal form so you can use it to write a verbal punch line. Base your descriptive phrases on the most prominent details of what you see, that is, the visual handles. For example, you might see "an overweight guy," "a guy playing Stratego on the sidewalk," and "a female fan."

4. Create punch lines from the associations of the location.

That is, plug your lists of associations, including the descriptive phrases you wrote at the location, into the Punch Line Maker techniques I covered in Chapter 5. The most useful technique for Location-Dependent Field Pieces tends to be a variation of Punch Line Maker #1: Take a phrase that describes something you see at the location and link it to some other association of the location. So shuffle those associations together until you find a combination that says something surprising that the audience will also agree is true.

To give you some examples, here are the punch lines from the Triumph *Star Wars* piece that I listed above, along with the associations of the location that were linked to create them:

- An overweight guy + *Star Wars* fan association ("nerd") = "Huge nerd."

- A guy playing Stratego on the sidewalk + *Star Wars* fan association ("no social life") = "Spends his life playing Stratego at home."

- A female fan + *Star Wars* fan association ("sexually inexperienced") = "All these guys have no idea how to please you."

- A guy in line + *Star Wars* fan association ("doesn't date") = "Imaginary girlfriend."

- A little girl in costume with her parents + *Star Wars* fan association ("dresses weirdly") = "What parent forced you to do this?"

314

- A pregnant woman + *Star Wars* fan association ("sexually inexperienced") = "That's the last time he'll ever see female genitalia."

- A guy in a wizard costume + *Star Wars* fan association ("doesn't date") = "Have you ever talked to a woman without having to give your credit card number?"

- A guy mentions spoilers + *Star Wars* fan association ("no social life") = "Here's a spoiler. You will die alone."

- A fan with buttons on his Darth Vader costume + *Star Wars* fan association ("lives with his parents") = "Which of these buttons calls your parents to pick you up?"

- A wedding between fans + *Star Wars* fan association ("loves video games") = "Spending their honeymoon in an arcade."

- A groom kisses his bride + *Star Wars* fan association ("doesn't date") = "Practiced kissing on his sister."

Punch Line Maker #2 is also frequently used in writing Location-Dependent Field Pieces. That technique suggests that you link an association of the location to something that the association suggests in pop culture. For instance, when correspondent Biff Henderson visited Yankees Spring Training on *LSWDL* he walked up to a ballplayer holding a bat and asked, "Is a bat the only thing you've ever choked up on?" That punch line links an association of the location—"choking up on a bat"—with something that the association suggests in pop culture—"masturbation." Note that that joke could have been, and probably was, written ahead of time because it was based on something that was sure to be seen at the location—some ballplayer holding a bat.

5. Polish each punch line for maximum impact.

Even when you write a punch line at the location, on the fly, take a few moments to craft it so it'll be as funny as possible. Use the same Joke Maximizer techniques I discussed in Chapter 6. In particular, make sure each punch line ends on the laugh trigger. It's a little funnier to have Triumph say, "That's the last time he'll ever see female genitalia" than to say "That's when he'll see female genitalia for the last time."

6. Write an on-camera introduction.

Either ahead of time or out on location, write a few introductory sentences for the host or correspondent to deliver on camera. This introduction should explain where the host is and either state or imply what his task is. The introduction can also include a joke. For example, Triumph's on-camera introduction began, "It's premiere night here for *Attack of the Clones,* but outside the Ziegfeld Theatre is the real show: Return of the Dorks."

You can edit the introduction onto the top of the piece, if you want the finished video to be self-contained, or you can leave it off and let the host introduce the piece from his desk. But it's better to have a taped intro and not need it than to need it and not have it.

7. Supervise post-production of the video.

Post-production is the process of turning the raw footage you bring back from the location into an airable comedy piece. I'll cover that process at the end of this chapter.

HIDDEN CAMERA PRANKS

Ever since Allen Funt's *Candid Camera* debuted in 1948, TV shows have been getting laughs by pulling pranks on unsuspecting civilians and recording their reactions with hidden cameras. Hidden Camera Pranks have had entire shows devoted to them, like *Punk'd*, but also appear regularly on many comedy/talk shows and on the Internet. Like a lot of the Audience Games I talked about in Chapter 12, Hidden Camera Pranks confirm the Superiority Theory of Laughter: the audience laughs because they suddenly feel superior to the prank victim.

Hidden Camera Pranks tend to be Location-Dependent. In other words, most of the time a particular prank will only work in a certain type of location. For example, *Candid Camera* once aired a prank in which civilians reacted to a fake bar of soap that had been planted in a public restroom. The same prank wouldn't have worked if the fake soap had been placed, say, on a sidewalk.

Because most Hidden Camera Pranks are Location-Dependent you can consider the location, the public restroom in the scenario above, to be the topic of your prank. The angle of the prank consists of putting a twist on a key element—a handle—of the location, like replacing the real bar of soap with a fake. The punch lines of the prank are the civilians' reactions to the angle.

In some Hidden Camera Pranks nobody on-camera is in on the joke. For example, the civilian in the soap prank reacted to an inert bar of fake soap, not to a human performer. But Hidden Camera Pranks on comedy/talk shows almost always involve either the host or a correspondent interacting on-camera with the civilian "mark" in some way. I'll refer to the performer interacting with the mark as the prankster.

Two Types of Hidden Camera Pranks

In Hidden Camera Pranks on comedy/talk shows the prankster usually interacts with the mark in one of two basic ways: either he pretends to be a different person or he gives human characteristics to something nonhuman. I'll discuss each of these scenarios in more detail.

1. The prankster pretends to be a different person.

In this type of Hidden Camera Prank the prankster pretends to be someone who would naturally be at a particular location. But instead of behaving the way that person would normally behave the prankster does things to provoke a reaction from unsuspecting civilians.

Here are some examples:

"Howie Mandel at a Hardware Store" [*TSWJL*]—In this installment of a recurring piece called "Hidden Howie," comedian Howie Mandel pretends to be an irritating salesman in a large hardware store. Howie wears a disguise consisting of a baseball cap and eyeglasses that house a video camera. Sample scenes are: Howie apparently drinks paint from a can, follows a customer around while belching repeatedly, and discusses a customer's toilet habits.

"Conan Runs a Focus Group" [*TSWCO*]—Conan, wearing makeup that renders him unrecognizable, moderates a focus group of elderly people. Conan shows video clips of himself hosting *Late Night* and gets the participants to share their frank opinions about him. Sample comments by the civilians are: "I can't imagine that the studios with all their talent scouts and people that can recognize talent could possibly have advanced a man like this." "I'm wondering...is he mentally off?" "I think he's a sociopath."

"Dave and Rupert Annoy People" [*LSWDL*]—Deli owner Rupert Jee wears a concealed microphone and earpiece along with eyeglasses containing a video camera. Dave, in a nearby van, gives instructions to Rupert through the earpiece and Rupert obeys. In one installment Rupert pretends to be an obnoxious server at a sidewalk café. Sample scenes are: Rupert insists on putting "fresh ground pepper" on a customer's bread, writes down a customer's salad order as "a bowl of chili," and delivers a glass of water with his thumb in it.

2. The prankster gives human characteristics to something nonhuman.

In this second type of Hidden Camera Prank the prankster provokes reactions from civilians by making a nonhuman object at a location talk like a human, move like a human, or both.

Here are a few examples:

"Tonight Show Photo Booth" [*TSWJL*]—An automated photo booth is equipped with a hidden video camera and a two-way audio system that lets an unseen female comedian talk with patrons inside. The comedian's robotic voice greets patrons as they enter with, "Welcome to the Free Photo Booth," then startles them with her unexpected remarks. Sample scenes are: When a girl raps on the photo booth with her knuckles the comedian exclaims, "Ow! Don't do that!" After a boy has his photo taken the comedian tells him, "You are a very beautiful girl." Two guys sit on the bench in the booth and the comedian warns, "Please do not sit down. The paint is still wet on the bench."

"Pumpcast News" [*TSWJL*]—A male comedian portrays a news anchor seen on a TV screen mounted atop a service station gas pump. Hidden cameras record the fake news anchor startling customers and then joking with them. Sample scenes are: The news anchor segues from a story about fashion dos and don'ts to criticism of the particular outfit worn by a woman pumping gas. The anchor convinces a couple of Beatles impersonators to improvise a new theme song for "Pumpcast News." The anchor persuades a male customer to put on a cape that's hanging at the pump and pretend to be a new superhero.

"Chevy at the Hollywood Wax Museum" [*The Chevy Chase Show*]—Chevy, made up to look like a wax replica of himself, sits among mannequins of celebrities on display in the Hollywood Wax Museum. He startles tourists by suddenly coming to life as they walk by.

How to Create a New Hidden Camera Prank

Follow these three steps to create a successful Hidden Camera Prank:

1. Pick a promising location. Two factors play the biggest role in determining whether a location is promising:

> **a) The amount of foot traffic**—A promising location has a steady stream of unsuspecting civilians passing through it. This is important because a Hidden Camera Prank is like a Found Comedy Piece and, as I pointed out in Chapter 8, a Found Comedy Piece depends for its success on having plenty of raw material to work with. For a Hidden Camera Prank the raw material is civilians minding their own business. So if one civilian doesn't give you the kind of entertaining reaction you're looking for, you want plenty of other civilians right around the corner who you can mess with.
>
> I say that the civilians should be "passing through" the location for an important reason: you want the marks to leave after

I was crouching in a nearby alcove of the Hollywood Wax Museum watching Chevy on the monitors; the museum staff had cleared out a fake torture chamber to make room for our little "video village." But I was in a writer's kind of torture chamber: we could only tape Chevy for about an hour and a half until he had to leave and I was afraid we wouldn't get enough good footage to fill out a piece. Finally a pair of girls came through with a reaction huge enough to end the piece with. Their torrent of laughter and crying was riveting. Even when Chevy tried to calm one girl down she was barely able to summon the courage to touch his hand. The girls were in their early teens, too young to give permission to air the footage, but fortunately we were able to track down their parents and get signed releases from them. If we hadn't gotten those releases one of the most successful comedy pieces in the short life of the show would probably never have aired.

And that would have been a shame because we had flown in actor William Christopher all the way from Phoenix to provide this final surprise for the piece: After the encounter with the hysterical girls a bell rings and Chevy breaks for lunch. He saunters over to an exhibit of wax mannequins of the characters in the TV show *M*A*S*H* and asks "Bill" if he wants to go get a bite to eat. William Christopher, made up as his Father Mulcahy character, steps out of the tableau and strolls off with Chevy. The audience loved it.

That Father Mulcahy bit is a good example of how you can insert scripted jokes into a Semi-Scripted Field Piece. But if you also include in your piece the reactions of civilians to your scripted jokes be sure those reactions are spontaneous. Civilians in general are bad actors, so directing them to react a certain way won't give you the genuine emotional display you need. If we had brought those two teenage girls over to the *M*A*S*H* tableau and directed them to scream again when Father Mulcahy came to life their terror would have looked phony, casting doubt over the authenticity of the rest of the piece. The audience, suspecting that the entire piece had been staged, couldn't feel superior and wouldn't laugh.

they've seen your prank because otherwise they may spread the word about it and make it impossible for you to get spontaneous reactions from other civilians in the vicinity. The day we taped Chevy's wax museum prank we got lucky. The flow of visitors through the room he was stationed in was steady but sporadic enough that we could usher each group of marks out in time to surprise the next group.

b) The presence of a Mark Magnet—A promising location either has or can have what I call a Mark Magnet. A Mark Magnet is someone or something that civilians will feel compelled to interact with. A Hidden Camera Prank location needs a Mark Magnet so civilians will have a hard time avoiding the prank. If civilians can easily avoid the prank you may not collect enough raw material for your piece.

A Mark Magnet could be something attractive, like a bowl of candy labeled: Free Candy. Or a Mark Magnet could be a something that channels physical movement, like a sidewalk or doorway. Or often it's a person in some position of authority. For example, a salesperson walking up to you in a hardware store is hard to ignore.

2. Modify a Mark Magnet at the location in a surprising way. If you think of the location as the topic of the prank, the angle of the prank is the modification you make to a Mark Magnet at the location. The modification usually involves changing just one of the Mark Magnet's characteristics in an unexpected way, like this:

a) If the Mark Magnet is a person, have the prankster pretend to be that person but adopt an extremely inappropriate trait. For instance, it's extremely inappropriate for a salesman in a hardware store and a server in a café to be obnoxious instead of pleasant. It's extremely inappropriate for the moderator of a focus group to be the subject of the focus group instead of being an impartial third party.

b) If the Mark Magnet is something nonhuman, have the prankster radically change one of its key properties. The prankster could alter some physical characteristic of the object in an unexpected way, as the *Candid Camera* pranksters did when they made a bar of soap out of some material that looked like soap but didn't clean. Or the prankster could make the nonhuman object talk or move like a human, the way pranksters caused a photo booth and a gas pump TV screen to converse like real people. And Chevy Chase made what appeared to be his wax replica spring to life.

Note that modified Mark Magnets, whether they're people or things, should blend in with the location so they don't tip off the marks that a prank is being pulled. Just as the topic of a Monologue joke has to be true, the topic of a Hidden Camera Prank has to be true-to-life. That is, the location can't look phony or rigged in any way. For example, Howie has to wear a convincing disguise when he annoys hardware store customers. If he doesn't, the customers will recognize him and know the same thing that the audience knows—that he's Howie Mandel. Because that would mean the audience couldn't feel superior to the customers, the audience wouldn't laugh.

3. Write provocative things for the prankster to do or say. I call those things stimuli. The prankster, acting through the Mark Magnet, will use those stimuli to get an entertaining reaction from civilians.

Many stimuli can and should be written ahead of time, before the prank is even underway. As with any Semi-Scripted Field Piece, the more writing that's done ahead of time, the less pressure on the writers and performers on the day of the shoot. For example, when preparing the "Tonight Show Photo Booth" prank it was easy to predict that, at some point, a boy would sit in the booth. That means the stimulus line "You are a very beautiful girl" could easily have been written beforehand.

But other stimuli can only be written when the writers and/or prankster see the location and the actual marks. For instance, there was little way to predict that someone would rap on the photo booth with her knuckles. So the stimulus line "Ow! Don't do that!" was probably improvised on the spot.

To write stimuli that the prankster can use to provoke reactions from civilians, follow these steps:

a) Research the location. Do your research the same way you would for any Location-Dependent Field Piece. That is, scout the location, draw on your knowledge of similar locations, go online, or phone a contact. In the case of the "Tonight Show Photo Booth," any one of those research methods would probably have been satisfactory.

b) Draw on your research to list a lot of handles of the location. Similar to the handles of a Monologue joke topic, the handles of a location are elements of the location that stand out. The handles of a photo booth include a curtain, walls, a light, instructions, photos, a place to insert money, a camera lens, and a seat.

c) Brainstorm associations for each handle. For example, one of the associations of "a seat in a photo booth" is "dry."

d) Write stimuli that tell the mark he's totally wrong about an association. Continuing with the photo booth example, this stimulus line tells the mark that the seat is not dry: "Please do not sit down. The paint is still wet on the bench." As another example, one handle of a hardware store is "paint," which has the association "undrinkable." But the stimulus of Howie Mandel apparently drinking paint from a can says that association isn't true. In each example the mark is startled by the unexpected stimulus and the audience members, who feel superior because they know the truth, laugh.

So far in this chapter I've talked about one basic type of Semi-Scripted Field Piece, the Location-Dependent Field Piece, which includes Hidden Camera Pranks. Now I'll turn to the other basic type of Semi-Scripted Field Piece.

LOCATION-INDEPENDENT FIELD PIECES

As I mentioned earlier in this chapter, the comedy in a Location-Independent Field Piece depends mainly on the reactions of civilians to things the host says and does. That's why a Location-Independent Field Piece can be shot at almost any location where there are enough civilians.

How to Create a New Location-Independent Field Piece

While the first step in creating a successful Location-*Dependent* Field Piece is to pick a promising location, the first step in creating a successful Location-*Independent* Field Piece is to pick a promising task for the host or correspondent. Most civilians aren't funny or entertaining on their own; they need a stimulus to react to before they'll give you any usable material. In this type of piece, that stimulus is some task the host performs which involves the civilians.

Two general types of tasks tend to produce entertaining reactions: asking people a question and getting people to play a Pedestrian Game. I'll talk about each type of task in turn.

1. Ask people a question.

In this type of Location-Independent Field Piece the host asks people to do something or to tell him their thoughts about something. Here are several examples:

"Jay Looks at Desks" [*TSWJL*]—Jay needs a new desk when he returns to the *Tonight* show after hosting his short-lived show at ten o'clock. So he does research by going into random civilians' homes and asking if he can try out their desks. Sample scenes are: Jay sees a little girl eating KFC fried chicken in the kitchen and remarks, "Mommy's a good cook, huh?" Jay sits at a family's desk in their living room and introduces his "next guest," comedian Adam Corolla, who enters and takes a seat next to the desk.

"Internet Dating" [*TSWJL*]—Jay asks pedestrians about their experiences with online dating. A sample exchange: A woman tells Jay that online dating didn't work out for her. He asks the woman how far she'd travel for an Internet date. She answers, "Five miles." Jay then asks how far she'd travel for a shoe sale. She replies, "Fifty miles." Jay comments, "Okay, I think I see the problem."

"Joke Run" [*TSWJL*]—Jay says he wants to test jokes for his Monologue to see if they're funny enough to perform on the show. So he cruises around Hollywood in one of his vintage convertibles, pulls up alongside pedestrians, reads jokes to them, and asks them for their opinions.

"YouTube Parents' Challenge" [*JKL*]—Jimmy turns his viewers into correspondents for his show: he asks them to record a video of themselves performing a task and upload it to YouTube, labeled so that his staff can find it. In one edition Jimmy assigns parents the task of lying to their children by claiming they ate all of the children's Halloween candy. The parents' unspoken question to the children is, "How do you feel about that?" The children react.

How to Create a New "Ask People a Question" Piece

Here are some tips:

a) Think of a question that's likely to generate a lot of usable responses. Since a Location-Independent Field Piece is a kind of Found Comedy Piece you'll need a lot of raw material to make it successful. In an "Ask People a Question" piece, the raw material is how civilians react to the question. So you want a question that most people can respond to in some way. For example, most people have a desk at home so they could let Jay try it out. And most people have an opinion about whether a joke is funny or not, so they'd be able to respond to Jay. By contrast, "What do you think about that new subatomic particle they found with the Large Hadron Collider?" would not be a good question to ask pedestrians.

b) Make sure the question is likely to grab viewers' attention. So the piece will be entertaining, make sure that viewers are apt to be interested in how civilians respond to the question. You want to put the Superiority Theory of Laughter to work here, the same way you would with an Audience Stories Piece (discussed in Chapter 12). So choose a question that encourages pedestrians to reveal something private about themselves because viewers will feel superior when they learn the pedestrians' secrets.

For example, most viewers will be amused to see the desks inside strangers' homes or to hear other people's humiliating Internet dating stories. Or if you really want to test the limits of the Superiority Theory of Laughter you could choose a question that will probably make children cry, as Jimmy Kimmel did with his "YouTube Parents' Challenge."

Another way to hook viewers' interest is to ask a topical question, a question tied to a current event that's on people's minds. For example, on one Friday the thirteenth Jay asked pedestrians questions about their superstitions and invited them to walk under ladders.

c) Pick a well-populated location for taping the piece. Remember, the more pedestrians the host interacts with, the more likely it is that you'll find enough comedy gold to fill a full-length piece (about four to ten minutes long). The piece will also be more entertaining if the pedestrians have varied looks and the location is visually interesting.

For the above reasons, these types of locations tend to be the most productive when you're shooting Location-Independent Field Pieces:

- A sidewalk with a lot of pedestrian traffic. On *TSWJL* Jay frequently taped pieces on trendy, colorful Melrose Avenue in Hollywood, which harbors a lot of quirky pedestrians.

- A popular tourist attraction. Jay also shot at the Universal Studios Hollywood theme park. For pieces on *LNWDL*, Dave often visited Times Square, which draws visitors from all over the world.

- An apartment building or a residential neighborhood where people are apt to be home. The host goes door-to-door.

Note that because the video clips for "YouTube Parents' Challenge" are crowdsourced, the "well-populated location" for taping the piece is every home where *JKL* is viewed.

d) Write provocative questions and activities for your host ahead of time. To do that, think of associations of the main question your host is asking people. Then use those associations to generate additional questions and activities the host can use to provoke reactions at the chosen location. As usual, the more of this writing you do ahead of time, the less panic at the shoot about what to do next.

Here's an example of how writing a Field Piece in advance can really pay off. We had already aired a few editions of the "Joke Run" piece on *TSWJL* so I wanted to take the next edition a step farther. I thought of associations of "ask a pedestrian about jokes" and came up with "prostitute." If Jay was trying out his Monologue jokes on pedestrians, why not hookers? I asked around and found out that they tended to congregate in a taco stand parking lot near the corner of La Brea and Santa Monica in Hollywood. (In case you're thinking of swinging by there to shoot your own comedy piece I should tell you that the streetwalkers are long gone, displaced by a huge shopping mall.)

The night of the "Joke Run" Jay wheeled into the taco stand parking lot in his vintage Buick convertible and, sure enough, was greeted by several ladies of the evening. Jay had only told them a few jokes when the location paid us another dividend, this one unexpected: An unmarked police car sped over and disgorged three or four plainclothes cops, eager to bust what seemed to be a hapless john trying to do business. Once the cops recognized Jay and learned he was just telling jokes everybody shared a laugh. And our alert camera operator captured everything on tape. The incident was a terrific way to end the piece.

This next type of task a host can perform in a Location-Independent Field Piece is a variation of asking people a question.

2. Get people to play a Pedestrian Game.

In this type of piece the host asks people questions in connection with playing a Pedestrian Game. Adding a game element to an "Ask People a Question" piece amps up its entertainment value because viewers at home can usually play the game, too. This "play-along" factor is one reason game shows are a perennially popular television genre.

There are two basic types of Pedestrian Game: games where the pedestrians are the players and games where the viewers are the players.

a) Games where the pedestrians are the players

In this type of Pedestrian Game, civilians guess the correct answers to questions. Here are a few examples:

> **"Complete the Country-and-Western Lyrics"** [*TSWJL*]—Jay asks patrons of a cowboy bar to fill in the blanks in some country-and-western song lyrics. A sample joke: Jay asks a cowboy to complete the line, from a Jimmy Buffet song, that begins, "If the phone doesn't ring..." The cowboy responds, "Don't answer it."

> **"Jaywalking"** [*TSWJL*]—Jay asks pedestrians general knowledge questions that should be easy to answer and we hear their comically incorrect responses. For example, Jay asks one man, "What countries border the United States?" The man responds, "Australia...and Hawaii." Often a "Jaywalking" piece will have a theme; for example, during Earth Week Jay asked questions about the earth.

> The "Jaywalking" pieces on *TSWJL* were very popular, validating the Superiority Theory of Laughter. Plus "Jaywalking" was a dream from a production standpoint. If the writers ever needed a

surefire Field Piece fast they could just write some quiz questions (which didn't even have to be jokes), have the questions read to pedestrians for an hour or so, and put together what amounted to their own truTV "World's Dumbest Pedestrians" video. I've been out on plenty of "Jaywalking" shoots and nothing about them is faked. Dumb pedestrians really are that easy to find.

"Lie Witness News" [*JKL*] – This is another entry in the "People are Dumb" category. In one edition, a correspondent goes to the Coachella Valley Music and Arts Festival and asks attendees for their opinions about bands that don't really exist. The attendees pretend to have heard of the fake bands. In one scene, the correspondent asks a group of attendees, "Are you guys as excited as I am about The Obesity Epidemic?" One of the attendees responds, "I just like their whole style. Like, their whole genre is great." In this piece the pedestrians are playing a game you could call "Guess Which Bands are Real" but they don't even know they're playing it.

b) Games where the viewers are the players

In this second type of Pedestrian Game the players are the viewers watching the pedestrians. More specifically, the audience is challenged to answer questions about some characteristic of the pedestrians. Here are some examples:

"Good Dancer or Bad Dancer?" [*TSWJL*]—Jay asks pedestrians general questions about themselves like: What do you do for a living? Are you married or single? What's your idea of an ideal date? After chatting briefly with each pedestrian Jay invites viewers to guess whether the pedestrian is a good dancer or a bad dancer. Then the pedestrian dances on the sidewalk in full view of passersby so that Jay and his viewers can judge for themselves.

"Bald or Not?" [*TSWJL*]—Jay wants to test his theory that many men wear hats because they want to cover up their baldness. He chats with men wearing hats and invites the audience to guess whether each man is balding or not. Then each man removes his hat and reveals the answer.

"Drunk or Not Drunk?" [*TSWJL*]—Jay banters with a series of pedestrians. The video clip of each pedestrian is paused and the studio audience is invited to shout out whether they think the pedestrian is "drunk" or "not drunk." Then the video starts up again and the pedestrian is seen blowing into a Breathalyzer. An on-screen graphic reveals his Blood Alcohol Content and whether he is in fact drunk or not drunk.

How to Create a New Pedestrian Game Piece

Here are a couple of tips:

1. Think of a personal characteristic that most people would rather not reveal publicly about themselves. It could be something intimate, like whether they're hiding a bald spot ("Bald or Not?"). Or it could be something embarrassing, like their degree of inebriation ("Drunk or Not Drunk?"), or how physically uncoordinated they are ("Good Dancer or Bad Dancer?"), or how dumb they are ("Jaywalking," "Lie Witness News"). Then base a game on learning that personal characteristic of pedestrians. When the pedestrians expose the characteristic to the world, and possibly humiliate themselves, the Superiority Theory of Laughter will ensure that the audience is entertained.

Note that people are more willing to open up to a TV camera than you might think. *Lopez Tonight* on TBS once aired a Pedestrian Game in which George asked a pedestrian whether he had ever been in jail; the pedestrian admitted that he had. Just make sure you get your participants to sign releases.

2. Pick a location that will make the game challenging. That is, play the game in a place where any random pedestrian has both a good chance of having and a good chance of not having the characteristic that the game is based on. For example, "Drunk or Not Drunk" could have been played anywhere but was more challenging because it was played at the St. Patrick's Day Parade in New York City, where many spectators were liquored up. And "Bald or Not" was shot at a cowboy bar in Houston where virtually all the males wore cowboy hats, whether their hair was thinning or not.

HYBRID FIELD PIECES

It's also possible to create a Semi-Scripted Field Piece that blends several types of Semi-Scripted Pieces. One example from *TSWJL* is "Jay at the Time Trials of the Indianapolis 500." It was basically a Pedestrian Game where Jay asked some of the top Indy car drivers in the world questions from the Indiana Bureau of Motor Vehicles driver's test booklet. But the piece was also a Location-Dependent Field Piece because it included jokes based on the Indianapolis Motor Speedway. And it ended with the Stunt of Jay driving the official pace car around the track and a scripted visual joke: Jay's hair artificially blown back with hair gel.

A cautionary tale from the Indianapolis Motor Speedway: I forgot to remind our camera operator to check the tape until we had already recorded Jay quizzing many famous drivers. When we did check we discovered that a camera defect had rendered the footage unusable. We couldn't shoot those drivers again because by that time they were out zooming around the track. So we had to wait until the local NBC affiliate sent over a replacement camera and then reshoot the quiz with other drivers. The audience never knew the difference and the piece played great. But I learned not to go too long on a Field Piece without checking the footage.

THE POST-PRODUCTION PROCESS

So far in this chapter I've talked about how to create Semi-Scripted Field Pieces of all kinds. But the creation process doesn't end after the raw footage for a piece is shot. The last step for the writer of any Semi-Scripted Field Piece is to supervise the post-production process.

Post-production is the editing of the raw footage—also known as source material—into a finished, airable comedy piece that's as entertaining as possible. Here's the typical process that a writer on a comedy/talk show would follow:

1. Start by logging all your raw footage. Logging means watching the source material you brought back from the location and listing all the shots. Write down a brief description of each shot and where it is in the footage. Logging is easy if you've received the raw footage with the time code (those black-and-white numbers at the bottom of the video) burned into it. Also note in your log the moments where you think the audience might laugh; if you're lucky there are a lot of those.

2. Do a paper cut, also known as a paper edit. That is, before you sit down with your editor make a written list of what shots you want in the piece and in what order. I start a paper cut by writing a few words describing each shot that I like on a separate sticky note. Then I arrange those sticky notes in an effective order, the same way I'd arrange the jokes in any comedy piece: start with a strong joke, end with the strongest joke, and order the jokes in between so that the momentum of the piece builds. I add the host's on-camera intro to the top and his outro, if he recorded one, to the end. When I've decided on my shot list, I usually transcribe it onto sheets of paper in case my sticky notes come unstuck. Those sheets of paper represent my paper cut.

3. Work with your editor to translate your paper cut into a rough cut. A rough cut is the editing together of the actual shots listed in your paper cut into a crude approximation of the finished video. If the first version of your rough cut is longer than you want the finished video to be—and it should be longer, so you'll have choices—take out the weakest jokes. That is, "cut to the funny." Also take out any jokes that seem too mean; you want the viewer to feel superior, not too guilty to laugh. Then show your rough cut to the head writer and possibly the host and get their opinions about it if that's part of the post-production process on your show.

4. Work with your editor to prepare a fine cut. Start by making any requested changes to the rough cut. Then supervise your editor in smoothing out all the video and audio edits. As part of that process, come into each shot as late as possible and get out of each shot as soon as possible, all without hurting the joke. In other words, begin and end each shot as close to the important action in the shot as you reasonably can. With Field Piece jokes, as with any other jokes, shorter is better.

5. Consider including "comedy helpers." What I call a comedy helper is a joke that isn't in the raw footage; it's created in post-production. I mentioned one commonly used comedy helper in the previous chapter: cut to a shot of bystanders apparently reacting blankly to some lame thing the host is doing even if the bystanders weren't actually reacting that way to the host at the time. Steal the shot of the deadpan bystanders from somewhere else in your raw footage.

Other comedy helpers involve adding on-screen graphics to your fine cut. Here are a few examples: a counter that keeps a tally of some silly, repeated action, like somebody blinking; superimposed text, like a subtitled "translation"; or a flashing arrow pointing at an incongruous detail.

6. Get comments on your fine cut from the people who have to approve it. Those people usually include the head writer and the host. Revise the fine cut as necessary with your editor until the host tells you the piece is finished. The final cut of your Semi-Scripted Field Piece is now ready to be rolled into the show.

SUMMARY

In a Semi-Scripted Field Piece (often dubbed a "Remote" or a "Field Piece") a camera crew records the host performing a task somewhere outside the studio that involves unpredictable civilians. Semi-Scripted Field Pieces can be divided into two basic types: Location-Dependent, which includes most Hidden Camera Pranks, and Location-Independent.

Location-Dependent Field Pieces

These depend for their comedy on the particular location where the pieces are shot. To create one, follow these seven steps:

1. Pick a location with a lot of associations.

2. Research the location ahead of time. Scout it, draw on your knowledge of similar locations or events, go online, or phone a contact at the location.

3. List a lot of associations of the location. At the location, also make a list of associations that consists of brief descriptions of what you see there.

4. Create punch lines from the associations of the location. A variation of Punch Line Maker #1 is apt to be particularly useful: take a phrase that describes something you see at the location and link it to some other association of the location.

5. Polish each punch line for maximum impact. Use the Joke Maximizers.

6. Write an on-camera introduction.

7. Supervise post-production of the video.

Hidden Camera Pranks

On comedy/talk shows the prankster usually interacts with the mark in one of two ways: either he pretends to be a different person or he gives human characteristics to something nonhuman. Follow these three steps to create a Hidden Camera Prank:

1. Pick a promising location. You want a steady stream of unsuspecting civilians passing through it and also a Mark Magnet that will make it hard for the civilians to avoid the prank.

2. Modify a Mark Magnet at the location in a surprising way. If the Mark Magnet is a person, have the prankster pretend to be that person but adopt an extremely inappropriate trait. If the Mark Magnet is something nonhuman, have the prankster radically change one of its key properties.

3. Write provocative things for the prankster to do or say. Write as many of those stimuli as possible ahead of time by following these steps:
- Research the location.
- Draw on your research to list a lot of handles of the location.

- Brainstorm associations for each handle.
- Write stimuli that tell the mark he's totally wrong about an association.

Location-Independent Field Pieces

These depend for their comedy mainly on civilians' reactions to things the host says and does while performing a task. Two tasks that tend to produce entertaining reactions are asking people a question and getting people to play a Pedestrian Game.

Do this to create an "Ask People a Question" Piece:

- Think of a question that's likely to generate a lot of usable responses.
- Make sure the question is likely to grab viewers' attention.
- Pick a well-populated location for taping the piece.
- Write provocative questions and activities for your host ahead of time.

Do this to create a Pedestrian Game:

- Think of a personal characteristic that most people would rather not reveal publicly about themselves. Base a game on learning that personal characteristic of pedestrians.
- Pick a location that will make the game challenging.

The Post-Production Process

For a writer this process consists of the following steps:
1. Log all your raw footage.
2. Do a paper cut, also known as a paper edit.
3. Work with your editor to translate your paper cut into a rough cut.
4. Work with your editor to prepare a fine cut.

5. Consider including "comedy helpers."

6. Get comments on your fine cut from the people who have to approve it.

Now you have all the tools you need to write like a staff member of a late-night comedy/talk show. You can also use what you've learned to create comedy for the Internet or for print media like magazines. You can craft jokes for your Twitter feed, fake commercials for radio, or sketches for YouTube. You can make just about anything funnier, from a corporate speech to a real commercial to a spec sitcom.

But what if you want to get a job actually writing for a late-night comedy/talk show? I'll take up that subject next.

SUBMISSION PACKETS

U NLESS YOU'RE A close personal friend of the host, to get hired as a writer on a comedy/talk show you'll almost certainly have to submit a writing sample. And not just any writing sample, a comedy/talk show submission packet.

In that respect comedy/talk shows are different from sitcoms and one-hour shows. A sketch writer from *Saturday Night Live* might be able to land a staff job on a sitcom without ever having written a sitcom script. A playwright may be able to parlay her stage plays into a staff job on a one-hour television drama. But writing for a comedy/talk show requires a very specialized set of skills, like the ability to write Monologue jokes, Audience Games, and Semi-Scripted Field Pieces. So to land a staff job on a comedy/talk show you'll have to prove you can write the kind of material the show needs. That means putting together a comedy/talk show submission packet.

Most writers don't have a comedy/talk show submission packet, so if you do—and the packet is fantastic—you'll have a huge advantage when one of those shows is looking to hire. How you prepare your packet depends on what type of show you'll be submitting it to:

- If you'll be submitting it to a show that's currently being broadcast, tailor it to that show.

- If you'll be submitting it to an upcoming show that's not being broadcast yet, make an educated guess as to what kind of comedy the show will emphasize and reflect that in your packet.

- If you're not aiming to submit it to any particular show right now but you want to be ready when the opportunity presents itself, write a generic packet.

I'll cover each of these situations in turn.

WRITING A SUBMISSION PACKET FOR A CURRENT SHOW

The best packet to submit to a comedy/talk show that's currently being broadcast is one you've written specifically for that show. That's because the people who hire writers for a comedy/talk show want to see packets containing material they could use on their show right away. Packets like that prove that the writers who submitted them could start contributing to the show immediately. And that's a valuable ability for a writer to have because the head writers and producers of daily comedy/talk shows don't have much time for rewriting and handholding.

You may have heard different advice about submitting writing samples to shows in other TV genres, like sitcoms and one-hour dramas. The conventional wisdom is that if you're applying for a writing job on Sitcom XYZ you shouldn't send that show a spec episode of Sitcom XYZ. Instead, you should submit to Sitcom XYZ a spec episode of a different sitcom that's similar in tone. The thinking is that if you submit a Sitcom XYZ spec to the staff of Sitcom XYZ they'll be able to find fault with it too easily. Staff writers know their own show inside and out so any little missteps in your spec will loom large in their minds and make your spec seem worse than it is.

So why are comedy/talk shows different from other shows as far as spec material goes? Why couldn't you submit a packet you wrote for one late-night laffer (as *Variety* calls them) to a similar late-night laffer? Because it's easier to write an excellent submission on spec for a comedy/talk show than for a sitcom. For one thing, a typical sitcom episode has one or more story lines; multiple main characters, each with a layered personality and an established backstory; and a complex weave of character interactions. Comedy/talk shows don't. For another thing, a typical sitcom script is at least thirty pages long, compared with eight to ten pages for a comedy/talk show submission packet. Since it's perfectly possible, then, for a prospective writer to put together a terrific submission packet that's tailored to a given comedy/talk show, the people who hire writers for that show will expect to see one.

So how do you write a submission packet that's tailored to a comedy/talk show currently being broadcast, the show you'd love to work for, your Target Show? The process starts with research.

Find out your Target Show's submission guidelines.

The head writer of any comedy/talk show usually has a clear idea of what a prospective writer should include in a submission packet to demonstrate that he can turn out useable material for the show. And the head writer wants to find writers who can turn out useable material. That means the head writer has a strong incentive to give detailed submission guidelines to prospective writers. (WGA rules say that detailed guidelines are okay as long as the show only intends to use your submission as a writing sample. If the show actually airs material you've submitted they have to pay you according to the WGA contract.) So call up the head writer of your Target Show and ask what his submission guidelines are.

Here's how to do that, step by step:

1. Find out the name of the head writer (or a head writer, if there's more than one). You can acquire that information with a little Internet research or just watch for it in the crawl—the list of credits—at the end of the show. Union rules dictate that a show has to list the names of all of its writers in the crawl on a regular basis. Sometimes the head writer is called the "writing supervisor."

2. Find out the name of the studio where the show is produced, that is, the production facility you'd go to if you had a ticket to sit in the audience. This information is available online, on the show's own website among other places. Wherever the studio audience is, the writers' offices aren't far away.

3. Conduct some online research and find out the main telephone number of the studio. Dial that number and ask the operator to connect you to the production offices of your Target Show.

Try calling on days when your Target Show is "dark" (not being produced) because the writers may be in their offices but not particularly busy. You can find out when the show is dark by checking the show's website to see what days tickets are unavailable. If you have to call when the show is in production, the best times are around lunch time and in the early evening, after the show has been taped; those are times when the head writer is apt to have a free moment.

4. Ask the person who answers the phone at the show's production offices to put you through to the head writer; ask for the

head writer by name. If questioned, explain that you're a writer and you're interested in submitting material to the show. The staffs of most comedy/talk shows are used to getting calls like that.

5. If you're able to talk with the head writer, tell him that you're a writer, you think his show is amazing, and you'd love to write for it. Ask him what type of material he'd like to see in a submission packet. Most head writers are decent people and will answer you.

If you aren't able to talk with the head writer but you are transferred to someone else, say the writers' assistant, explain to him who you are and why you are calling. Ask him if he can tell you the show's submission guidelines or could connect you with someone who can.

Whomever you wind up talking with, be charming and don't sound like a weirdo and eventually you'll get the information you need. After all, it's in the staff's best interest to hire writers who will be an excellent fit with the show so it makes total sense for them to tell a prospective writer what material they'd prefer to see.

6. Write down in detail whatever you learn about the submission guidelines because they can be quite specific.

It's definitely worth making the effort to find out what your particular Target Show is looking for in a submission because each show wants to see different types of material. Even if you've learned what one show wants, another show might want something very different. I know because I've spoken with head writers of all the top late-night shows. Some shows like to see a page or two of Monologue jokes; others don't. Some shows like to see ideas for new Desk Pieces; others don't. Some shows like to see a fully scripted sketch; others don't. But if I were to write in this book what I've learned about the submission guidelines of various shows, that information could become dated very quickly. So it's a good idea for you to call up your Target Show yourself.

Learn the unwritten rules of your Target Show.

Once you've found out the stated guidelines for what to submit to your Target Show, learn what the unspoken guidelines are. Here are three ways to do that:

1. Watch your Target Show a lot.

That's what I did before I wrote a submission packet for the first television show I ever worked on, *Late Night with David Letterman*. First I bought a videocassette recorder; consumer VCRs were still fairly new and expensive at the time but staying up every week-night until 1:30 a.m. to watch the show wasn't an attractive option. Then I taped and studied the show for a few weeks.

Today DVRs and video on demand have replaced VCRs but the principle is the same: get to know your Target Show very well. If you're a regular viewer of the show you probably have enough of a feel for it already. If you haven't been watching the show regularly, record and binge-watch at least a month of episodes. What you're looking for are the answers to questions like these:

- **What types of comedy pieces does the show do?** Desk Pieces? Story Sketches? Audience Pieces? Does the host perform characters? Does the show do Semi-Scripted Field Pieces? If so, who goes out on location, the host or a correspondent? Not every show does all the types of comedy pieces covered in this book.

- **What is the host's persona?** Chapter 1 lists questions you should be able to answer about the host. You need to know the host's on-camera character intimately because everything you write for the host must be consistent with it.

- **How big a budget does the show seem to have?** A show's budget affects how the comedy pieces are written. Does the show do Parody Sketches with lots of speaking parts and elaborate sets, props, and costumes, or does it stick to less costly pieces? If the show does Desk Pieces, are they more expensive Prop Pieces or less expensive Text Pieces?

- **Are celebrities enlisted to participate in the show's comedy?** If so, are they A-listers or C-listers? If you pitch an idea that requires a celebrity, you want to suggest someone who's gettable.

- **What audience does the show seem to be aimed at?** All adults, like Dave Letterman's show? Younger adults, like Jimmy Fallon's show? It's important to have a good sense of who the show is for: what they know, what they care about, how they feel about various topics. That's the only way you can write comedy that that show's particular audience will laugh at. For example, if they've never heard of the latest viral video, they won't get a joke about it unless you describe it to them first.

2. Research your Target Show online.

In addition to watching complete episodes of your Target Show, study video clips of the show's comedy pieces on YouTube, Facebook, and the show's own website. Videos of hundreds of comedy/talk show pieces, including many of the ones mentioned in this book, can be viewed online.

You can also read online articles about the shows. For example, the Wikipedia article "List of *Conan* Sketches" contains brief descriptions of dozens of comedy pieces that have appeared on *Conan* and provides an easy way to acquaint yourself with what the writers have been up to.

3. Research other comedy/talk shows.

One unwritten rule of any comedy/talk show is to broadcast only comedy material that no other show has broadcast. So research other comedy/talk shows too, to make reasonably sure that your material will seem original to its readers on your Target Show, who have seen a lot of late-night comedy. Have some idea of what comedy pieces other shows have aired so you'll know what not to include in your submission packet.

Aim to write the same, but different.

As I've said, you should research comedy/talk shows other than your Target Show to help you keep your material original. But you should also research those other shows to get inspiration for creating your own pieces. In other words, research other shows so you can write material that's "the same, but different."

"The same, but different" is a paradoxical principle that governs the production of most forms of American mass entertainment. What it means is that a new television show, say, has to be in many ways the same as other, successful television shows. That's because that sameness reassures the television executives who approve the production of the expensive new show that it will be successful, too.

Originality is highly prized on comedy/talk shows. A staffer on one top show is assigned the daily task of transcribing the Monologues and summarizing the comedy pieces of several other comedy/talk shows. The host relies on these reports to make sure he doesn't repeat a joke or a comedy bit from another show.

The possibility of that happening accidentally is real. One night I saw a host who apparently doesn't watch his competition repeat a joke almost word for word that Jay Leno had told a couple of days before. I'm sure that the other host's writers didn't steal Jay's joke. It's just that, with every topical Monologue writer in television writing jokes the same way—the way I've described in this book—different writing staffs will occasionally turn in the same joke independently.

Another example of this phenomenon occurred in December 2010. *Conan* and *Jimmy Kimmel Live* each aired a parody video promoting a fake TV Christmas special in which former Vice Presidential candidate Sarah Palin shoots Rudolph the Red-Nosed Reindeer. Conan's parody aired two weeks after Jimmy's, which led Conan to issue an apology online. But the similarity of the two comedy pieces was certainly accidental. On the December 5, 2010, episode of *Sarah Palin's Alaska*, Ms. Palin shot a caribou. Obviously what happened then was that both shows' writers seized on that well-publicized topic and applied Punch Line Maker #1. They associated "caribou" with "Rudolph the Red-Nosed Reindeer" and *Sarah Palin's Alaska* with "Sarah Palin's Christmas Special" and linked those two associations to generate the idea for the parody.

But a new television show also has to be different in some significant ways from every other television show because those differences will make the show seem somewhat fresh and therefore more attractive to viewers. Those differences will also make it harder for some production company to win a copyright infringement lawsuit against the producers of the new show.

The principle of "the same, but different" also explains why movie producers like to hear new movie ideas pitched to them as versions of other movies. For example, the movies *Olympus Has Fallen* and *White House Down* could both have been pitched as "*Die Hard* [the same] in the White House [but different]." The fact that both those movies were released less than four months apart is also evidence that the entertainment industry isn't particularly strict about the "different" requirement; many additional factors also play a role in the decision of whether to make a feature film.

In the case of your submission packet, "the same, but different" means to use your research to inspire you to write similar comedy but not virtually identical comedy. In other words, use comedy pieces you see as springboards for creating your own new material but don't plagiarize those pieces. They are copyrighted, so imitate them, don't steal them.

Does it still seem strange that I'm telling you to write comedy that's similar to other comedy that's already been on national television? If so, understand that I'm only recommending that you do what professional writers on comedy/talk shows do every day. Yes, those writers try to create as much totally brand-new comedy as they can. But the fact is that dozens of similar shows have aired so many thousands of jokes and comedy pieces over the years that it's virtually impossible to come up with a new idea that's one-hundred-percent original. And it's completely impossible to stock five shows a week, week in and week out, year in and year out, with one-hundred-percent-original comedy.

That's why the staff writers on a show will often create a new comedy piece by taking an existing comedy piece and changing one element of it. If *LNWDL* did the Graphic/Prop Piece "New Valentine's Day Cards" in

February and it played well, the show will probably do "New Mother's Day Cards" in May. The same, but different.

Here are a few more examples of "the same, but different" pieces on comedy/talk shows:

- Steve Allen, the original host of the *Tonight* show, gets covered with hundreds of teabags and jumps into a big vat of hot water. Years later, Dave Letterman is lowered into a tank of water while wearing a suit covered with Alka-Seltzer tablets.

- On *LNWDL* Dave performs a Desk Piece called "Dumb Ads," which involves holding up real advertisements from magazines and pointing out misspellings and other inadvertent humor. On *LNWCO* the writers put a spin on that piece and create "Actual Items," in which Conan displays supposedly real magazine advertisements to which the staff has added jokes.

- *LNWDL* airs a Taped Joke Basket Sketch called "New Cable Channels," composed of short, scripted video clips. Years later, *LNWCO* does a similar piece called "Satellite TV," which also consists of scripted clips from fake TV channels. Then the writers on *LNWJF* translate the idea from TV to smartphone to create "New iPhone Apps."

So every comedy piece in your submission packet should be (1) like what your Target Show already does but (2) not too much like what your Target Show already does and (3) not too much like pieces that other comedy/talk shows have done. How are you supposed to write pieces that meet all three requirements?

Don't drive yourself nuts. Research your Target Show thoroughly but understand that you can't know every comedy piece that the show has ever aired. Have a good working knowledge of what similar shows have done. Resolve to keep your submission material at least as original as the new pieces that pop up on your Target Show. As I'll recommend later in this chapter, run your submission packet past a few trusted, knowledgeable friends. If they flag any material as being too familiar, remove it. Then take comfort in knowing that you've done as much to hit the "same but different" sweet spot as any writer could be reasonably expected to do.

Decide what comedy pieces to include in your submission packet.

Now you know something about the submission guidelines and unwritten rules of your Target Show. Your next step is to take that information into account and brainstorm lots of ideas for new comedy pieces for your Target Show that are "the same, but different." Then you'll have to decide which of those pieces to include in your submission packet. Remember that your overall goal is to submit material that's as close as possible to being immediately useable on your Target Show.

Sometimes a show's submission guidelines will tell you exactly what types of comedy pieces to include. If that's the case, just refer to the relevant chapters in this book and follow the steps there to create new pieces of whatever types you need.

But often the submission guidelines will be vague, asking for something like "new ideas for the show." When you're faced with that kind of open-ended task it's easy to feel overwhelmed. But don't. Simply break the task down into smaller, more manageable tasks. Here are two approaches to doing that:

Start with a category of comedy piece.

This approach takes advantage of the way I've sorted the comedy pieces on comedy/talk shows into categories. The steps are as follows:

- Pick a category of comedy piece that your research tells you your Target Show does a lot of, like Desk Pieces.

- Pick a subcategory of that type of piece, maybe one you haven't seen on the show very often, say an Art Card Piece.

- Pick a topic for that subcategory using the tips I list in the chapter covering that type of comedy piece. For example, the section on "How to Create a New Art Card Piece" in Chapter 7 might spark the idea for an Art Card Piece consisting of vanity license plates.

Start with a topic.

You can use this second approach to create a comedy piece around a topic of your choice. Here are the steps:

- Pick a topic that has lots of associations, that is, many people, places, and things that the audience would mentally connect with it. The topic could be a current event, a pop culture phenomenon, or anything else you think most viewers would be interested in. Let's say, for example, that the circus is in town. The circus has lots of associations so you decide to create a comedy piece about it.

- Generate an idea for a new comedy piece by considering all the categories of pieces that your Target Show does and picking a category that will allow you to easily make jokes about your chosen topic. Staying with the circus topic, you could create a new Prop Piece called "Circus Souvenirs." Or a new Art Card Piece called "Rejected Circus Acts." Or a Remote Camera Piece called "Pedestrian Ringmaster," where a pedestrian is recruited to lead a surprise circus parade into the studio.

I've personally used both of these approaches to create new comedy pieces for shows. Use either or both of them yourself to come up with more than enough promising ideas for new pieces for your submission.

Write jokes for each new comedy piece.

Take each idea you have for a new comedy piece and write at least a half-dozen jokes for it using the techniques I've suggested for that type of piece. To write jokes for your "Circus Souvenirs" piece, for instance, you'd consult the section on "How to Create a New Prop Piece" in Chapter 7.

As you polish the wording of each joke, use the Joke Maximizer techniques I discussed in Chapter 6. Also be sure to follow the unwritten rules of your Target Show that you learned while doing your research. Based on what you've heard the host say in the past, would he really be willing to utter the words "elephant doo-doo"?

Write up each new comedy piece idea in the proper format.

When you include an idea for a new comedy piece in your submission packet, don't script out the entire piece. That is, don't write up the piece in complete detail as if you were on the staff of the show and actually putting the piece into production. If you do, you'll be wasting your time and your readers' time. Instead, provide only enough detail about the idea to convey the premise and to demonstrate how the piece would be funny.

Specifically, submit each idea for a new comedy piece in the format recommended by every head writer I've ever talked with. This is the same format that staff writers on comedy/talk shows use to submit their own new ideas to their head writers. The format consists of these three elements for each idea you submit:

- **Title**: Give the comedy piece a good title, one that the host could use when introducing the piece on the show. A good title is descriptive, punchy, and short.

- **Premise**: State the basic concept of the piece in, at most, a couple of short paragraphs, briefly describing the participants and what they do. Also include any key production details. Your goal here is to get your readers to quickly visualize how the piece would play out on the show and to convince them that it's producible. Keep your description straightforward. Don't embellish your description with little quips, which will just distract and annoy the reader. Save your comedy for the sample jokes.

- **Sample jokes**: Provide your best three or four sample jokes for the piece, with each joke comprising at most a few sentences. The reason to include these jokes is to convince your readers that the piece would get laughs. In the case of a sketch idea, the sample jokes should be funny things that happen ("beats") in the sketch, including how the sketch ends.

The comedy professionals who will be reading your submission are used to seeing ideas presented in this stripped-down format and will be able to easily judge the quality of those ideas. For examples of how to write up various comedy piece ideas using this format, see the Generic Comedy/Talk Show Submission Packet that I've included in Appendix A.

Make sure your Monologue jokes seem fresh.

Some comedy/talk shows ask to see a page of Monologue jokes in your submission packet. The fresher those jokes seem when they're read, the more impressive they'll be. But if a show's staffers look at your submission at all, they may not look at it until weeks after it was written. So if you're submitting Monologue jokes, how do you make sure you don't get penalized because they seem dated and stale by the time they're read?

Here are three ways:

1. The Best Way—Write all your Monologue jokes within a week of when you submit your packet to the show. Doing that has the following advantages if your submission is read right away:

- Your jokes are as fresh and funny as they can be.

- You've demonstrated you can write fast and haven't labored over your jokes for months. The ability to "churn it out" is, of course, highly valued on a daily comedy/talk show.

Even if your submission packet is read months after you submit it, the fact that all the Monologue jokes were written during the same week will be apparent to your readers because of the topics you've used. You'll still have shown your writing speed and your dedication to your craft and, even though your jokes may seem dated, your readers will still be able to judge the skill that went into creating them.

2. The Second-Best Way—Every day, month after month, write one Monologue joke that you're proud of. This routine has a couple of benefits:

- It sharpens your skill at writing Monologue jokes and other topical comedy. The more you write, the better you get.

- It builds a stockpile of reasonably fresh jokes that you can draw on at a moment's notice. On any given day you can submit a page of solid Monologue jokes, none of which was written more than two weeks ago.

To discipline yourself to write one good topical joke a day you may want to commit to posting a daily joke on Twitter. That would also give you practice in keeping your jokes short because Twitter limits posts to 140 characters or less, including spaces. I'll talk more about Twitter in the "Networking" section of the next chapter.

3. The Third-Best Way—Write half of your Monologue jokes within a week of when you submit your packet and fill the rest of your quota with jokes you've written about evergreen topics over the past weeks and months. As I mentioned in Chapter 3, in the section on "Topicality of the Writing," an evergreen topic is one that stays fresh over time and therefore has a long shelf life.

Incorporating evergreen jokes into your submission packet has two benefits:

- It allows you to respond more quickly to a request for your submission packet, since you don't have to write as many brand-new Monologue jokes.

- It allows you to include jokes that you know for sure are top-quality since you've spent weeks writing them and testing them out on your friends.

The best evergreen topic for a Monologue joke is one taken from an obscure, "odd news" story. Because the news story is true, your topic will have the ring of authenticity. But because few people read the story when it first came out, your joke about it won't seem dated for months, if ever. As I mentioned in the section "The Six Characteristics of a Good Topic" in Chapter 5, you can easily find "odd news" stories online.

Trim your submission packet to the requested length.

A show's submission guidelines will almost always specify a requested page count or number of comedy pieces. Take the weakest pieces and jokes out of your packet to bring it down to the requested length. If you don't have enough strong material to get to the requested length, write more until you do.

If your Target Show doesn't specify a length for submission packets, keep yours to eight to ten pages.

Put your comedy pieces in an effective order.

You want to maximize the likelihood that your packet will get read and will impress your readers. With that in mind, order the comedy pieces in it this way:

- The piece you think is funniest should go first. That way you'll entice readers who had only planned to glance at your packet to keep reading.

- The piece you think is second-funniest should go second. You want to convince your readers that your first piece wasn't a fluke and to hook them into reading even more of your material.

- The piece you think is third-funniest should go last, so your readers will read something strong right before they have to decide what to do with your submission.

- Arrange the remaining pieces so that each page features a different category of piece. Doing that will help keep your packet surprising and stimulating.

Yes, just like a collectible car auction, your submission packet should have "a beginning that gets you excited, a middle that grips you and an end that delivers."

Make your submission packet look professional.

You can't judge a book by its cover? Sure you can, up to a point, and readers judge submission packets by their appearance all the time. You want to come across as a low-maintenance professional who will make your reader's life easier and not a time-sucking amateur who will need constant rewriting and sow chaos. So make sure your submission packet looks its best by doing these things:

- Type it in regular 12-point Courier. Other fonts and font sizes occasionally find their way into comedy/talk show scripts but regular 12-point Courier is the show business standard. So why not use that and send the message that you're a member of the club? Don't switch to smaller characters so you can cram more material onto a page. Instead, cut all unnecessary words and maybe a few of your weaker ideas and stick with regular 12-point Courier.

- Type any fully-scripted sketches (like Parody Sketches) in something close to a standard script format. I recommend using feature film format (i.e., with dialogue single-spaced) to help keep each sketch to two pages maximum. You don't have to buy a full-featured screenwriting program. Free options are available online; just search for "free screenwriting software."

- If seeing a particular photo or graphic is necessary to understand a joke, show the actual photo or graphic on the page; don't just include a link to where it appears online. You want a reader who only has a printout of your submission and no Internet access to be able to appreciate the joke. Similarly, if a joke relies on seeing a video clip, describe the important elements of the clip in your submission in addition to providing the link.

- Lay out each page so that it's easy-to-read and inviting. Don't fill your pages with long, intimidating blocks of text; build in plenty of white space. And make it obvious where one comedy piece idea ends and the next one begins.

- Number your pages in case they get separated. Your packet looks more professional that way, too.

- Double-check for typos and grammatical errors. Don't just rely on your computer to check your spelling and grammar because it won't catch every all your mistakes. For example, my computer didn't flag the superfluous word "every" I left in the previous sentence. Instead, have your packet read by a conscientious human. Again, you want your readers to think you'd behave like a professional on staff instead of a speed bump.

- Don't make any handwritten corrections. Instead, take a few minutes to print out a revised page. But it is okay to include hand-drawn illustrations if, for example, you're describing the props for a piece; that's what the staff writers on a show do.

- Don't put a cover on your submission, just a title page laid out like the one in the sample packet in Appendix A. Be sure to include your name, address, phone number, and e-mail address (or the contact information for your agent or other representative, if you have one). You want to be easy to find.

- Attach the pages together with one staple in the upper left-hand corner. That's what comedy/talk shows do to their scripts.

- If you e-mail your submission packet, send it as a PDF file so the formatting won't get accidentally messed up. Sending a PDF file as opposed to, say, a Microsoft Word document also makes it a little harder for someone to steal your material. I'll talk more about theft in the next chapter.

Appendix A contains an example of a professional-looking submission packet. It's a compilation of material I've written over the years. I'll discuss it in more detail below.

I recommend that you do everything you can to tidy up the appearance of your submission packet even before you give it to your friends for feedback. That way your friends won't have to waste their time giving you "notes" (comments) on little mistakes you'd probably have fixed eventually anyway and they can instead focus on the important stuff—the comedy content. A professional-looking packet also tells your friends that you've worked hard on it and that you'd appreciate their taking it seriously, too.

Ask some friends for feedback.

Comedy/talk shows get plenty of so-so submission packets. You want your packet to be the one that jumps out of the stack and shouts, "This material is good enough to be on tomorrow's show! You should hire this writer!"

To help you get your submission packet to that level of quality, ask a few trusted friends to read it and to give you their notes. Ideally they'll be friends who at least occasionally watch the show you plan to send your submission to. They'll also be friends who will be honest with their feedback. Nobody likes to hear their material criticized but the alternative is sending your Target Show a weak packet and having it tossed into a trash can or deleted.

If a couple of your readers give you the same note about something in your submission, or if even one person gives you a note that you agree with, edit your material to fix the problem. Reword jokes, swap in new comedy piece ideas, do whatever it takes to get your readers to agree that your packet is really strong all the way through.

Yes, putting together a submission packet is a ton of work. The good news is that you might have months to do that work. As long as none of your jokes seems dated when you send your packet out, and none of the new comedy pieces in it has coincidentally appeared on some show, nobody who reads your packet will know that it's been worked over many times by you and your friends.

If you don't have any friends whose opinions about comedy/talk shows you respect, consider joining a writers' group or starting one of your own. You can get as much feedback on your material as you want from the fellow writers in your group and not have to worry about whether you're imposing on them. Just return the favor by being generous with your own time.

So that's how to write a submission packet for a show that's already being broadcast. Now I'll talk about what to do if a show you're interested in hasn't launched yet.

WRITING A SUBMISSION PACKET FOR AN UPCOMING SHOW

If you're serious about the entertainment industry you routinely read online blogs and websites like Deadline, HollywoodReporter, and Variety. You probably also subscribe to an e-mail publication like the

ones sent out by Cynopsis Media. However you get your show business news, let's say you read that some performer has been given a
new talk show. The talk show is expected to debut in, say, one year. A
new talk show in development represents a great opportunity for writers because, at least in the beginning, all of the writing slots are wide
open. If you'd like to be considered for a comedy writing job on that
upcoming talk show, what kind of submission packet should you put
together?

To answer that question, first answer these questions:

- Is the prospective host a stand-up comedian or a comic actor?
- Do any news articles about the show mention that it will have
  comedic elements?
- Do any news articles compare the show to other shows that have
  comedy?

If the answer to all of those questions is "no" then it's unlikely that the
new show will have any comedy. That means you'd probably be wasting
your time to prepare a submission packet for it. But if the answer to any
one of those questions is "yes," the new show will probably have some
comedy and some jobs for comedy writers and you'll need to submit a
packet if you want to work there.

You prepare a submission packet for an upcoming show almost exactly
the same way you'd prepare one for a current show; I covered how to do
that in the previous section. The only difference in the process is how
you decide what comedy pieces to include in your packet.

What Should Be in a Submission Packet for an Upcoming Show

Since the show isn't being broadcast yet you have to do your research a
little differently. Follow these steps:

- **Find out as much as you can about the show.** Search online and read everything that's been written about it. If the host is on Twitter, follow him and study what he's saying. Read between the lines and try to pick up clues about the show's content.

  For example, years ago I read somewhere that the upcoming *Caroline Rhea Show* was going to have a format similar to *The Rosie O'Donnell Show*. I researched the latter and learned that Rosie played a lot of Audience Games. So when I wrote some submission material for Caroline Rhea I made sure to include ideas for new Audience Games.

- **Find out as much as you can about the host.** Based on the host's background, draw some conclusions about what kind of comedy he'll be inclined to perform. For example, a stand-up comic like Jay Leno will probably gravitate toward joke baskets like Desk Pieces. A comic actor like Jimmy Fallon will probably want to do Story Sketches and Parody Sketches.

  Before Seth Meyers took over hosting duties on *Late Night* he was quoted in *The New York Times* as saying this about the upcoming show's format: "I have to draw on my background in improvisational comedy and sketch comedy and stand-up comedy and try to find some mix of that." A quote like that from a host gives prospective writers clues about what sort of comedy pieces to submit to him.

- **Find out whether an executive producer has been hired.** You can learn this information online; the entertainment industry websites will mention it. If an executive producer is onboard, call the production company of the show, say you're a writer who's interested in submitting material, and ask to speak with the executive producer. Find out from the executive producer, or from whomever you wind up talking to, when the show will be accepting writing submissions and what type of material they'd like to see.

Taking all the above input into account, choose pieces for your submission packet that reflect what you think will be the comedy needs of the new show. If the input you've gathered isn't giving you much guidance, write a generic submission packet.

WRITING A GENERIC SUBMISSION PACKET

A generic submission packet for a comedy/talk show is one that isn't tailored to any particular show. There are several reasons to put one together:

- It can serve as a writing sample for an upcoming show when you have no idea what types of comedy the show will be doing.

- It can be customized for multiple shows and submitted in various forms as writing opportunities present themselves.

- It gives you an opportunity to hone your comedy writing skills. Like anything else, the more you do it, the better you get at it.

What Should Be in a Generic Submission Packet

You write a generic submission packet almost the same way you'd write a submission packet for a current show; see the steps earlier in this chapter. The only difference is that you aren't thinking of a specific show when you choose what comedy pieces to include; you're thinking of comedy/talk shows in general. So, to be most useful, a generic submission packet should contain the types of pieces that comedy/talk shows tend to request most often in submission packets.

Over the years I've spoken with head writers of most of the top comedy/ talk shows and found out what they'd like to see in submission packets. I've refined that information using my own experience as a head writer and come up with these recommendations for what you should include in a generic submission packet:

1. Monologue jokes; one page—That works out to about ten jokes. As I mentioned in Chapter 5, on some shows every writer is expected to contribute to the Monologue. Therefore, proving that you can write Monologue jokes demonstrates your versatility and makes you more valuable as a writer. Not only that, it gives the impression that you'd be skilled at writing the many joke basket pieces that consist of Monologue-style jokes, like Desk Pieces.

2. Desk Pieces; two pages of new ideas—Many comedy/ talk shows do Desk Pieces; in Chapter 7 I listed the reasons for that. And because so many Desk Pieces have been done before, relatively fresh Desk Piece ideas are rare. So Desk Pieces are popular but original Desk Piece ideas are hard to come by. That's why more than one head writer has told me that a great, new Desk Piece idea is "worth its weight in gold." Impress your readers by supplying two pages' worth.

3. Audience Pieces; one page of new ideas—Audience Pieces such as Audience Games are a regular feature of several late-night comedy/talk shows and are also common on daytime comedy/talk shows.

4. Parody Sketch; one fully-scripted parody—Your script should parody a TV show promo, a commercial, a movie trailer, or a PSA. Most comedy/talk shows air those types of parodies. Submitting a fully-scripted parody proves that you know how to properly structure a sketch, flesh it out with jokes, and present it

366

in a professional format. Keep your parody to a maximum of two pages to ensure that your readers get through the whole piece.

5. Semi-Scripted Field Pieces; one page of new ideas—Many comedy/talk shows send the host or a correspondent out on these pieces.

6. Other live pieces; one page of new ideas—Live pieces like Story Sketches, Live Joke Basket Sketches, Remote Camera Pieces, and Stunt Pieces often appear on comedy/talk shows.

How Long Should a Generic Submission Packet Be?

A generic submission packet should be eight to ten pages long, not including the title page. That's short enough to entice people to read it but also long enough to prove you can do the job. The material I recommend above for your generic packet will take up eight pages, assuming a two-page Parody Sketch.

What Does a Generic Submission Packet Look Like?

Unlike a spec script that you'd submit to get a job on a sitcom or a one-hour drama, a submission packet for a comedy/talk show has no standard format. But staff writers on comedy/talk shows do tend to use certain roughly-defined formats when they submit their own ideas to their head writers. So if you stick to those formats when you prepare your submission packet you'll give the impression that you'd fit right into the writing staff, which is what you want.

What are those formats? You can see them in use in Appendix A, which contains a generic submission packet I put together from material I've written. You'll notice that this sample packet consists of the same types of material I recommend that you include in your own generic packet.

Many of the jokes in the sample packet in Appendix A are dated; obviously it's impossible to keep current any topical jokes that are printed in a book. Before you submitted a packet like that to a show you would, of course, make sure all your topical jokes seem up-to-date. You'd also use the first name of your Target Show's host in your packet instead of the generic name "Host." In other words, consider my sample packet to be an example of proper formatting only and not an example of material you'd actually submit to a show.

SUMMARY

To get hired as a writer on a comedy/talk show you'll almost certainly have to present a writing sample, specifically, a comedy/talk show submission packet. How you prepare that packet depends on what type of show you plan to submit it to: a show that's currently being broadcast, an upcoming show, or some show you haven't identified yet.

Writing a Submission Packet for a Current Show

The best packet to submit to a comedy/talk show that's currently being broadcast is one you've written specifically for that show. Here's how to write a submission packet that's tailored to a current show, your Target Show:

- **Find out your Target Show's submission guidelines.** Do that by phoning the show.
- **Learn the unwritten rules of your Target Show.** Watch the show a lot and research it online. Also research other comedy/talk shows to make sure the material in your packet is as original as possible.

- **Aim to write the same, but different.** Draw on your research to write comedy that's similar to comedy you've seen on your Target Show but not virtually identical to it (and also not virtually identical to material you've seen on other shows).
- **Decide what comedy pieces to include in your submission packet.** As you brainstorm ideas, take into account what you've learned about your Target Show's submission guidelines and unwritten rules. If you're asked to come up with "new ideas for the show," break the task down by picking either a category of comedy piece or a topic to start with.
- **Write jokes for each new comedy piece.** Use the writing techniques I suggested for each category of piece in the preceding chapters. Polish your jokes using the Joke Maximizers in Chapter 6 and keep in mind the unwritten rules of your Target Show.
- **Write up each new comedy piece idea in the proper format.** That format consists of three elements: a good title, a brief statement of the premise, and three or four sample jokes. For detailed examples, consult the Generic Comedy/Talk Show Submission Packet in Appendix A.
- **Make sure your Monologue jokes seem fresh.** Write at least half your jokes within a week of when you submit your packet. The rest of your jokes can have evergreen topics.
- **Trim your submission packet to the requested length.** If no length is specified, aim for eight to ten pages.
- **Put your comedy pieces in an effective order.** Begin and end with funny pieces and mix up the categories of the pieces in the middle.
- **Make your submission packet look professional.** Neatness and proper formatting count.
- **Ask some friends for feedback.** Ideally they're familiar with your Target Show and willing to be candid with their comments.

Writing a Submission Packet for an Upcoming Show

An upcoming show may need comedy writers if any of the following is true:

- The prospective host is a stand-up comedian or a comic actor.
- Articles mention that the show will have comedic elements.
- Articles compare the show to other shows that have comedy.

If you'd like to write for the upcoming show, prepare a submission packet for it almost exactly the same way you'd prepare one for a current show. But follow these steps to decide what comedy pieces to include:

- **Find out as much as you can about the show.** Try to pick up clues online and elsewhere about the show's content.
- **Find out as much as you can about the host.** The host's background will suggest what types of comedy he's likely to be most interested in.
- **Find out whether an executive producer has been hired.** Phone him or her and ask about any guidelines for submitting a writing packet.

Choose pieces for your submission that your research tells you are likely to meet the needs of the new show.

Writing a Generic Submission Packet

A generic submission packet for a comedy/talk show is one that isn't tailored to any particular show. Write a generic packet almost exactly the same way you'd write a customized packet but include these comedy pieces:

- one page of Monologue jokes
- two pages of new ideas for Desk Pieces
- one page of new ideas for Audience Pieces
- one fully-scripted Parody Sketch (two pages maximum)

- one page of new ideas for Semi-Scripted Field Pieces
- one page of new ideas for other live pieces like Live Joke Basket Sketches

To see what a generic submission packet looks like, go to Appendix A.

Now you know how to write a comedy/talk show submission packet, whether it's for a show currently being broadcast, for a show soon to be broadcast, or for no show in particular. But once you've finished your packet, what do you do with it?

I'll talk about that next.

15

HOW TO GET A WRITING JOB ON A COMEDY/TALK SHOW

To get hired onto the writing staff of a particular comedy/talk show you'll have to accomplish three tasks:

- Write an amazing submission packet.
- Get information about a job opening.
- Get your packet read by someone who can get you hired.

The first task, to write an amazing submission packet, is what this book has been about up to this point. The only advice I'll repeat here is to make your packet as strong as you reasonably can before you try to use it to get a job. Once you send it out into the world you'll never know what path it will take and you want to favorably impress everyone who reads it along the way. The more fans you attract with your material, the more likely it is that one of those fans will hire you, if not for a comedy/talk show, then for something else.

After you've made your submission packet as bulletproof as you can, do something else before you share it with anyone but your trusted friends: register it.

REGISTER YOUR SUBMISSION PACKET

Register your packet with the Writers Guild of America (WGA). You can find out how on their website, www.wga.org.

Registration with the WGA proves that your submission existed as of the date you registered it. So if you submit your registered packet to a show and later see one of your jokes or ideas performed on that show, you have some evidence that the show may have stolen your material. But you'd want to think twice, even three times, before taking any action against that show for the following reasons:

> 1. The show almost certainly didn't steal your material. Even if you could prove the show had received your WGA-registered packet, that doesn't mean that anybody on the staff read it; many writing submissions only get glanced at, if that. What probably happened is that the staff writers independently wrote material similar to yours. As I mentioned in Chapter 14, similar jokes pop up on different comedy/talk shows fairly often because all the writers on all the shows are reading the same news and turning it into jokes the same way.

> 2. You'd need a lawyer and lawyers are expensive, probably more expensive than any damages you could ever hope to win.

> 3. You'd get the reputation of being a writer who sues TV shows and it's hard enough getting hired without having that kind of baggage.

4. The show may have actually stolen your material or your idea, in which case they might eventually decide that any writer who is worth stealing from is worth hiring.

So if you'd almost never take any action against a show that you suspect stole your material, why even bother to register your submission packet with the WGA? There are three reasons:

1. Registration does give you some small feeling of security. If that sketch you wrote is stolen and developed into a major motion picture, it's nice to know that you could, if you wanted, go after a share of the profits. This feeling that you have some protection may give you the confidence to distribute your packet more freely, which will increase the odds that somebody in a position of power will read it and fall in love with it.

2. Registration is fast, easy, and relatively inexpensive.

3. Sometimes (very infrequently) a reader will ask you for the WGA registration number of your submission; supplying the number means you've officially claimed that you wrote the material so you probably haven't stolen it yourself. But don't print the registration number on your title page; doing so would make you look like an insecure amateur.

I always register with the WGA any new work I've written before I distribute it.

In addition to registering your submission packet with the WGA you could also register it with the U.S. Copyright Office, which takes a little more time and costs a little more money. Registration with the Copyright Office conveys certain additional benefits but those benefits don't mean much in the case of low-stakes material like a comedy/talk show submission packet. That's why I personally wouldn't bother registering one of those with the Copyright Office. I would, however, take that additional step if I were circulating a spec pilot or a spec feature film. In that case I think the higher stakes would make registration with the Copyright Office worth the extra trouble.

Now that your submission packet is registered and ready-to-go I'll talk about the other two tasks standing between you and a writing job. Because getting information about a job opening is hard, I'll first discuss getting your packet read.

GET YOUR PACKET READ

Your goal is to get your packet read by somebody who can get you hired. But who exactly is that? Whose hands should you be trying to get your submission packet into?

The ideal person to read your packet is the host of the show. If the host wants to hire you, you'll have a job. But getting your submission packet to the host without first going through somebody else on the show's staff is almost impossible. So instead your goal should be to have the head writer read your submission. If he loves your material he'll almost certainly be able to convince the host and any relevant producers that you should be the next writer who is offered a job.

How do you get your material read by the head writer? Don't just send your submission to him without getting his permission first. Unsolicited material that comes into a show or production company will almost certainly never get read, for two reasons:

- Most shows have a strict policy against reading unsolicited material. That way they can easily defend themselves against writers who claim the shows stole their stuff.

- The people who work for shows are usually very busy, so reading submissions from writers they never heard of is at the bottom of their to-do list.

The best way to have your packet read by a head writer is to convince someone the head writer knows to give it to him. The head writer can't ignore your material in that case; it goes to the top of his reading pile. And how do you get someone the head writer knows to do you that favor? You network.

NETWORK

Networking means making a deliberate effort to meet people who can help you or can refer you to other people who might help you. In that respect landing a job in show business is no different from landing any other job; it's not only about how well you can do the work—although that's a big part of it—but also about who you know.

Let's say you're trying to decide which of two contractors to hire to build your swimming pool. Both contractors seem equally qualified. They both quoted you the same cost for the job. They're both licensed and insured. They've each shown you handsome photographs of other swimming pools they've constructed. But in addition, one of the contractors was recommended to you by your good friend, whose swimming pool the contractor built. Isn't the contractor who was endorsed by someone you know and trust the one you would hire?

So while you're writing, devote some energy to networking, too. Take advantage of the "six degrees of Kevin Bacon" phenomenon to meet people who can help you get your material to your Target Show's head writer. Contact anyone you know who has any connection to show business and ask them to read your submission packet. Tell them what show you're trying to get hired by. Then hope that the high quality of your writing will persuade your readers to refer you to people more closely connected to your Target Show, ideally to someone who works for the show.

Here are some ways to expand your circle of potentially valuable contacts:

Get a non-writing job on the staff of a comedy/talk show.

Obviously it's way better to be one degree away from Kevin Bacon than six degrees. And you'll only be one degree away if you photocopy scripts for Kevin Bacon every afternoon.

I was once on a show with a young man who got his internship because he was, I was told, the son of the host's Porsche dealer. As it turned out, that intern didn't get hired after his internship ended but he easily could have been because he was across the moat, past the gate, inside the castle.

If your circumstances allow it, try to land a job as a writers' assistant on a comedy/talk show. Writers' assistant positions are highly sought-after because they allow you to learn how to write for the show from the inside, to contribute informally to the comedy pieces, and to get the staff comfortable with having you around. When a writing slot opens up, if a writers' assistant has demonstrated interest and talent, he or she will be at the top of the list for consideration. I've known many writers' assistants, not just on comedy/talk shows but on sitcoms and one-hour shows, who have graduated to become writers on their shows.

I've also known writers' interns, talent department interns, talent coordinators, and segment producers who eventually joined the writing staff of the comedy/talk show they were working for. Being inside the castle grants you the ear of His Royal Highness Prince Head Writer and a huge advantage.

Get a day job in show business.

If you can't land a non-writing job on the staff of a comedy/talk show, the next best thing is to get some other kind of job in show business. Working in entertainment gives you direct access to people who can help you move toward your ultimate goal of being paid to write. Of course, the contacts you make aren't enough by themselves; you still need terrific writing samples to show them.

My first job in show business was solidly in the "business" camp: I was a financial analyst for Columbia Pictures. One of the reasons I took the job was to get closer to realizing my dream of being a television writer. By day I wore a suit and programmed spreadsheets but at night I wrote a spec episode of *Hart to Hart*, a light, one-hour mystery show I enjoyed. Coincidentally, *Hart to Hart* was produced by Columbia Pictures Television. As a Columbia insider I was able to make a phone call and get somebody at the studio to read my script.

My *Hart to Hart* script never went anywhere because I had broken two unwritten rules: (1) I had submitted my spec episode to the show it was written for, with the result that my reader spotted a flaw that might have sailed past someone who wasn't as close to the show, the flaw being that (2) I had made the murderer in my story a friend of the Harts, not realizing that the Harts would never, even unknowingly, be friends with a killer.

My spec script ended up serving a purpose, though. I mailed it to a few agents who had indicated to the Writers' Guild that they would accept unsolicited submissions and one of them actually responded with some positive comments about the writing. That feedback helped give me the confidence to leave the corporate world and try writing professionally when I got my big break. More on that later in this chapter.

How do you get a day job in show business or one of the non-writing jobs on a comedy/talk show that I mentioned above? The same way you get any other job: by networking and by exploring online. Search on "entertainment jobs" and you'll find lots of relevant websites. In addition, almost every entertainment company has its own career opportunities webpage. Comb those sites regularly for positions you're qualified for that are as close to the production of TV shows as you can get. If you're hired into one of those positions you might eventually be able to grab the attention of a writer who works on a show you like.

For example, one time when I was writing for the one-hour show *Monk* the staff saw a clever promo for the series that had been written by someone in USA Network's promotion department. The promo impressed our executive producer so much that he invited its writer to pitch story ideas for *Monk*. If the executive producer had liked one of those ideas, that promo writer would have gotten a freelance script assignment and a chance at a TV series writing career.

Participate in the comedy community.

Even if you're not in a position to get some kind of show business job you can still participate in the comedy community and do the following:
- sharpen your writing skills
- make potentially valuable contacts
- learn about possible job openings
- gain credibility in the eyes of people who can hire you to write
- have fun and remind yourself why you want to write comedy at all

Here are some examples of how you can participate in the comedy community:

- Take classes in writing comedy and in performing comedy—improv, sketch, or stand-up.

- Go to a comedy club and watch one of your favorite comics perform. After the show, introduce yourself to the comic as a fan and a writer. Ask the comic for advice on breaking into the business. After the comic gets to know you a little, ask whether she'd be willing to read some of your material. If she says yes, send her a page of jokes you think she might like; if she buys jokes from freelancers maybe she'll buy one of yours. If she does buy a joke, maybe she'll buy more and eventually be willing to recommend you to TV producers she knows. Many of Jay Leno's long-time writers on the *Tonight* show got their start in television by writing jokes for Jay's stand-up act before he got the late-night hosting job.

- Write and sell comedy in a medium other than television. For example, if you do an Internet search on "comedy prep services" you'll find companies that supply radio shows with jokes, parodies, and other comedy material; some of those companies buy from freelancers. *MAD Magazine* also accepts freelance material, as do comedy websites like CollegeHumor and Cracked; their submission guidelines are on their websites.

- Write and produce comedy videos and post them online, either on a website like YouTube, or Funny or Die, or on your own website. A comedy video, especially one that attracts a lot of views, can work together with your writing submission to get you in the door at comedy/talk shows. In fact, a funny series of Internet videos can even spawn a TV series, as the web series Annoying Orange did on Cartoon Network.

- Post jokes on Twitter on a regular basis. Tweeting jokes can expose your material to some of the many comedy professionals who use the service and could lead to your making a valuable contact. Writers have even parlayed their work on Twitter into job offers; as a (very rare) example, one writer's Twitter feed spawned the TV sitcom "$#*! My Dad Says."

- Write and publicize a comedy book or blog. A well-written book or blog can attract attention and help solidify your credentials as a comedy professional. Writers of books like "The Last Girlfriend on Earth" and Tumblr blogs like "Hollywood Assistants" have gotten TV pilot deals off them.

To recap, the best way to get your submission packet into the hands of a head writer on a show is to get someone he trusts to hand it to him. And the best way to make that happen is by networking as you expand your range of show business and comedy contacts.

But if networking doesn't seem to be getting you anywhere you could always try the direct approach. Sending a query letter to a head writer probably wouldn't work; letters and e-mails are too easy to ignore. Instead, do something that lets you showcase your winning personality: cold-call.

COLD-CALL

Cold-calling is phoning somebody you haven't been introduced to. It's equivalent to being a telemarketer except you're not selling something like chimney cleaning services; you're selling your submission packet.

Nobody likes to get calls from telemarketers. But the head writers of comedy/talk shows will often talk to writers who cold-call them for several reasons:

- One of a head writer's jobs is to help find writers who can make his life easier and make the show better.

- Taking a phone call is relatively easy compared with responding to a query letter or to a query e-mail.

- Most comedy/talk shows are open to hiring writers who don't have an agent. The head writers know that and understand that cold-calling is sometimes the only option available to those writers.

How to Cold-Call a Comedy/Talk Show

Your goal is to get someone on the writing staff of your Target Show, ideally the head writer, to invite you to send him your submission packet. To make that happen, follow these steps:

1. Call the production offices of your Target Show and ask to speak to the head writer. For tips on how to do this, see the section in the previous chapter on how to "Find out your Target Show's submission guidelines." If you get put through to the head writer, great. If not, ask to be connected with someone on the writing staff with whom you can talk about making a submission. Note that on some shows a particular writer is in charge of assembling the Monologue. So if you're interested in writing specifically for the Monologue, ask who the Monologue coordinator is and whether you could speak with him.

2. Pitch yourself to whoever agrees to talk with you. Your goal, again, is to persuade that person to invite you to submit your packet. To that end, do this:

- Identify yourself and make sure you know who you're talking to; you'll want to be able to follow up with that person later.

- Tell the person you're a huge fan of the show and you'd love to send him a writing submission.

- Reassure the person that you're a writer. In a charming, confident manner, briefly describe some credential you have that supports that claim. It doesn't have to be much of a credential. If you're participating in the comedy community, as I suggested above, you'll have something to say. Maybe you've sold a radio commercial parody or you perform in a sketch group. All you're trying to do now is pique your listener's interest and convey the impression that reading your submission wouldn't be a waste of time.

- Tell the person that you have a submission packet that's ready-to-go and ask if you can send it to him. If he says no, thank him for his time and go back to networking. But chances are that if you've gotten this far he'll say yes. In that case, proceed to the next step.

3. Ask the person, your contact, for the show's release form. Because you're not submitting your material through a representative like an agent you'll have to sign a release. A signed release tells the show's lawyers that you won't accuse the show of stealing your material.

4. Ask your contact how he'd like to get your submission packet, via e-mail or via the U.S. Postal Service. If he asks for it by e-mail, volunteer to send it by USPS also and confirm his mailing address. My feeling is that it's easier to overlook or ignore an e-mail than a printed copy, so why not put a printed copy in his hands?

5. Send your submission packet, with the signed release form, to your contact right away. Also include a brief cover letter or e-mail reminding him in a friendly way of your phone conversation. That way he'll remember that he invited you to submit.

It's important to send over your submission packet immediately so your contact doesn't forget who you are and feel free to toss your packet in the trash when it finally shows up at his office. That's why your material has to be perfected and ready for public consumption before you start marketing it.

One time I was head writer on a comedy/talk show and the writers' assistant asked me if I was willing to talk with an aspiring writer who was on the phone—a cold-caller. I had a minute so I said sure. The writer said she was a big fan of the show's host and would love to join the staff. Her credentials seemed marginal but I invited her to send in a writing sample. She did some verbal tap-dancing and it soon became clear that she didn't have a writing sample. I explained that we couldn't even consider hiring a writer without one and told her I'd be happy to read hers when it was ready. I gave her some suggestions about what kind of material to put together and the call came to a cordial end. I never heard from her again. She blew an opportunity to be considered for a staff writing job because she wasn't prepared when the opportunity presented itself.

6. Follow up with a phone call to your contact in a couple of weeks. Tell him you're just calling to make sure he got your submission packet, or leave him a message to that effect. Then wait a few more weeks. If he hasn't contacted you by then, follow up with one more phone call or message.

7. If your contact doesn't get back to you, assume he's not interested. Don't try to reach him again. Turn your attention to other shows.

There's a small possibility that, even after a couple of months have passed, your contact still hasn't read your submission. Maybe it's still sitting in its unopened envelope in a stack on his credenza, possibly because there are currently no openings on the writing staff. But if you follow up with him more than twice you risk annoying and alienating him. It's better to leave him alone and hope that one day when he's motivated he'll take a look at your submission packet, get hooked, read it all the way through, and want to meet you.

GET AN AGENT IF YOU'RE PREPARED FOR ONE

As I mentioned, many writers on comedy/talk shows (including me) landed those jobs without an agent. And even if you have an agent you'll still have to network to advance your career. You'll still have to market yourself; an agent can't and won't do everything. Plus, you'll have to pay your agent 10% of whatever gross (i.e., before-tax) compensation you earn while that agent is representing you.

But an agent will help you find work. And most writing positions in television get filled by writers who have agents. There are a few reasons for that:

- Having an agent gives you credibility. It tells potential employers that at least one show business professional believes that you deserve to be paid to write.

- Agents have more information about job opportunities for writers than you could ever gather by yourself. In particular, agents tend to know when comedy/talk shows are hiring. This information is hard for writers without agents to find out; I'll talk more about this below in the section "Get Information about a Job Opening."

- Agents will usually make sure their clients' writing packets are good enough before they submit them to potential employers. They don't want to get a reputation for sending out weak material.

So you may not need an agent right now. Or you may not be prepared yet to go after an agent. But if you are prepared and you seriously want to be a professional television writer, try to get an agent because you'll need one eventually.

I worked in my first TV writing job, on the staff of *LNWDL*, for six years without an agent. It was only when I decided to leave the show, and New York, for the unfamiliar turf of Los Angeles that I got an agent. I needed professional help to get established on the "Left Coast," where I didn't have many contacts of my own.

How to Get an Agent

How to get an agent is beyond the scope of this book but I'll give you some tips because the question comes up so often among writers.

The most surefire way to get an agent is to prove you can make money for her immediately by approaching her with a job offer already in hand. That is, first get a job offer yourself using the methods described earlier in this chapter. Then call around to find an agent who will negotiate the deal for that job and also agree to continue to represent you. Yes, you'd have to pay your new agent ten percent of your gross compensation from that job for basically doing nothing; your first writing job would probably be for the Writers Guild minimum salary so your new agent would have nothing to negotiate. But at least now you'd have an agent to help you get your next job.

The other ways to land an agent are similar to the ways you might land a writing job by yourself, which I covered above. Here's what you should do:

1. Prepare excellent writing samples. In addition to your comedy/talk show submission packet you'll also need a couple of spec scripts. The most useful spec scripts are probably an original pilot and an episode of a well-regarded show that's currently on the air and will probably stay on the air for another season or two. Having that variety of solid writing samples will help convince agents that you're talented, versatile, and highly motivated, that is, a writing factory who would consistently turn out a wide range of material that the agent could use to sell your services.

2. Network. Your goal is to get somebody who has an agent, or a relationship with an agent, to recommend you to her. Once you've been introduced to an agent and been invited to send over your writing samples, send them over immediately.

You could also try to find someone who will recommend you to a manager or to an entertainment lawyer. It's a little easier to get a manager or lawyer to represent you than an agent. You'd have to pay 5 to 10% of your gross compensation to each of those industry insiders as well but either one of them could help you land both an agent and a job.

3. If networking isn't productive, try cold-calling. Agents are highly accustomed to dealing with people on the phone, which is why written queries (letters and e-mails) are likely to be less effective with them. Don't just cold-call agents randomly, though. Target some agents who represent the type of writer you want to be. Here's how to assemble a list of them:

- Get the names of writers who work on the shows you'd like to work on. You can find their names online or in the shows' credits.

- Go to the Writers Guild website (www.wga.org), open up the "if you're an employer" drop-down menu, and click on "find a writer."

- Look up your list of writers and find out which agents, if any, represent them.

- Get the contact information for those agents from the Writers Guild website; an "agency list" of Writers Guild signatory agencies is accessible via the drop-down menu "writer's resources."

Once you've put together a list of your target agents, cold-call them using the techniques I covered in the previous section. If you can't get through to an agent, pitch yourself to the agent's assistant instead. As you might expect, your goal is to get the agent or her assistant to invite you to send them your writing samples.

If someone at the agency agrees to read your material, ask if they'd prefer snail-mailed hard copies or e-mailed PDF files. Send your material to them immediately, along with a brief cover letter and the release they'll require you to sign.

It's a numbers game, so try to get as many agents as possible to agree to read your writing samples. If you're striking out at the larger agencies, try smaller ones.

Wait about two weeks before calling your agency contact "to be sure they got the material." Then follow up with another phone call in a few more weeks. If you don't get a response, move on to other agents on your list.

And if an agent does offer to represent you, don't play hard to get. Just say yes.

GET INFORMATION ABOUT A JOB OPENING

Most hiring of writers for prime-time TV shows—sitcoms and so on—tends to take place in the spring. That's when the major networks announce what new shows they're airing in the fall. But there's no comparable hiring season for writers on comedy/talk shows, which are in production year-round. Writing slots on those shows open up almost at random as writers quit or get fired. A writing staff might even be expanded by a position or two if the studio and network decide to spend more money on the show.

Obviously you'll never get hired onto a show if there's no open slot for a writer, even if everybody on the staff loves your submission. So how do you know when your Target Show is hiring? Put another way, how do you know the best time to submit your packet?

There are three ways that someone who doesn't already work on a comedy/talk show can find out when that show is hiring writers:

1. You get hiring information from someone who works on the show. Maybe you cold-call the show and someone you chat with mentions an opening. Or maybe someone who works on the show tells somebody else, who tells you. Participate in the comedy community, as I recommended in the "Network" section above, and you'll be in a better position to pick up hiring news you can use.

> A tip from an insider is how I found out about upcoming openings on the writing staff of *LNWDL*. I knew the show's head writer, Jim Downey, from college; we were on the *Harvard Lampoon* together. Jim let me know that several writers were about to leave the show and invited me to submit a packet. I got hired and that was the start of my television writing career.

2. You get hiring information from your agent, manager, or lawyer. Either that or you get tipped off by a helpful friend who has an agent, manager, or lawyer.

3. You know that the show is still in development. If the show won't be on the air for at least six months or so it probably doesn't have a writing staff yet, which means it'll be hiring soon. For tips on how to gather information about upcoming shows see "Writing a Submission Packet for an Upcoming Show" in the previous chapter.

So if it seems as though it's hard to find out when your Target Show has open writing slots, it is. Learn whatever you can about when the show is hiring and time your submission accordingly. Otherwise, just submit your packet when it's ready and take your chances with the timing.

Even if a show isn't actively looking for a new writer when your packet lands on the head writer's desk, if the packet is fantastic it won't get tossed away. It'll most likely be at the top of the stack when somebody tells the head writer that the show is hiring. So, again, do what you can about the timing of your submission but focus mainly on what you can control: putting together a first-rate packet and getting it read by someone who can get you hired.

INTERVIEWING TIPS

Let's say you do get asked in to meet a head writer or another decision maker on a show. How do you prepare for the meeting? Should you write some jokes for the occasion? What do you wear?

Relax. If a head writer is going to devote time to meeting you it almost always means that he has read your material and really likes it. It means that he's already convinced that you could share his writing burden and make his job easier. You're very close to getting a job offer. The interview is just to make sure that he and the rest of the staff wouldn't mind spending up to twelve hours a day with you.

That means you don't have to go out of your way to be funny in the meeting. Don't prepare special material. Don't do a comedy routine or perform a kooky character. Just be casually witty, good-natured, and enthusiastic. Say some nice things about the writing on the show, maybe about a particular comedy piece that you liked recently. Tell your interviewer that you'd love to work on the show. You don't have to prove you're talented; your submission has already done that. You just have to demonstrate that you'd fit comfortably into the staff and not drive everybody nuts.

Be well-groomed. Dress casually, as if you were already on a television writing staff. What does that mean? Do a Google Images search on "television writers room" and see for yourself. Men can't go wrong with jeans, sneakers, and a long-sleeved, collared shirt; women should wear the equivalent. The idea is to look as though you already work there.

Dave Letterman liked the packet I had submitted to my friend, the head writer of *LNWDL*. When I got the call that Dave wanted to meet me I was working in a job that required a business suit. I was afraid that if I showed up in Dave's office dressed like that he wouldn't think I could ever be funny because I didn't look like a comedy writer. So the afternoon of my meeting I told my coworkers I was going out to lunch. I walked down to the *LNWDL* production offices about six blocks away, ducked into an empty room, and changed out of my pinstriped suit, wingtips, and silk tie into a pair of corduroys, sneakers, and a polo shirt I had brought in a gym bag. It was the first and last time I ever dressed down for a job interview.

SUMMARY

You'll have to do three things to get hired onto the writing staff of a particular comedy/talk show:

- Write an amazing submission packet.
- Get information about a job opening.
- Get your packet read by someone who can get you hired.

Register your packet with the Writers Guild of America before you give it to anyone but your trusted friends. Network to try to get your packet into the hands of somebody who can get you hired, ideally a head writer. Increase the odds that your networking will succeed by doing one or more of the following:

- Get a non-writing job on the staff of a comedy/talk show.
- Get a day job in show business.
- Participate in the comedy community.

If networking isn't producing results, try cold-calling your Target Show. Your goal is to get the head writer or another staff member to invite you to submit your packet.

If you're willing to do the necessary preparation, try to get an agent. You'll have to write excellent samples (including a couple of spec scripts), network, and possibly cold-call.

It's hard to know when a comedy/talk show has an open writing slot. So find out what you can about when your Target Show is hiring and time your submission accordingly. Otherwise, just submit your packet when it's ready and hope you get lucky with the timing.

A FEW PARTING WORDS

If you do get a job writing for a comedy/talk show, congratulations! The lessons you learned in this book will help you contribute from your very first day. They'll also help you leverage your talent and establish yourself as a key member of the writing staff. Then you can forge ahead beyond this book and blaze some exciting trails of your own through the wilds of the comedy/talk show genre. I can't wait to see where those trails go.

Have fun and keep writing!

Appendix A

A GENERIC COMEDY/TALK SHOW SUBMISSION PACKET

COMEDY/TALK SHOW WRITING SAMPLE

by

Joe Toplyn

Street Address
City, State, Zip Code
Phone Number
E-Mail Address

MONOLOGUE JOKES

Google is launching a network of high-altitude, Wi-Fi Internet balloons. Google says they're concerned that many remote areas of the world don't have access to fast, affordable lack of privacy.

Last weekend two Detroit police officers were arrested for armed robbery. City officials were shocked to find out there was still something in Detroit worth stealing.

On its opening weekend "The Lone Ranger" only sold about a million dollars' worth of tickets in all of South Korea. North Korea's Kim Jong-un is now threatening to retaliate with an even bigger bomb.

According to "USA Today," police departments around the country are thinking about raising money by selling advertising space on their patrol cars. So now the cars are going to read, "To protect and serve...delicious Sara Lee Coffee Cake."

In Pennsylvania a woman was arrested for walking through a Walmart naked. Customers were outraged that she wasn't wearing a bathrobe like they were.

A food scientist in Oregon has developed a disinfectant made from wine. So, ladies, be careful...if a guy invites you back to his apartment for a glass of chardonnay, he may just want you to clean his bathroom.

Tomorrow is Mickey Mouse's eighty-fifth birthday. To celebrate, Disneyland is lowering the price of a pair of Mickey Mouse Ears to only eighty-five dollars.

Michelangelo's statue of David is being washed for the first time since 1873. Isn't that just like a man? You think he's perfect, then it turns out he hasn't had a bath in over a hundred years.

An English craftsman just made a diamond iPhone worth fifteen million dollars. It's the perfect gift for someone who has everything except a story about how they were robbed.

It's the day after the Fourth of July and drivers in New York City are politer than usual. That's because some of them accidentally blew off their middle fingers.

PRODUCT IMPROVEMENTS (Desk Piece)

Host holds up real products like grocery items, sporting goods, and household appliances. To each product we've affixed a brightly colored, starburst-type sticker with the joke.

WEBSTER'S NEW COLLEGIATE DICTIONARY: "Kim Kardashian edition! No words over two syllables!"

SMUCKER'S GRAPE JELLY: "Now with 50% more Smuck!"

EX-LAX LAXATIVE: "Now in Fashion-Model Strength."

ASK DINGLE (Desk Piece)

Host demonstrates a new search engine that's better than Bing and Google; it's called Dingle. Host "types" questions, which appear on-screen. Then the possible answers, Dingle's search results, appear on-screen one at a time as Host reads them out loud. The search result could also be a photo or a short video clip.

1. Question: What would Donald Trump do first if he were elected President?

Answers: Review the budget...Restructure the Executive Branch...Rename his ride "Hair Force One." [HOST CLICKS ON THE LINK "HAIR FORCE ONE" TO DISPLAY A DOCTORED PHOTO OF AIR FORCE ONE WEARING TRUMP HAIR ON THE FRONT.]

2. Question: Physicists just discovered a new subatomic particle. What cosmic mystery do they hope it will explain?

Answer: [WE SEE A PHOTO OF SNOOKI, PREGNANT.]

3. Question: Russia plans to build a nuclear power plant that floats. What are experts afraid might happen as a result?

Answers: A catastrophic meltdown...a terrorist hijacking...a new Michael Bay movie.

STRIP TRIVIA (Audience Game)

Host is in the audience along with a celebrity guest who is wearing six tee shirts, one over the other. On the top tee shirt is printed a pop-culture trivia category like movies.

Host asks an audience member a trivia question about the movies. If the audience member answers correctly, the celebrity removes the tee shirt to stripper music. This reveals the next tee shirt, on which is printed another trivia category like music.

The contestant answers questions in this way until the last tee shirt is exposed. Printed on it is her prize, a show tee shirt.

SIT ON IT (Audience Game)

Three contestants stand next to seven chairs. On each chair seat, covered with a cloth, is a different item. Host has the contestants play a variation of musical chairs. Each time the music stops—"Sittin' on the Dock of the Bay"—the contestants race to find a specified item by feel using only their butts.

If a contestant finds the item, that item is removed. If a contestant guesses incorrectly, she has to miss the next round. The contestant who finds the most items gets to keep them all.

Possible items to identify: a hammer, a banana, a pine cone, a bobble head doll of Sigmund Freud, a nutcracker, a toothbrush, an autographed photo of Meryl Streep, a Hostess Twinkie.

STUDIO ISLAND (Desk Piece with Audience)

The camera shows a series of unsuspecting audience members. We see their first names and (fake) occupations as Host recaps what they've supposedly been up to on a studio audience reality show.

[A CONSERVATIVE-LOOKING GUY] "Jim is an assistant to New Jersey Governor Chris Christie. Jim narrowly avoided being voted out of the studio when Governor Christie ate the ballot box."

[AN ATTRACTIVE WOMAN] "Sarah is a bartender. Sarah won the ice tea drinking competition but then refused to give up her seat to go to the bathroom. (beat) Can we get a mop over there?"

[AN ATHLETIC GUY] "Todd is a member of the U.S. Olympic track and field team. Todd alienated many women in the studio when he invited them to pole vault in his pants."

HEIMLICH'S RESTAURANT (Commercial Parody)

                    HOST
          New York City has a lot of theme
          restaurants. Here's a new one.

VIDEOTAPE PLAYBACK:

EXT. UPSCALE RESTAURANT - NIGHT

Host and his date (attractive, 30s) enter through front door.

                    ANNOUNCER (VO)
          Tired of the same old dining
          experience? Looking for a taste of
          excitement? Maneuver your way over
          to Heimlich's, where the world-
          famous poster comes to life.

Sign next to front door reads: Heimlich's.

INT. UPSCALE RESTAURANT - NIGHT

Host and his date sit at a table. They admire the food that a
dapper waiter serves them: chunks of meat and cheese, small
sausages, pieces of melon, and other throat-sized items.

                    ANNOUNCER (VO)
          At Heimlich's, all of our mouth-
          watering and windpipe-plugging
          specialties are spiced with a
          thrilling reminder of your own
          mortality.

We see a plate of baby carrots, then chicken nuggets.

                    ANNOUNCER (VO)
          Heimlich's has trachea-sized
          appetizers and entrees for small
          throats...large throats...and even
          the most experienced prostitute.

We see a plate holding a large cucumber.

                    ANNOUNCER (VO)
          Pop on over to Heimlich's for a date
          you'll never forget...

Host pops cork out of champagne bottle, then goes to his choking date and Heimlichs her, popping a meatball out of her mouth.

> ANNOUNCER (VO)
> ...because your life will flash
> before your eyes. At Heimlich's, we
> know that nothing is more romantic .
> than cheating...the Reaper.

Host's Heimlich maneuver turns into caressing his adoring date.

> ANNOUNCER (VO)
> Heimlich's is perfect for
> celebrating birthdays...

A semi-chewed chunk of veal plops onto a birthday cake.

> ANNOUNCER (VO)
> ...celebrating engagements...

A diamond ring lands in a champagne glass.

> ANNOUNCER (VO)
> ...and even celebrating that large
> insurance policy your husband just
> took out naming you as beneficiary.

A gorgeous woman (30s) holds out a huge hunk of steak on a fork to a worshipful man (70s, distinguished) who has his mouth open.

Host tries to catch in his mouth hunks of bread his date playfully tosses at him. Other gobs of food fly in and hit them.

> ANNOUNCER (VO)
> So go toward the light...to
> Heimlich's. Our food will take your
> breath away.

SUPER TITLE: Heimlich's. Our food will take your breath away.

> ANNOUNCER (VO)
> (quickly)
> All checks must be paid in advance.

A wad of food splats onto the camera lens.

END OF VIDEOTAPE PLAYBACK

PAWN GUY (Live Sketch in Studio)

A (fake) audience member, call him Pawn Guy, keeps trying to sell stuff to Host. Host says that the guy must be confusing this show with "Pawn Stars." Pawn Guy tries to sell Host an antique Civil War sword. Host refuses to play along and tries to continue with the show.

Then Pawn Guy puts on a fake mustache and claims to be a Civil War buff who would pay a ton of money for an antique Civil War sword. Host says that Pawn Guy is just trying to trick him into buying Pawn Guy's sword.

Next Pawn Guy offers to sell Host some celebrity memorabilia: Host's own leather chaps that Pawn Guy stole from Host's dressing room. Host is annoyed at this violation of his privacy.

Finally Host agrees to buy something—a ball gag. Pawn Guy happens to have one. Host wants to be sure it works so he has Pawn Guy gag himself. Host says he'll pay Pawn Guy after the show if the gag holds up until then. Pawn Guy nods in agreement and sits quietly.

STAFF'S GOT TALENT (Live Sketch in Studio)

Host says that some of the show's staff members are planning to send in audition tapes to "America's Got Talent." The staff members demonstrate their talents.

Staffer #1 says that he can sing notes so high that they're beyond the range of human hearing. Staffer #1 sings higher and higher notes until they become inaudible. Lots of (fake) bats fly around, crashing into the scenery, squeaking and disoriented.

Staffer #2, with one trouser leg rolled up above his knee, holds a chain saw. Staffer #2 says that he can drop nineteen pounds in ten seconds. Host asks to see that. Staffer #2 sets the chain saw down on a nearby scale and announces how much the saw weighs: nineteen pounds.

Staffer #3, showing three tennis balls, says that he can juggle three balls. Staffer #3 tosses just two of the tennis balls from hand to hand as he shakes his hips. Host does the math and comments on Staffer #3's apparent anatomical quirk.

CRUISIN' FOR MRS. CRUISE (Field Piece)

Host says it looks like Tom Cruise will be shopping for Wife Number Four soon. To help Tom out, Host will audition some potential wives for him—some pedestrians.

Host has a tall woman crouch and walk next to a life-sized photo of 5'7" Tom, to make sure they'd look good in·photos together.

Host asks a woman to prove she loves Tom by jumping, "Oprah"-style, on a sofa placed on the sidewalk.

Host asks a woman to try on all of the wedding jewelry that Tom would be giving her: a diamond ring...a diamond tiara...and a diamond ankle bracelet GPS tracker.

SPIT-TAKE SUPERSTAR (Field Piece)

Host wants to find someone who can add entertainment value to the show by doing spit-takes. Host goes out and auditions pedestrians. Host hands each pedestrian a cup of water, reads a short joke from one of his past monologues, and comments on the pedestrian's spit-take performance.

Host tries to teach the technique to a tourist who can barely speak English. Host asks a lawyer if spit-takes on the sidewalk, unlike actual spitting, are legal. Host has two pedestrians compete in a spit-take contest for distance.

Host picks the winning pedestrian. Host brings him into the studio, live, to do spit-takes during the rest of the show.

GETTING LUCKY (Field Piece)

Host visits various real Manhattan businesses with "Lucky" in their names. (There are plenty of these.) He finds out how lucky the employees are in their sex lives. Also:

At Lucky Cleaners, Host asks an employee which dry-cleaned outfit on the garment conveyor a guy should wear to get lucky.

At Lucky Food Market, Host asks a clerk what kind of food a guy should feed a woman to get lucky. Has it worked for the clerk?

At Lucky Wang (a clothing store), Host asks a male employee if he has a lucky wang. How often does his wang get lucky?

SHOCKING CELEBRITY SECRETS (Desk Piece)

For each celebrity, Host reads a shocking secret as he holds up
a doctored photo depicting the secret.

KRISTEN STEWART: "One time, when she tried to change her
expression, a chunk broke off her face." [PHOTO SHOWS KRISTEN
WITH A CHUNK OF SKIN OFF HER FACE, REVEALING SKULL UNDERNEATH.]

ALEC BALDWIN: "As a wedding present he gave his wife a fur coat
made entirely of his own chest hair." [PHOTO SHOWS FULLY DRESSED
ALEC PUTTING DARK FUR COAT ON HIS WIFE.]

ARNOLD SCHWARZENEGGER: "He's actually two little people, named
'Schwarz' and 'Egger'." [PHOTO SHOWS ARNOLD HOLDING HIS TRENCH
COAT OPEN, REVEALING HE'S ONE LITTLE PERSON STANDING ON ANOTHER
LITTLE PERSON'S SHOULDERS.]

MEL GIBSON: "He got so worked up about this photograph that he
punched one of our stagehands in the face." [PHOTO SHOWING MEL'S
ANGRY FACE IS SPLATTERED WITH BLOOD AND HAS A HUMAN TOOTH
STICKING TO IT.]

TRAVEL SOUVENIRS (Desk Piece)

Host displays a selection of fake travel souvenirs.

"Souvenir stands at the base of Mount Rushmore will let you
scoop up a bucket of this for only forty dollars. They call it
LINCOLN'S DANDRUFF." [HOST SHOWS A TRANSPARENT PAIL OF ORDINARY
ROCKS CRUDELY LABELED "LINCOLN'S DANDRUFF."]

"Here's the perfect souvenir of your trip to Alaska, lovingly
handcrafted by Eskimos. It's a PEZ BLUBBER DISPENSER." [HOST
SHOWS AN OVERSIZED PEZ DISPENSER WITH THE HEAD OF A WHALE. HE
TIPS THE HEAD BACK, TAKES OUT A CUBE OF BLUBBER, AND EATS IT.]

"You'll want this souvenir if you go to the Winter Olympics in
Sochi, Russia. It's a SNOW GLOBE FILLED WITH AUTHENTIC DRUG TEST
URINE." [HOST SHOWS A SNOW GLOBE. INSIDE ARE THE OLYMPIC RINGS
LOGO AND "SOCHI 2014." IT'S FILLED WITH A CLOUDY YELLOW LIQUID.]

Appendix B

JAY VS. DAVE: TURNING THE TIDE OF THE LATE-NIGHT WAR

I N AUGUST 1993 *Late Show with David Letterman* debuted on CBS. For the first time Dave was competing head-to-head with Jay Leno, host of *The Tonight Show with Jay Leno* on NBC. Dave's domination was immediate and decisive. As Bill Carter writes in his excellent book *The Late Shift*, "David Letterman's show became the talk of the television industry before the end of his first week on the air. It wasn't just that he was drawing monster ratings; it was the show itself." Late-night television had a new king and for the first time in decades he wasn't sitting behind the desk at the *Tonight* show.

But only two years later the *Tonight* show was beating *Late Show* in the ratings every single week. Jay's show was also earning critical respect; it won the 1995 Primetime Emmy Award for Outstanding Variety, Music or Comedy Series.

What happened?

Here's my insider's perspective on one of the biggest turnarounds in television history.

My first job in television was writing for *Late Night with David Letterman*, the NBC show that Dave hosted at 12:30 a.m. before he relocated to CBS. Most of what I learned about comedy writing for late-night television—most of the contents of this book—I learned while working for Dave. The job was one of the best I've ever had and led to my winning four Emmy awards. But after six years I wanted to try something different. So in February 1990 I left *Late Night* and New York and moved with my family to Los Angeles.

My main goal was to write sitcoms. I wanted to create characters and tell stories, to take what I knew about short-form comedy and apply it to a larger canvas. But I found out that even though the sitcom canvas was larger, it tore easily; a couple of the sitcoms I wrote for only lasted a few episodes. I was drawn to the idea of returning to late night and putting everything I had learned on *Late Night* to work again.

That's why in April 1993 I accepted an offer to become co-head writer of the upcoming late-night comedy/talk show *The Chevy Chase Show*. Late-night television was undergoing an upheaval and I wanted to be part of the action. Jay had taken over the *Tonight* show on May 25, 1992. He had the 11:35 p.m. comedy/talk show arena all to himself for over a year until Dave launched his new *Late Show* on August 30, 1993. A week later, on September 7, 1993, *The Chevy Chase Show* premiered. Up until the taping that day, in the newly-christened Chevy Chase Theater on Sunset Boulevard, I thought we had a real chance against the biggest heavyweights in late night. Working for Dave had spoiled me. He had made it all look too easy.

The Chevy Chase Show was only on the air for five weeks. Even so, about nine years later, *TV Guide* would place it at #16 on its list of "Worst TV

Shows of All Time." Word spread at Chevy's fiftieth birthday party at the Beverly Hilton hotel that the show had been cancelled. I wasn't surprised but I was frustrated. Working in late night again, experimenting, helping to create something new, had been fun. I felt as though I had unfinished business.

So when Jay Leno contacted me his timing was perfect. I was packing up my office at the Chevy Chase Theater and tossing the script for that day's show in the trash when Jay called and asked if I'd be interested in joining the *Tonight* show. I liked Jay; I had met him briefly a few times when he had been a guest on *Late Night*. And I admired his talent and work ethic. The invitation flattered and intrigued me. I'd be on the front lines of the Late-Night War again, this time serving under a seasoned general.

It was October 1993, and Dave and *Late Show* had been clobbering Jay and the *Tonight* show in the ratings for about two months. Bill Carter, in *The Late Shift*, deftly sums up the public's perception of the late-night matchup this way: "Letterman was cool; Leno was square. Dave was hot; Jay was not. Letterman and CBS were winning; Leno and NBC were losing." The legendary *Tonight* show franchise was getting pounded into the dirt and hundreds of millions of dollars were at stake.

I started work on the *Tonight* show in November 1993, a few weeks after *The Chevy Chase Show* had crashed and burned. Jay had never had a formal head writer before but a veteran member of his writing staff, Joe Medeiros, and I became co-head writers. I understood that appointing head writers was part of a new emphasis being placed on the "bits," the comedy other than the Monologue. Jay and his Monologue team would continue to focus on the Monologue while Joe, the bit writers, and I would concentrate on other ways to get laughs. Jay didn't give us any specific guidance about what he was looking for so we just dove right in.

I have an MBA and my first job after business school was in marketing for a consumer packaged goods company. That background gave me a way to think about how we could put the *Tonight* show back on top. Getting more people to watch our show was really no different from getting more people to buy any product. To me, that meant that we had to start airing more comedy that had three characteristics: (1) the audience liked it (of course); (2) it played to our strengths, so we could execute it well; and (3) our competition—*Late Show*—wasn't providing it.

Jay and his Monologue writers were already in the process of adding comedy that met those three criteria by lengthening the Monologue. The audience seemed to like the barrage of topical jokes at the start of the show; the ratio of laughs to jokes was consistently high. What's more, the Monologue had always been a relative strength of the show, especially compared to the handful of jokes that opened Dave's show. My main task, as I saw it, was to help add other comedy to the show that met those three criteria the way the Monologue did.

My task was made easier by me being the new guy. I hadn't seen many of the comedy pieces the show had done before so I may have been freer to consider other possibilities. I put into practice all the techniques I cover in this book and started pitching and writing new comedy pieces. The process was a little like putting together a thick submission packet for an upcoming show that hadn't quite figured out what it wanted to do yet; I discussed that process in Chapter 14.

As we started airing more and more varied comedy, the show's strengths became even clearer. At the top of the list of those strengths was Jay himself: not only was he an outstanding host, he was easy to work with and very accessible. At any time Joe or I could stroll into Jay's office, which was right next to ours, and pitch him an idea. Jay's open door policy eliminated a lot of wasted time and energy and made the comedy machine much more efficient.

That efficiency was essential because we were trying to pack a lot of comedy into each show. Our goal was to get to midnight before bringing out the first guest because ratings almost always dipped when the first guest arrived. That meant writing and producing about twenty minutes of comedy—practically the amount of scripted material in a weekly sitcom—every single night.

Another strength Jay brought to the show was his willingness to give new ideas a shot. Often you don't know whether a new comedy piece will work unless you try it. So it was a huge plus to have a host with the self-confidence to take even an offbeat piece out there in front of an audience and sell it.

A good example of Jay being up for almost anything is his character Mr. Brain, which I mentioned in the "Joke Basket Characters" section of Chapter 9. Here's how Mr. Brain came about. In April 1994 I wrote a joke for the show which involved a video effect that enlarged Jay's chin. During a rehearsal, the show's technical director started experimenting with a similar effect that expanded the top of Jay's head. Jay noticed the effect on a monitor and, amused, improvised an insulting character from a superior extraterrestrial race, barking out exclamations like, "You puny earthlings...you're all idiots!"

I thought the character was hilarious and, right then and there, suggested to Jay that we could use it to deliver jokes, the way Johnny Carson had used characters like Carnac the Magnificent. Jay agreed to try the idea, even though he had never performed a character on the show before, much less a character that depended in large part on a video effect that made him look silly.

The night Mr. Brain was to make his debut I was more nervous than usual. Jay would be sitting onstage in a lab coat. To see the comical "egghead" effect the audience would have to ignore the real Jay in front of them and look up at the monitors. Would they look up? And if they did, would they laugh? Well, they did laugh. They laughed as soon as they saw the effect. And they laughed so much throughout the piece that Jay didn't have time to deliver all the jokes we'd written for it.

As I said in Chapter 7, on Desk Pieces, a successful and refillable comedy piece is a godsend when you're trying to produce five shows every week; a piece like that is "comedy crack." So the first question we writers asked ourselves was, "How soon can we do Mr. Brain again?" Because we didn't want to burn out the abrasive alien too soon, we decided to limit him to one appearance every six weeks.

Meanwhile, we fed our new addiction to special effects Joke Basket Characters by creating more of them. Iron Jay was a slow-witted physical fitness expert with an enormous neck. And Beyondo was a disembodied head from the spirit world who predicts the future. Mr. Brain and his cousins seemed to earn the writing staff some additional credibility around NBC Burbank. They also helped distinguish the *Tonight* show from its competition because Dave Letterman almost never performed comic characters.

Another relative strength of the show was Jay's desire to do Semi-Scripted Field Pieces. As I mentioned in Chapter 13, there are several reasons Semi-Scripted Field Pieces are good for a comedy/talk show. And Jay wanted to do one every week. Every Wednesday night after taping the show he'd take a camera crew out and have some fun with pedestrians. By that time Dave had stopped going out on Field Pieces himself, so popular segments like "Jaywalking" set the *Tonight* show even farther apart from *Late Show*.

The *Tonight* show Field Pieces probably seemed particularly fresh to late-night audiences at the time because they offered a playful look at Los Angeles. We tried to shoot comedy pieces at iconic local landmarks to help give the show a distinctive visual flavor. Jay taped pieces on the Hollywood Walk of Fame and at the Chinese Theater; in the Earthquake, King Kong, and Backdraft attractions at Universal Studios Hollywood; at the La Brea Tar Pits; all throughout Disneyland; and at the foot of the Hollywood Sign, among other locations.

On one memorably busy day I directed three separate comedy pieces with Jay at Disneyland. One of them, in which Jay seemed to climb the Matterhorn, I described in Chapter 9. That same day Jay also apparently flicked the fedora off Indiana Jones's head with a bullwhip (to present the hat as a souvenir to an audience member) and cleaned off an audience member's eyeglasses by wearing them on Splash Mountain.

The fact that we returned to Burbank with the footage for three ambitious sketches was a tribute not only to Jay's stamina but also to the professionalism of our production staff, which was another strength of the show that the writers took full advantage of. I appreciated the fact that the production staff was willing to play along with a lot of new comedy ideas, even ones that seemed a little risky, because I believed that new ideas could help attract a larger audience.

Sometimes, though, getting to yes took some negotiation. For example, I wanted Jay to go on an Excursion where he tells the audience that because it's such a beautiful day there's something he just has to do. Jay hurries up to the sunny roof of the studio building, where he twirls around blissfully as he lip-syncs a gorgeous tenor voice singing, "The hills are alive...with the sound of music..."

I pitched the idea to our executive producer, who raised the reasonable question of whether Excursions were a type of comedy piece so closely identified with *Late Show* that we'd be accused of stealing our competitor's material. I didn't think viewers who saw Jay lip-syncing would ever claim that Dave was famous for that so I made the case that airing the Excursion was worth the risk. The executive producer agreed that we could do the piece.

"Jay Sings 'The Sound of Music'" played well on the show and we never caught any flak about it, so the writers were able to add Excursions to their comedy repertoire. It wasn't long before Jay was ducking into a bathroom on the nearby set of *Days of Our Lives*, riding a motorcycle through the studio building, and stealing flowers from a Tournament of Roses Parade float.

The road to an expanded comedy repertoire sometimes went through dicey neighborhoods, however. The writing was under a microscope. About five months after I arrived at the show Joe and I were summoned to a meeting with an NBC executive. He presented us with a report card on the comedy material in which he and a fellow executive had assigned every comedy bit from the previous three months a letter grade from A to F.

Here are some sample grades: Jay's "Joke Run" Field Pieces got As. The Remote Camera Piece "Chinese Theater Twister" (which I described in Chapter 12) earned a C+. What got an F? A bit listed as "Multiple Choice Test," whose subject I mercifully forget. Copied on the report card, which rated our comedy overall as only "Good," were other high-ranking executives at NBC. Joe and I got the unspoken message: "We have a lot riding on the *Tonight* show so don't screw it up with crappy comedy pieces."

The other writers and I forged ahead, reprising bits that worked, retiring those that didn't, and continuing to try new material. And NBC must have gotten more comfortable with the direction the show was moving in. In May 1994 the network ponied up the extra funds to have us do a week of shows in New York City, Dave's backyard. It was the first time that Jay's entire show had ever gone on the road. We made sure that those New York shows featured the best of the new comedy we'd developed, like Mr. Brain. Our ratings for that week were higher than usual, which was encouraging.

Something else good came out of those New York shows. After a week of performing closer to the audience, in the studio from which *Saturday Night Live* is broadcast, Jay realized he needed a new studio. So, back in Burbank, NBC built him one. In late September 1994 Jay's *Tonight* show moved out of Johnny Carson's old haunts into a brightly colored new facility across the hall.

The new studio positioned Jay practically within arm's reach of the audience when he performed his Monologue. The radically different setting played to Jay's strengths as a nightclub comic and his persona as an approachable Everyman. It also seemed to send a message: This is a new *Tonight* show. This is Jay's show. Why not take another look at it?

More and more viewers were taking another look at the *Tonight* show thanks to the prime-time ratings success of its network, NBC. A network's prime-time ratings can boost the ratings of its late-night programming because some viewers tend to stay tuned to whatever network they happen to be watching at 11:00 p.m. A network can also more effectively promote its late-night shows in prime time when its prime-time ratings are higher. And in 1994-1995, NBC's prime-time ratings were growing.

Spearheading this growth was *E.R.*, which debuted the same month Jay moved into his new studio and was immediately a huge hit for NBC on Thursday night. Thanks in part to the lead-in provided by *E.R.*, the *Tonight* show started to beat *Late Show* regularly on Thursday nights, and by a lot. In fact, about a month after *E.R.* hit the airwaves I happened to talk with a top NBC executive; he was in the hallway outside the *Tonight* show studio, taping a comedy bit for us. The executive told me that, thanks mostly to *E.R.*, he thought the *Tonight* show could start winning entire weeks in the ratings. I thought to myself that that goal seemed very ambitious but if this experienced executive believed it was achievable, why not keep on plugging?

Meanwhile something had happened that nobody could have predicted. On June 17, 1994, actor and former football star Orenthal James "O. J." Simpson was arrested in Los Angeles for the murder of his ex-wife Nicole Brown Simpson and her friend Ron Goldman. The arrest took place after O. J., in his white Ford Bronco, led the L.A.P.D. on a riveting low-speed chase that was covered nationally on live television. After O. J.'s arrest the police found in the Bronco his passport, $8,000 in cash, a loaded .357 Magnum, and a fake goatee and mustache.

The O. J. story attracted an enormous amount of media coverage, particularly in the Los Angeles area where it was unfolding and where, of course, the *Tonight* show was produced. The O. J. trial itself, which began in January 1995, was called "The Trial of the Century" and gripped the attention of the American public. For well over a year, the O. J. story could not be ignored and was therefore Potential Topic Number One for comedy.

The question facing the *Tonight* show was...what comedy? Two people had been brutally murdered, slaughtered in their prime. How could Jay's writers create comedy about the O. J. case when the underlying reality was so horrifying? To find an answer to that question Jay used the Monologue. One night he gauged the mood of the audience by performing a joke about the O. J. case and seeing how it went. The audience reaction was positive, so the next night Jay told a few more jokes on the topic. He and the Monologue writers felt their way, probing the audience the way a doctor presses his fingers on your abdomen and asks, "Does it hurt when I do this? How about this?"

Monologue jokes led to other comedy about the O. J. case. You may remember from Chapter 5 that one of the six characteristics of a good topic is that your audience will let you joke about it. Jay and his writers soon managed to discover which aspects of the case were acceptable as topics for comedy. Those acceptable aspects were peripheral ones like Judge Ito, prosecutors Marcia Clark and Chris Darden, O. J.'s "Dream Team" of lawyers, the jury, O. J.'s slacker houseguest Kato Kaelin, the media circus, and so on. Sticking to those aspects steered clear of the graphic, disturbing details of the crime itself and provided "ways into" the problematic but huge O. J. story. (Chapter 5 recommends that same technique for dealing with tricky but hard-to-ignore topics in general.)

Once we figured out how to do comedy about the case we did more and more of it. How could we not, when the audience devoured it? Before long the *Tonight* show was doing one or two O. J.-related comedy pieces a night in addition to multiple Monologue jokes, and virtually all of that material went over big. The audience cheered the Dancing Itos, a team of five Asian-Americans made up and costumed to resemble Judge Ito. They roared with laughter at "O. J.'s Island," a Parody Sketch based on the *Gilligan's Island* opening and theme song that featured look-alikes of Judge Ito, Marcia Clark, Kato Kaelin, and the rest. They went crazy for "The O. J. Bunch," a twist on a scene from *The Brady Bunch* that not only featured our O. J. trial look-alikes but also Florence Henderson, who played Mrs. Brady on the actual sitcom. Brilliant writing? Maybe not. But those *Tonight* show comedy pieces became part of the culture. They effectively went viral before the term even existed.

One time we writers palpated the audience's metaphorical abdomen and the audience yelped in pain. Here's what happened. The scene from "The O. J. Bunch" played so well that, comedy crack addicts that we were, we decided to produce another one about a week later. To this second scene we added a new member of the O. J. Bunch—the character of O. J.

himself. Big mistake. As soon as the O. J. look-alike entered the scene I heard the audience gasp, clearly taken aback and creeped out. The actor playing O. J. did a great job but he must have reminded the audience of the ugly crime at the center of the trial. The laugh-free sketch limped to a conclusion and we resolved never again to portray O. J. himself in a comedy piece.

But that one "ouch" from the audience didn't stop the writers from probing. We also aired a joke showing the O. J. trial characters having a cookout where the infamous bloody knife made an appearance. That's right—we used the murder weapon, the blade that O. J. allegedly used to hack two innocent people to death, as a punch line. Still, the audience laughed. So you never know.

The O. J. case was one of the main engines powering our comedy during the *Tonight* show's first year in its new studio. It was a particularly effective engine because only our show had it under the hood. Jay's main competitor, Dave, was barely doing any O. J. comedy. The reason Dave gave on his show at the time was that he wasn't amused by double homicides. Yet less than two years earlier, in 1993 and 1994, Dave had frequently joked about another high-profile murder trial, that of Erik and Lyle Menendez. The Menendez brothers had been accused of the brutal shotgun slaying of their parents. Whatever was holding *Late Show* back from doing O. J. comedy, we were glad we had that particular topic mostly to ourselves.

In early 1995 the O. J. trial wasn't the only media spectacle with possible implications for *Late Show*. On March 27 Dave hosted the Academy Awards for the first time. As I watched it on television I was surprised that so many of his jokes and comedy pieces seemed to fall flat. Although the ratings for the show turned out to be the highest in twelve years, some critics tore into Dave's performance. A review in *The New York Times* said, "The winner isn't David Letterman. As the stars glittered,

Dave fizzled." Reviews like that may have encouraged more late-night viewers to consider watching Jay.

Meanwhile the *Tonight* show had begun to close in on *Late Show* in the ratings, thanks to the addition of more crowd-pleasing comedy, the new studio, and NBC's prime-time success, among other factors. An article in the *Los Angeles Times* on May 25, 1995, bore the headline "The Nice Guy Gets an Edge: Jay Leno Begins His Fourth Year Behind 'The Tonight Show' Desk...and He's Gaining on Letterman." The article continues, "After being bashed in the ratings ever since David Letterman premiered his 'Late Show' on CBS nearly two years ago, Leno has finished just .1 of a ratings point behind Letterman for three weeks running, while routinely dominating such large markets as Los Angeles and Chicago." The *Tonight* show was building momentum.

Then on Monday, July 10, 1995, fate granted the *Tonight* show another opening. Actor Hugh Grant graciously honored his agreement to appear on the *Tonight* show only two weeks after his highly publicized arrest with a prostitute. It was Grant's first talk show appearance since the incident and the *Tonight* show staff expected viewer interest to be enormous.

My marketing training from years earlier kicked in. After a packaged goods company improves a product it often distributes a high-value coupon to entice consumers to sample it. The hope is that consumers will try the improved product, like it, and become regular purchasers. Well, it seemed to me that Hugh Grant was our high-value coupon. Lots of viewers would be sampling The New and Improved *Tonight* Show and I wanted to be sure they liked what they saw and became regular viewers.

So we scheduled a surefire Main Comedy Piece for the Hugh Grant episode, an appearance by Beyondo, that character of Jay's who appears as a disembodied head. We hoped the piece would favorably impress viewers who hadn't tuned into the *Tonight* show in a while. We also slot-ted in some of our best comedy pieces for the rest of that week, like Jay performing his popular bodybuilder character, Iron Jay, with action star Steven Seagal. We wanted to persuade new viewers that the Hugh Grant episode wasn't a fluke, that the show was now strong every night, and that they should keep tuning in.

The tactic paid off. Jay interviewed Grant skillfully, leading with the memorable question, "What the hell were you thinking?" Jay's *Tonight* show earned its third-highest rating to date that night and also scored ratings victories on two other nights that week. The result: that week, for the first time ever, the *Tonight* show beat *Late Show* in the weekly ratings. Apparently viewers came for Hugh Grant but stayed for *The Tonight Show with Jay Leno*. And two months later, in September 1995, the *Tonight* show won the Primetime Emmy Award for Outstanding Variety, Music or Comedy Series, besting four other nominees including *Late Show with David Letterman*.

The turnaround was complete. After that, the *Tonight* show attracted more viewers than *Late Show*, both young and old, almost every week that the two shows went head-to-head for the next eighteen years. Even during that long period in the new millennium when CBS was crush-ing NBC in prime time and crippling its late-night lead-ins, the *Tonight* show came out on top. What Jay said about the Late-Night War on more than one occasion back then turned out to be true: "It's a marathon, not a sprint."

INDEX

Made in the USA
Lexington, KY
23 June 2018